A GUIDE FROM THE
FIRST AMENDMENT CENTER

The First Amendment in Schools

CHARLES C. HAYNES

SAM CHALTAIN

JOHN E. FERGUSON JR.

DAVID L. HUDSON JR.

OLIVER THOMAS

Association for Supervision and Curriculum Development
Alexandria, Virginia USA

FIRST AMENDMENT CENTER
FUNDED BY THE FREEDOM FORUM

®
Association for Supervision and Curriculum Development
1703 N. Beauregard St. • Alexandria, VA 22311-1714 USA
Telephone: 800-933-2723 or 703-578-9600 • Fax: 703-575-5400
Web site: http://www.ascd.org • E-mail: member@ascd.org

FIRST AMENDMENT CENTER
FUNDED BY THE FREEDOM FORUM
1207 18th Avenue South
Nashville, TN 37212 USA
Telephone: 615-727-1600 • Fax: 615-727-1319
Web site: www.firstamendmentcenter.org • E-mail: info@fac.org

ASCD Staff: Gene R. Carter, *Executive Director;* Nancy Modrak, *Director of Publishing;*
Julie Houtz, *Director of Book Editing & Production;* Darcie Russell, *Project Manager;*
Georgia McDonald, *Senior Graphic Designer;* Barton Matheson Willse and Worthington, *Typesetter;*
Eric Coyle, *Production Coordinator.*

This book is not meant to provide legal advice. It is general information on First Amendment issues,
printed with the understanding that the authors are not providing legal advice or other professional
services. If the reader has specific legal questions, the reader should seek the services of a qualified,
licensed attorney.

All Web links in this book are correct as of the publication date below but may have become inactive
or otherwise modified since that time. If you notice a deactivated or changed link, please e-mail
books@ascd.org with the words "Link Update" in the subject line. In your message, please specify the
Web link, the book title, and the page number on which the link appears.

Printed in the United States of America.

November 2003 U.S. member book (pc). ASCD Premium, Comprehensive, and Regular members
periodically receive ASCD books as part of their membership benefits. No. FY04–2.

ISBN: 0-87120-777-X   ASCD product no.: 103054
ASCD member price: $21.95   nonmember price: $25.95

Library of Congress Cataloging-in-Publication Data

The First Amendment in schools / Charles C. Haynes . . . [et al.].
    p.   cm.
  Includes bibliographical references and index.
  ISBN 0-87120-777-X (alk. paper)
  1. Educational law and legislation—United States.   2. Civil rights—United States.   3. United
States. Constitution. 1st Amendment.   I. Haynes, Charles C.   II. Association for Supervision and
Curriculum Development.

  KF4124.5.F57 2003
  342.73'085—dc21   2003002637

13 12 11 10 09 08 07 06 05 04 03   12 11 10 9 8 7 6 5 4 3 2 1

This book is not meant to provide legal advice. It is general information on First Amendment issues, printed with the understanding that the authors are not providing legal advice or other professional services. If the reader has specific legal questions, the reader should seek the services of a qualified, licensed attorney.

Note that the law concerning the First Amendment in public schools changes with new court cases and legislation. For legal updates on this area of the law—including revisions to this publication—consult the resources page at www.firstamendmentschools.org.

THE FIRST AMENDMENT IN SCHOOLS

Foreword. vii

Acknowledgments xi

How to Use This Book. 1
    About Specific Legal Questions 1
    A Brief Introduction to the U.S. Court System 2
    Decoding a Legal Citation 4

The Birth of the First Amendment. 9
    The Call for a New Government. 10
    The Role of James Madison. 11
    The Adoption of the First Amendment 12

Part I: First Amendment Schools: Educating for Freedom and Responsibility . . . 17
    Vision Statement 18
    Frequently Asked Questions. 21
    Project Schools. 24

Part II: Core Issues for All Schools to Consider. 34
    Religious Liberty: The Establishment Clause 35
    Religious Liberty: The Free Exercise Clause. 38
    Accommodating the Religious Needs and Requirements of Students. . . . 39
    School Prayer and Student Religious Expression. 42
    Student Extracurricular Clubs and Activities 47
    Teaching About Religion 51
    Religious Holidays 55
    Use of School Facilities by Outside Groups 57
    Cooperative Agreements Between Public Schools
        and Religious Communities 58
    Released-Time Programs. 59

Free Expression Rights of Students 59
Speech Codes 69
Student Distribution of Literature 73
Student Dress and School Uniforms 74
Students and the Internet 81
Student Publications 86
Teacher and Administrator Rights and Responsibilities 92
Book Selection and Other Decisions About the Curriculum 104

Part III: 50 Key Legal Cases 116
Case Directory 117
Supreme Court Case Summaries 119
Lower Court Case Summaries 143

Part IV: Resources 167
Selected Programs and Organizations 167
Selected Education Groups 177
Selected Advocacy Groups 181
Selected Bibliography 186

Index 190

About the Authors 203

FOREWORD

The notion that students should learn more about the Bill of Rights, and especially about the First Amendment, is hardly new. Roughly 40 years ago, three events focused national attention on this educational priority. A group of social studies teachers and curriculum developers, lawyers, and others gathered in Williamstown, Massachusetts, late in 1961 to prepare a report that became a blueprint for law-related education. The next year Supreme Court Justice William J. Brennan Jr., soon to be the most prominent jurist on free speech issues, took a leading role at a Washington-area conference on Bill of Rights education; that fall he gave the keynote address to the National Council for the Social Studies on the same theme. A few months later, the Ford Foundation commissioned a seminal study of law-related education by Chicago lawyer Alex Elson, whose report gave further momentum to curricular emphasis on civil rights and civil liberties.

These efforts had a disquieting antecedent. During the 1950s, several surveys of high school students and recent graduates revealed an appalling lack of knowledge about the Bill of Rights. Such a discovery was the more alarming because it came at the height of the Cold War, when the nation was challenged by fears of Communism and subversion on one hand and by the excesses of McCarthyism on the other. At a time when freedoms were being sorely tested and when judgments were being made about civil rights and liberties in the courts, in Congress, and even in state and local councils, educators were startled to learn how little the nation's schools were doing to prepare future citizens to shape and protect these basic values.

Many groups responded to the call and began to develop law-related materials, with special emphasis on freedoms of expression and religion protected by the First Amendment. The American Bar Association created new committees for this purpose. Regional and local bar groups followed suit, most notably the Chicago Bar Association, which collaborated with the Chicago Board of Education to found Law in American Society. State educational agencies, especially the California State Board, established programs to provide law-related materials to the schools of the state. California also became the home of two successful and durable Bill of Rights projects, Law in a Free Society and the Center for Civic Education, which rank high on a now-substantial roster of programs devoted to overcoming the gap in student understanding of civil liberties.

Along the way there were bound to be a few disappointments. In Chicago, for example, it proved far more difficult than either the lawyers or the teachers had expected to find entry points in the established social studies curriculum for the new law-related units. Eager individual teachers found a niche for the new materials, but the structure remained largely impermeable there and in many other communities where the will existed, if not always the way. There were bound to be excesses, as with any good cause. The supreme irony was the experience of a Burbank, California, public school superintendent who was effectively forced from office for failing to add enough Bill of Rights material to satisfy a committed but intransigent group of parents and citizens. During these years there was more of an emphasis on law-related material, and especially on the study of the First Amendment, both in the schools and in the published materials for teaching social studies.

Although recent surveys do not reveal the alarming ignorance of the 1950s, they do indicate that much remains to be done. If the entire text of the Bill of Rights, or simply that of the First Amendment, were circulated on the streets as a petition, many would resist approving it—either because they did not recognize their own Constitution as the source or, even worse, because they could not accept the principles reflected in these basic guarantees. Thus the time is ripe, and the need urgent, for everyone to understand the deeper meaning of free expression and religious liberty.

Such urgency surely existed by early March 2001, when the First Amendment Center and the Association for Supervision and Curriculum Development (ASCD) launched "First Amendment Schools: Educating for Freedom and Responsibility." Yet the events of Sept. 11, 2001, dramatically raised the stakes. The official response to the horrific attacks of that day raised the stakes with regard to free expression—in a host of ways of which we cannot even be completely aware until measures adopted in the War on Terrorism are more fully tested in the courts. Meanwhile, the scope and character of our nation's religious freedom stand as a special beacon against the conviction—not only of certain Islamic militants, but of many others as well—that government and religion should be partners, with the state essentially subordinate to a clerical orthodoxy.

It is in this context that the First Amendment Schools project offers such high hope for enhancing appreciation and understanding of our most basic liberties. The project promises to recognize and support the efforts of individual schools and teachers to expand exposure to First Amendment values, and to make materials widely available for teachers and students who wish to know more about their heritage of free expression and worship. Those who convened the Williamstown workshop, launched the Bill of Rights initiatives of the 1960s, and prepared materials for an earlier generation of students would applaud what is today being done under First Amendment Schools auspices.

The First Amendment is the oldest and most durable of the world's guarantees of expressive and religious freedom, surpassing even the constitutional safeguards adopted more recently by nations much older than the United States. It is also unique in several important ways. Although some other countries expressly protect freedom of worship and belief, only Australia insists on a separation between government and religion—and Australian judges have interpreted an identical textual provision less rigorously than have U.S. courts.

When it comes to expression, the First Amendment reaches freedom of assembly and petition, as well as speech and press. It has also been expanded to protect freedom of association, symbolic or nonverbal communication, and most recently speech in totally new media such as the Internet. Moreover, U.S. courts insist that expression be freer than just about anywhere else on earth. As you will learn in the pages that follow, such acts as wearing antiwar insignia or burning a flag in protest may be protected here as "speech" even though few other legal systems reach that far. We also insist that deeply offensive, militantly racist, sexist, and homophobic rhetoric must be tolerated to a degree that few, if any other, nations demand. In the United States we sometimes pay a high price for our freedom of speech—in wounded feelings, in uncivil discourse, even in public disorder—but we believe deeply that such costs are in the long run worth paying in order to preserve the First Amendment values that have served us so well for more than 210 years.

This book provides a clear understanding of what First Amendment values mean and how they operate in very practical as well as abstract terms. It should not only fill that critical gap for the next generation of national leaders, but along the way it should make fascinating reading for anyone who cares about our liberties and our legal system.

Robert M. O'Neil
Professor of Law, University of Virginia
Director, Thomas Jefferson Center
for the Protection of Free Expression

ACKNOWLEDGMENTS

During the development of this book, several outstanding legal scholars and First Amendment experts read and critiqued the manuscript. For their thoughtful evaluations and constructive suggestions, the authors wish to thank the following people:

Ron Collins, First Amendment Center
Bernard James, Pepperdine University School of Law
Paul McMasters, First Amendment Center
Rachel Moran, Boalt School of Law, University of California at
    Berkeley
Jamin Raskin, Washington College of Law, American University
David Schimmel, School of Education, University of Massachusetts

We also appreciate the valuable help of Mabel McKinney-Browning, director of the Division for Public Education at the American Bar Association, and Robert O'Neil, director of the Thomas Jefferson Center for the Protection of Free Expression.

Our collaboration with ASCD on the First Amendment Schools project inspired the writing of this book. We are grateful for the leadership of Gene Carter, executive director; Diane Berreth, deputy executive director; Mike Wildasin, former director of the First Amendment Schools project; and the other members of the ASCD team.

Special thanks to Nancy Modrak and Darcie Russell of ASCD for their help in developing this project and preparing the manuscript for publication.

Finally, this book would not have been written without the support and encouragement of Ken Paulson, executive director of the First Amendment Center.

HOW TO USE THIS BOOK

This book is part of a larger school reform initiative—"First Amendment Schools: Educating for Freedom and Responsibility." Sponsored by the Association for Supervision and Curriculum Development (ASCD) and the First Amendment Center, this program calls on all schools to reaffirm First Amendment principles and put them into action. A central goal of the initiative is to help schools become laboratories for democratic freedom—places where students learn how to exercise their rights with responsibility.

An important starting point for becoming a First Amendment School is to know how the principles of the First Amendment should be applied in a public school under current law.[1] This book provides a civic and legal framework for giving all members of the school community—students, parents, teachers, administrators, and community members—a real voice in shaping the life of the school.

About Specific Legal Questions

In this book, we offer a straightforward and concise synthesis of how the courts currently understand and apply the First Amendment in public education. Keep in mind, however, that the answers given here include general information on the subject of First Amendment expression and practice in schools. For answers to specific legal questions about an incident or issue in your school, consult your school board lawyer or another qualified, licensed attorney in your community.

This publication is designed to answer only the most *frequently asked questions* on how the courts interpret the First Amendment in schools—not all possible questions and answers about a large and complicated area of the law. School districts drafting policies in the areas discussed in this book will want to consult their state statutes and education codes for a fuller understanding of what the law does or does not permit under a properly crafted policy.

A Brief Introduction to the U.S. Court System

A brief description of the courts in the United States may be useful background for understanding the cases mentioned in this book.[2]

U.S. courts can be divided into two groups: state and federal. Generally, federal courts hear claims based on alleged violations of federal statutes or the U.S. Constitution. State courts hear cases involving state statutes or common (court-made) law or a state's constitution. For example, a First Amendment claim charging public school officials with censorship is typically brought in federal court because the First Amendment is part of the U.S. Constitution. A lawsuit claiming that a principal has violated a state's student free-expression law will typically be brought in state court.

Federal and state courts are divided into trial courts, which hear the case initially, and one or more levels of appellate court. Although the specific names of state courts vary, all federal trial courts are called *district courts*. There are 94 district courts in the country, at least one in each state. No district overlaps two states. Each federal district court has jurisdiction to hear cases within its geographic area. Someone who loses a case can appeal from a federal court to a *circuit court of appeals*. There are 13 of these around the country—11 circuit courts covering different geographic boundaries (see Figure 1), a D.C. Circuit Court, and the U.S. Court of Appeals for the Federal Circuit. All but one have *jurisdiction*, or legal standing, over district courts within the geographic boundaries of their circuit.

There are no juries at the appeals court level—only judges. Usually, a panel of three judges will decide a case. A litigant who loses before a three-judge panel may petition for *en banc*, or full panel, review of the case. The number of judges who sit for an en banc review varies from state to state, although it is usually between 11 and 15.

FIGURE 1

Geographic Boundaries of the United States Courts of Appeals and United States District Courts

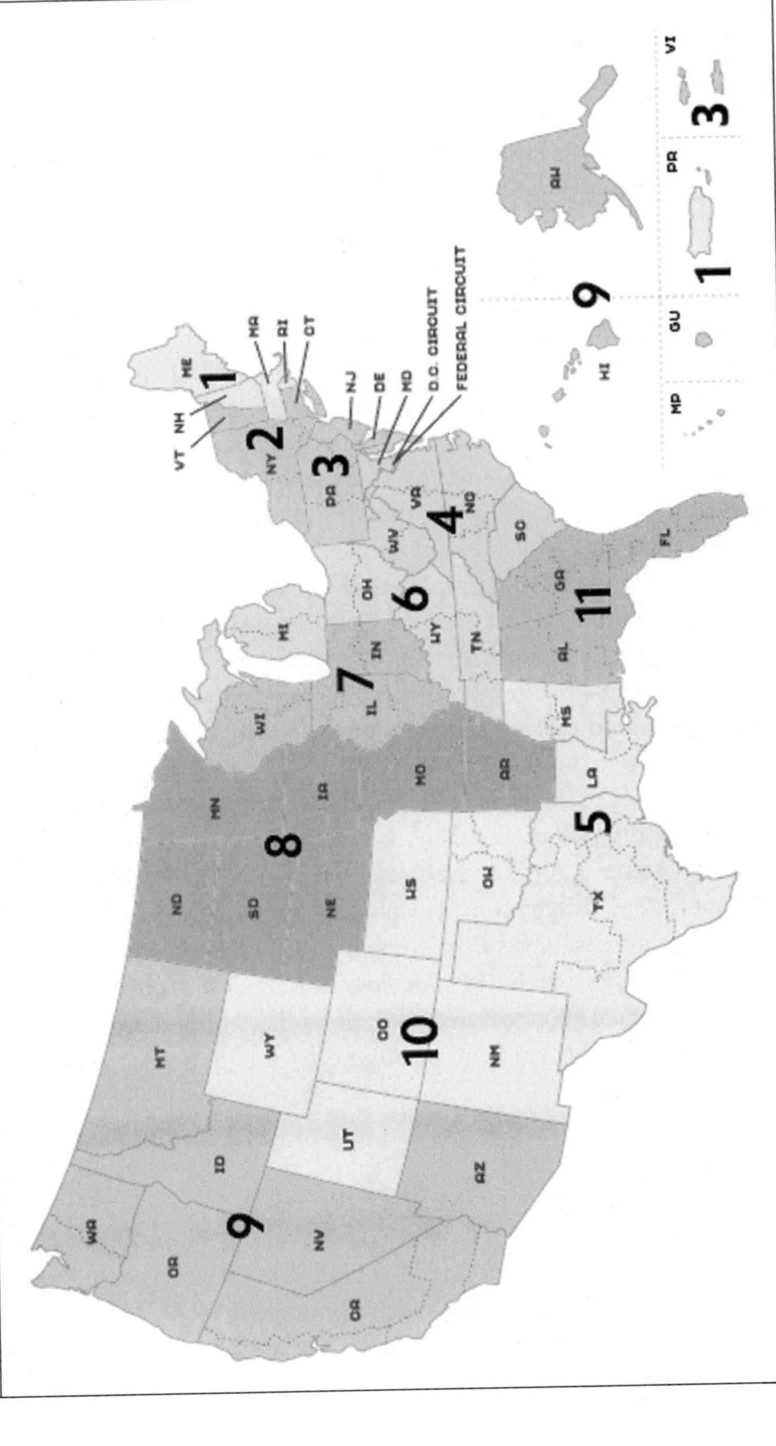

Parties to a lawsuit decided by an en banc review in a federal court of appeals can ask the U.S. Supreme Court to review their case. However, the Supreme Court typically can choose the cases it wants to consider. If the Court does accept a case for review, it issues a writ of *certiorari*—a directive to the lower court to deliver the case for review.[3] There is no appeal beyond the U.S. Supreme Court.

Decisions of a federal court of appeals must be followed by all the district courts located within that circuit. (For more information on the Federal Courts outreach contacts in your area, see Figure 2.) District courts outside that circuit, however, are not bound by such decisions. Further, one district court does not have to follow the rulings of any other district court. A court is bound only by the decisions of higher courts that have direct jurisdiction over it. This is the concept of *precedent*. Because the U.S. Supreme Court is the highest court in the country, all courts must follow its precedent. Note, however, that state courts do not have to follow the rulings of federal courts on matters solely based on state law, and vice versa. For example, although the U.S. Supreme Court significantly reduced the amount of First Amendment protection available to most high school journalists in the 1988 case of *Hazelwood School District v. Kuhlmeier*—a ruling based only on federal law—a state court may, nevertheless, find that high school journalists in its state remain protected by state law.

If a court refuses to follow precedent or misinterprets a precedent, its decision may be reversed by the court above it. A court has the option, rarely exercised, to reverse its own precedent, although usually such precedent is *distinguished*, meaning that the court decides that the facts in the present case are so different from the facts in the past case that the court need not reach the same conclusion. Courts can be creative in finding differences between fact situations that allow them to distinguish the case in front of them from what might seem, to everyone else, to be binding precedent.

Decoding a Legal Citation

Citations have been provided for all the cases discussed in this book. These citations are not difficult to understand.

Citations are used for locating the *decisions*, or judicial opinions, of any given case. These opinions are published in sets of books called

---

FIGURE 2

Contact Information for Federal Courts

National Contact
Rebecca J. Fanning
National Outreach &
   Public Education Manager
Administrative Office,
   U.S. Courts
One Columbus Circle, N.E.,
Suite 7-400
Washington, DC 20544
202-502-2611

First Circuit
Gary Wente
Circuit Executive/
Outreach Contact
U.S. District Court
One Courthouse Way
Boston, MA 02210-3002
617-748-9613

Second Circuit
Stephen Young
Outreach Contact
U.S. Court of Appeals
40 Centre Street, Room 2904
New York, NY 10007
212-857-8708

Third Circuit
Theresa Burnett
Outreach Contact
U.S. Court of Appeals
601 Market St., Rm. 22409
Philadelphia, PA 19106-1790
267-299-4203

**Eastern District
of Virginia
In the Fourth Circuit**
Hilarie Gaylin
Outreach Contact
U.S. District Court
401 Courthouse Square
Alexandria, VA 22314-5798
703-299-2180

**Northern District
of Illinois
In the Seventh Circuit**
Daniel J. Lehmann
Outreach Contact
U.S. District Court
219 S. Dearborn Street
Chicago, Il 60604
312-435-5607

**Eastern District
of Missouri
In the Eighth Circuit**
Sherry Compton
Outreach Contact
U.S. District Court
111 South Tenth Street
Suite 3.300
St. Louis, MO 63102
314-244-7917

Ninth Circuit
David J. Madden
Outreach Contact
U.S. Court of Appeals
95 Seventh Street, Suite 429
P. O. Box 193939
San Francisco, CA 94119-3939
415-556-6177

D.C. Circuit Court
Robin D. Tabora
Chief Deputy for Administration
U.S. District Court District of Columbia
333 Constitution Avenue, NW
Washington, DC 20001
202-354-3012

Revised June 7, 2002

---

reporters. All decisions from the federal circuit courts are published in the *Federal Reporter.* There are now three series of the *Federal Reporter* books. All decisions from the federal district courts are published in *Federal Supplement* books. There are now two series of those books. All decisions for the U.S. Supreme Court are officially cataloged in a set of books called the *United States Reports*. Supreme Court cases may, however, also be found in the *Lawyers' Edition United States Supreme Court Reports* or in the *United States Supreme Court Reporter.*

Knowing about these different books is essential if you are interested in learning about how to decipher a legal reference. For example, take a look at the following citation:

Thomas v. Board of Education, 607 F.2d 1043, 1051 (2nd Cir. 1979)

In this case, several students sued their school when they were disciplined based on the content of a publication they had created and distributed off-campus. Let's break down the citation piece by piece:

Thomas v. Board of Education

The last name of the lead student, Thomas, is listed as the *plaintiff*, or petitioner, in the case.[4] The plaintiff is the party who has brought the case to court. Because the students were suing their school, their local Board of Education is listed as the *defendant*, or respondent, in the case. This is the party being sued.

607 F.2d 1043, 1051 (2nd Cir. 1979)

This part of the citation tells you that the *Thomas* case can be found in Volume 607 of the second series of the *Federal Reporter*. These books are listed as either F., F.2d, or F.3d. If the opinion was published in the *Federal Supplement*, it would be listed as F.Supp. or F.Supp.2d. For this particular type of note, known as a "pinpoint citation," two page numbers have been given (1043, 1051). The first number indicates on what page the decision begins; the second number indicates where the passage in question can be found. The parenthetical material (2nd Cir. 1979) indicates that this case was heard by the Second Circuit Court of Appeals, and that a decision in the case was reached in 1979.

Now let's briefly look at a citation from a Supreme Court case:

Wallace v. Jaffree, 472 U.S. 38 (1985).

For Supreme Court citations, U.S. stands for *United States Reports*. If the case was found in the *Lawyers' Edition United States Supreme Court Reports*, it would be listed as L.Ed. If it was found in the *United States Supreme Court Reporter,* it would be listed as S.Ct. By decoding this citation, we know the *Wallace* case will be found in Volume 472 of the *United States Reports,* beginning on page 38, and that a ruling was issued in 1985.

If a citation is identical to the previous citation, the word *Idem* (abbreviated as Id.) is used. If the case is the same but a different page number is being referenced, the format "Id. at 1056" or "Id. at 34" is used.

A cite to a scholarly journal or law review article should be read the same way as a court case citation. Citations to state statutes may vary, but they too are generally easy to decipher. If you are interested in reading more about some of the cases listed and discussed here, visit your local law school library, a local courthouse library, or a large public library with legal holdings. For online research, visit www.firstamendmentcenter.org.

Common Abbreviations

A., A.2d	*Atlantic Reporter*
A.L.R.	*American Law Reports*
F.	*Federal Reporter*
F.2d	*Federal Reporter, Second Series*
F.3d	*Federal Reporter, Third Series*
F. Supp.	*Federal Supplement*
F. Supp. 2d	*Federal Supplement, Second Series*
Fed. Reg.	*Federal Register*
L. Ed.	*Lawyers' Edition United States Supreme Court Reports*
LexisNexis	*Electronic, fee-based legal research tool*
Mass.	*Massachusetts Reports*
N.E.	*North Eastern Reporter*
N.E.2d	*North Eastern Reporter, Second Series*
N.W.	*North Western Reporter*
N.W.2d	*North Western Reporter, Second Series*
N.Y.S.	*New York Supplement*
P.	*Pacific Reporter*
P.2d	*Pacific Reporter, Second Series*
S.Ct.	*United States Supreme Court Reporter*
S.E.	*South Eastern Reporter*
S.E.2d	*South Eastern Reporter, Second Series*
So.	*Southern Reporter*
So.2d	*Southern Reporter, Second Series*

Stat.	*Statutes at Large*
U.S.	*United States Reports*
U.S.C.	*United States Code*
U.S.C.A.	*United States Code Annotated*

Notes

[1]Although the First Amendment applies only to the actions of public school officials (as state employees), the First Amendment Schools project invites all schools—public and private—to fulfill the spirit of the First Amendment by becoming laboratories for democratic freedom.

[2]This discussion of the court system is adapted from *Law of the Student Press*, published by the Student Press Law Center (www.splc.org) in 1994 and is used with permission.

[3]*Certiorari* is a Latin word meaning "to be more fully informed." Thousands of cases are appealed to the Supreme Court each year; only about 80 to 120, however, are actually accepted, or "granted cert"—shorthand for certiorari.

[4]Sometimes, however, the petitioner in a U.S. Supreme Court case will be the defendant and not the plaintiff. This is because in a Supreme Court case the petitioner is the person who appeals the Court for review.

THE BIRTH OF THE
FIRST AMENDMENT

Winning democratic freedom was a momentous struggle for the American people in 1776—just as it is today for many people around the world yearning to be free.

Yet ordering freedom—making it work—is an even greater challenge.

Today many of us take the Constitution with its Bill of Rights for granted. But consider this: Between 1971 and 1990, 110 of the world's 162 national constitutions were either written or extensively rewritten.[1] An average of five new constitutions are adopted somewhere in the world each year. Canada's most recent version was adopted in 1982. France, a country whose first attempt at constitution writing mirrored the timing of our own, had to begin rewriting less than three years after they finished. Since 1789, the French have written and rewritten a total of 15 times.

By contrast, the U.S. Constitution has endured for more than 200 years, making it the oldest—and shortest—written constitution in the world. Why has it succeeded, when so many others have failed? One reason stands above the others, according to the famous French observer of American democracy, Alexis de Tocqueville:

> Let us look to America . . . less to find examples than instruction; let
> us borrow from her the principles, rather than the details, of her laws.
> The laws of the French republic may be, and ought to be in many
> cases, different from those which govern the United States; but the
> principles on which the American constitutions rest, those principles
> of order, of the balance of power, of true liberty, of deep and sincere
> respect for right, are indispensable to all republics.[2]

De Tocqueville understood that the principles on which the U.S. Constitution is founded are timeless because they affirm that government does not give us our rights; its role is to guard the rights we already have by birthright. And no part of the U.S. Constitution is more important to the protection of "true liberty [and a] deep and sincere respect for right" than the 45 words that make up the First Amendment.

But how did the First Amendment come to be part of the U.S. Constitution? That story begins in Philadelphia.

The Call for a New Government

It was 1785 and the United States, just four years removed from its stunning victory over the British, was already in trouble.

The Articles of Confederation, our first model of self-government, was a failure. Wary of the strong central power of the British monarchy, our leaders had instead created a form of government that gave lip service to the notion of a "United States" but provided no real ways of ensuring the unity of the new nation.

Under the Articles, the United States was hopelessly divided. Congress, the government's central legislative body, could call for taxes from the states, but it could not enforce their collection; it could not effectively regulate commerce between the states, or prevent them from competing against each other. Instead of being united states, America was close to becoming 13 separate nations.

In an environment of such discord, the United States of Congress Assembled—as it was then called—was vulnerable and weak. Something needed to be done, or else the nation Americans had fought for and died to secure could be lost.

In response, beginning in 1785, many of the country's leading figures began to consider how they could strengthen the Articles of Confederation. Eventually, they decided to hold a convention of all 13 states, in Philadelphia, in the late summer and fall of 1787.[3]

In its instructions to the delegates, Congress clearly stated that the purpose of the convention was to revise the Articles of Confederation—not to draft a new form of government—but the men who gathered in Philadelphia quickly realized that was exactly what they had to do. Once the delegates resolved to work for a much stronger central government—a resolution that did not come without a fight—the central question was whether the new constitution should contain a specific list of guaranteed rights for its citizens.

One group of delegates, who became known as the Antifederalists, insisted that it should. This group included George Mason, who had drafted Virginia's Declaration of Rights; this document had become a model for other states and was drawn on by Thomas Jefferson in drafting the Declaration of Independence. To omit such a list, Mason and others argued, would be to fail "to attend to the rights of every class of people."[4]

A majority of the delegates, however, disagreed—not because they thought individual rights weren't important, but because the purpose of their meeting was to draft a more effective form of government. This majority, who became known as the Federalists because of their belief in a stronger central government, had a point: After all, nearly every state already had some provisions concerning individual rights in their state constitutions,[5] so wouldn't a national list be repetitive?

This question remained unresolved when the Philadelphia convention concluded,[6] and the draft of the new constitution—minus a bill of rights—was distributed to all 13 states for consideration. Each state would now have to elect representatives to its own ratifying conventions, where the fate of the constitution would be determined.

At first, ratification appeared to be assured. But as more states debated the document's merits, it became clear that many citizens shared the fears of the Antifederalists. In fact, beginning in Massachusetts, and continuing through New York's narrowly won support, 8 of the 11 states that voted for ratification[7] did so only after being promised that adding a bill of rights would be Congress's first order of business. In anticipation of that meeting, the 13 state conventions produced a dizzying list of recommendations—210 different amendments to be precise, covering 80 different areas.[8]

Clearly, representatives at the First Congress would have their work cut out for them.

The Role of James Madison

James Madison of Virginia played such a key role in Philadelphia that he is often called "the Father of the Constitution." But he didn't participate in the debate over the inclusion of a bill of rights—and was unconcerned about its absence. In fact, Madison and others felt that to specify only certain rights might leave others unprotected. Moreover, including a bill of rights in the Constitution might imply that the federal government had the power to determine which rights to guarantee. Madison feared that such provisions might lead to use of the government by the majority to oppress the minority.

When the first federal elections were held in 1788–89, Madison and other Federalists were concerned that the Antifederalists would win enough power to amend the Constitution in ways that would weaken the new federal government—or even to call a second convention. Madison was determined to be elected to the First Congress, but first he would need to defeat Antifederalist James Monroe.

Although Madison continued to believe that a bill of rights was unnecessary if not dangerous, he also recognized that popular support for the Constitution among his constituents was linked to adding a bill of rights. With the Constitution safely ratified, Madison was now willing to support some amendments through congressional action, and not a second convention.

Madison's changed position was shaped by the opinions of his good friend Thomas Jefferson. Jefferson was in Paris and had not participated in the constitutional convention, but he had written Madison often to offer his thoughts on the issues. "Let me add that a bill of rights is what the people are entitled to against any government, general or particular," Jefferson wrote in one of his letters, "and what no just government should refuse."[9]

Jefferson's ideas had an effect on Madison, who came to see that the new Constitution would fail unless it could speak to the "great mass of the people." Perhaps, he thought, with the public outcry for its inclusion so strong, a federal bill of rights would protect against the "oppressive majority" he feared.[10]

The Adoption of the First Amendment

Madison's new willingness to consider amendments helped him win the election. And when he rose, on June 8, 1789, to address the House of Representatives at the first session of the First Congress, he urged his colleagues "not to disregard [the people's] inclination, but, on principles of amity and moderation, conform to their wishes and expressly declare the great rights of mankind secured under this constitution."[11]

Once he had made the case for their consideration, Madison moved on to present his draft of the amendments, drawing heavily on most of the rights-related amendments recommended by the various states.[12] There were nine in all, but it is in the language of the middle three that we can see the precursors to the five freedoms of the First Amendment. They read:

> 4. The civil rights of none shall be abridged on account of religious belief or worship, nor shall any national religion be established, nor shall the full and equal rights of conscience be in any manner, or on any pretext infringed.
> 5. The people shall not be deprived or abridged of their right to speak, to write, or to publish their sentiments; and the freedom of the press, as one of the great bulwarks of liberty, shall be inviolable.
> 6. The people shall not be restrained from peaceably assembling and consulting for their common good; nor from applying to the Legislature by petitions, or remonstrances for redress of their grievances.[13]

Madison had originally suggested that the language of the amendments be incorporated directly into the body of the Constitution, a proposal that was rejected. But a special House committee did suggest some language revisions to Madison's original list. His fourth, fifth, and sixth amendments were combined, so they now read like this:

> 3. No religion shall be established by law, nor shall the equal rights of conscience be infringed.
> 4. The freedom of speech, and of the press, and of the right of the people peaceably to assemble and consult for their common good, and to apply to the government for redress of grievances, shall not be infringed.

Gone was the reference to "the great bulwarks of liberty," but the wording still wasn't perfect, or so thought the members of the House. First came the recommendation that the first of the two amendments be revised to read: "Congress shall make no law establishing religion, or to prevent the free exercise thereof; or to infringe on the rights of conscience."[14]

During debate over how to revise the second, Theodore Sedgwick of Massachusetts raised a key question. To list both the freedom to speak and to assemble, Sedgwick argued, was unnecessary. After all, there are countless rights—"a man's right to wear a hat, to go to bed when he wants, to ride a horse in the afternoon."[15] If you're going to guarantee one of these, he continued, why not all of them? Madison, however, allayed the fears of his colleagues by urging that they "confine [them]selves to an enumeration of simple, acknowledged principles."[16] And finally, on August 24, the House approved a total of 17 amendments for the Senate to consider. Two of those read as follows:

ARTICLE THE THIRD.

Congress shall make no law establishing religion or prohibiting the free exercise thereof, nor shall the rights of Conscience be infringed.

ARTICLE THE FOURTH.

The freedom of Speech, and of the Press, and of the right of the People peaceably to assemble, and consult for their common good, and to apply to the Government for a redress of grievances, shall not be infringed.[17]

When the proposed amendments arrived at the Senate, the senators set about trying to streamline the House's longer list into one that was more manageable. In the process, not only did they remove certain phrases— such as "the rights of Conscience"—they also rejected a separate amendment Madison had urged them to keep. It had read, "No state should infringe on the right of trial by jury in criminal cases, nor the right of conscience, nor the freedom of speech or of the press." Madison's attempt to keep states from interfering with these basic rights failed in the Senate. It would not be until the 20th century that the Supreme Court would make the First Amendment applicable to the states through the 14th Amendment's due process clause.

Eventually, the Senate revised the House amendments to 12. On Sept. 25, 1789, Congress sent these amendments to President Washington for transmission to the states. Through the process of state ratification, however, the first two amendments were quickly considered unworthy of consideration, and several states approved only the final 10.

Thus on Dec. 15, 1791, when Virginia became the required 11th state to ratify the Bill of Rights, the first of those amendments, which had once been three separate amendments, then two, and then the third overall, now read:

Congress shall make no law respecting an establishment of religion, or prohibiting the free exercise thereof; or abridging the freedom of speech, or of the press; or the right of the people peaceably to assemble, and to petition the government for a redress of grievances.

It has not been revised since.

Today, more than 200 years after enactment, the First Amendment is the bedrock of freedom in the United States. Throughout our history, Americans have invoked their five "first freedoms" to work for a more free and just society. From the abolitionists to the suffragettes to the civil rights movement—indeed in every important struggle for social justice and civil liberties—all five freedoms of the First Amendment have been essential for expanding the promise of democratic freedom.

The challenge for the United States in the 21st century is to sustain and deepen our commitment to individual rights as our nation grows more complex and diverse. The place to meet this challenge is first and foremost in the public school—the place where most Americans learn the rights and responsibilities of democratic citizenship. We hope that the pages that follow will inspire students, educators, parents, and community members to understand and apply the First Amendment in every school community.

Notes

[1] Goldwin, R. A. (1997). *From parchment to power: How James Madison used the Bill of Rights to save the Constitution.* Washington, DC: AEI Press, p. 1.

[2] De Tocqueville, A. (1948). *Democracy in America.* New York: Knopf, cvi-cvii.

[3] Every state but Rhode Island agreed.

[4] Farrand, M. (Ed.). (1966). *The records of the Federal Convention.* Yale University Press: v. I, 49.

[5] New Jersey was the lone exception.

[6] In protest, three delegates—Elbridge Gerry of Massachusetts, Mason, and Edmund Randolph of Virginia—refused to sign the Constitution, largely because of the absence of a bill of rights.

[7] North Carolina and Rhode Island initially rejected the Constitution; but once the new national government got under way, they had little choice but to join.

[8] Wagman, R. J. (1991). *The First Amendment book.* New York: World Almanac, p. 32.

[9] Boyd, J. P. (ed.) (1950-1995). *The papers of Thomas Jefferson.* Princeton University Press: v. 12, 440.

[10] Goldwin, p. 73.

[11] Lloyd, T. (Ed.) (June 8, 1879). The Congressional Register: v. 1, 429-436.

[12] Although many of the 10 amendments that constitute the Bill of Rights were dramatically rewritten before they were finally ratified, there is nothing they protect that is not mentioned, in some form, in this first list of Madison's.

[13] Cogan, N. (Ed.). (1997). *The complete Bill of Rights: The drafts, debates, sources, and origins.* New York: Oxford University Press, pp. 1, 83, 129.

[14]This recommendation was first made by Samuel Livermore on Aug. 15, 1789, although the language quoted is taken from a later draft written and presented by Fisher Ames on Aug. 20.

[15]Wagman, p. 37.

[16]Cited in Wagman, p. 38.

[17]In 1868, Congress passed the 14th Amendment, which guaranteed, in part, that "no state shall make or enforce any law which shall abridge the privileges or immunities of citizens of the United States." However, it was not until the 1925 case of *Gitlow v. New York* that the Supreme Court affirmed the notion that states, and not just Congress, must be bound by the First Amendment.

⇒ PART I ⇐

FIRST AMENDMENT SCHOOLS:
EDUCATING FOR FREEDOM
AND RESPONSIBILITY

The nationwide initiative, "First Amendment Schools: Educating for Freedom and Responsibility," is designed to transform how schools model and teach the rights and responsibilities that frame civic life in our democracy.

Early in 2001, ASCD and the First Amendment Center joined forces to launch the project, which has four primary goals:

1. To create consensus guidelines for any school interested in creating and sustaining First Amendment principles in the school community.

2. To establish project schools at which First Amendment principles are understood and applied throughout the school community.

3. To encourage and develop curriculum reforms that reinvigorate and deepen teaching about the First Amendment across the curriculum.

4. To educate school leaders, teachers, school board members and attorneys, and other key stakeholders about the meaning and significance of First Amendment principles and ideals.

In its fulfillment of these goals, the First Amendment Schools (FAS) project serves as a national resource to all schools—K–12, public and private—committed to transforming how First Amendment principles are modeled and taught.

Vision Statement

First Amendment Schools are built on the conviction that the five freedoms protected by the First Amendment are a cornerstone of American democracy and essential for citizenship in a diverse society.

For more than 200 years, the First Amendment has been at the heart of history's boldest and most successful experiment in liberty. We readily acknowledge that the United States failed to live up to its founding principles in 1791, and that the nation still has a distance to go in the 21st century. But the history of the United States is the story of the ongoing struggle to extend the promise of freedom more fully and fairly to every citizen.

Today the need to sustain and expand our experiment in liberty is made more urgent by the challenge of living with our deepest differences in a diverse and complex society. The need to commit ourselves as a people to the rights and responsibilities that flow from the First Amendment has never been more vital—or more difficult. At a time in U.S. history when citizens most need to reaffirm what they share across their differences, the ignorance and contention now surrounding the First Amendment threaten to divide the nation and undermine our freedom.

The place to address this challenge is in our schools—the institutions most responsible for transmitting civic principles and virtues to each succeeding generation. Schools must not only teach the First Amendment, they must also find ways to model and apply the democratic first principles that they are charged with teaching. The rights and responsibilities of the First Amendment provide a much-needed framework for reaffirming and renewing the civic aims of education.

We envision First Amendment Schools as places where all members of the school community practice the civic habits of the heart necessary to sustain a free people that would remain free. Schools may carry out this mission in ways that vary greatly, depending on the age of the students, the size of the school, the needs of the local community, and whether the school is public or private. What unites First Amendment Schools is not one view of democratic education or the First Amendment, but an abiding commitment to teach and model the rights and responsibilities that undergird the First Amendment.

We propose the following four principles as foundational for creating and sustaining a First Amendment School:

I. Create Laboratories of Democratic Freedom

The future of the American republic depends upon instilling in young citizens an abiding commitment to the democratic first principles that sustain our experiment in liberty.

First Amendment Schools educate for freedom by providing students and all members of the school community with substantial opportunities to practice democracy. Knowledge of our framing documents and the structure and functions of government is important, but preparation for citizenship also requires virtues and skills acquired through participation in decision making. By practicing democracy, students confront the challenges of self-government, including the difficult task of balancing a commitment to individual rights with a concern for the common good.

First Amendment Schools create organizational structures, allocate time and resources, and develop policies and curricula designed to support and promote democratic learning communities. Pedagogical decisions, including instructional and assessment practices, extend opportunities for authentic learning that inform a citizen's understanding of the world beyond the classroom.

First Amendment Schools include administrators, teachers, staff, students, parents, and community members when making decisions about organization, governance, and curricula. When everyone is given a meaningful voice in shaping the life of the school, each has a real stake in creating and sustaining safe and caring learning communities. All members of the school community should have opportunities to exercise leadership, negotiate differences, propose solutions to shared problems, and practice other skills essential to thoughtful and effective participation in civic life.

II. Commit to Inalienable Rights and Civic Responsibility

Freedom of religion, speech, press, assembly, and petition are fundamental and inalienable rights. Every citizen has a civic responsibility to guard these rights for others.

First Amendment Schools are dedicated to educating for citizenship by teaching and modeling the democratic principles of the Constitution of the United States. Schools take this mission seriously by providing all members of the school community with daily opportunities to exercise their constitutional rights with responsibility.

First Amendment Schools uphold the principles of freedom and democracy when they protect religious-liberty rights, encourage freedom of expression, promote academic freedom, ensure a free student press, and support broad-based involvement in school governance. Acting responsibly, students, teachers, administrators, staff, parents, and community members can do much to uphold the rights of every citizen.

III. Include All Stakeholders

The First Amendment provides the civic framework of rights and responsibilities that enables Americans to work together for the common good in schools and communities.

First Amendment Schools affirm the importance of modeling the democratic process and upholding individual rights in the development of policies and curricula. Decisions are made after appropriate involvement of those affected by the decision and with due consideration for the rights of those holding dissenting views.

First Amendment Schools recognize that parents have the primary responsibility for the upbringing and education of their children. Everyone, however, shares an important stake in educating students for responsible citizenship in a free society. Students and schools benefit greatly when parents, students, educators, and community members work closely together to promote a shared vision of the First Amendment throughout the school culture and across the community.

IV. Translate Civic Education into Community Engagement

A society committed to freedom and justice for all requires citizens with the knowledge, virtues, and skills needed for active engagement in public life.

First Amendment Schools encourage active citizenship by giving students opportunities to translate civic education into community engagement. Active citizens are willing to participate in public life by addressing problems and issues in their communities, their nation, and the world.

First Amendment Schools provide opportunities for students to learn civic virtue and moral character throughout the school culture and across the curriculum. Students are encouraged to demonstrate an active concern for the welfare of others through service learning and civic problem solving. First Amendment rights are best guarded and civic responsibilities best exercised when citizens are actively engaged in building a more just and free society.

These guiding principles are offered as a shared vision for schools seeking to fulfill the promise of freedom under the First Amendment. Learning about freedom and justice, however important, can never be enough; educating for democratic citizenship must be more than an academic exercise. If we are to sustain and expand the American experiment in liberty, young citizens must acquire the civic skills and virtues needed to exercise their freedom *with* responsibility.

We invite all schools and every citizen to join us in affirming these principles and putting them into action. The time has come for all citizens to work together to renew their shared commitment to the civic principles and virtues vital to democracy, freedom, and the common good.

Frequently Asked Questions

The following five questions are among the most frequently asked about the First Amendment Schools project.

1. How can the First Amendment Schools project serve as a national resource?

The project's Web site, www.firstamendmentschools.org, is designed to provide resources that can help all schools implement the guiding principles of the First Amendment. These resources include instructional materials designed to enhance the teaching of the First Amendment; helpful information about other civic-minded organizations and programs; strategies to promote active citizenship; and First Amendment research tools, complete with primary sources and U.S. Supreme Court opinions. Additionally, the Web site provides access to consensus guidelines that inform schools of the contours of First Amendment case law and suggest how student rights can best be understood and affirmed.

2. What is the First Amendment Schools Grant Award Program?

In spring 2002, the First Amendment Schools project awarded grants to 11 schools—K–12, public and private—from communities across the country to participate in a multiyear collaboration. These project schools are working to teach and model more completely the democratic principles of the First Amendment. The grant awards are designed to support these efforts and to promote the knowledge, skills, and virtues required for thoughtful and effective participation in civic life.

The first network of First Amendment Schools will work to generate models of educating for democratic citizenship that other schools can adapt to their own communities. Other project schools will be added through subsequent grant programs in the coming years. Visit www. firstamendmentschools.org to find out more information about future rounds of grant awards.

3. What is required to successfully implement the guiding principles of the First Amendment Schools vision statement?

A school's commitment to democratic first principles and its capacity to act in accordance with the vision statement are important indicators of success. Factors that provide evidence of a school's readiness to engage in the project include

- How closely the school's core values align with the vision statement,
- How well ongoing schoolwide initiatives complement the project, and
- How extensively diverse voices are heard.

For example, how well do the guiding principles align with existing school programs such as character education, law-related education, and service learning initiatives? In addition to capacity and commitment, schools need to have a supportive infrastructure to extend their efforts. For that reason, central office administrators and school board members need to endorse and support the school's work with the project.

Schools must also give voice to students and teachers. The project's guiding principles affirm the centrality of the perspectives of students and teachers on the important issues of teaching and learning, school governance, and community building. The project affords schools a vehicle to address student alienation; to challenge the achievement gap with schooling that relates to students' experiences; and to champion students, who too often are an untapped resource in the community.

4. What is the role of the community in a First Amendment School?

The community, especially the parents, must understand what it means to live up to the guiding principles of the vision statement. They must be involved in discussions that result in policy changes and new school practices. Setting the boundaries on student freedom, creating a climate of respect for the rights of others, and learning to live with deep differences cannot be an assignment left to the school alone. Rather, community support for First Amendment Schools must start in the homes of students and spread across the neighborhoods. Then a commitment to the civic framework that flows from the First Amendment can be widely shared.

5. What evidence demonstrates a First Amendment School's success?

There are multiple measures of success. Progress can be measured by members of a school community against goals they have set for themselves. Indicators of successful implementation of the guiding principles of the FAS vision statement include the extent to which

- School policies align with the guiding principles.
- School leadership has been shared.
- Student exhibitions are part of a balanced assessment program.
- Service learning is a curriculum requirement.
- Survey results reveal both a heightened understanding of First Amendment principles and evidence of a deeper commitment to civic engagement.
- Parents and community members are involved in the life of the school.
- Students and faculty members value project goals.
- Central office administrators and school board members support the work of the school to model and teach First Amendment principles.

To realize success as a First Amendment School, all communities must be deliberate in their planning, execution, and evaluation. Schools need to organize a diverse FAS team that is dedicated to keeping the project moving forward amid the press of competing claims on time, energy, and resources. Schools must work to keep the community informed and engaged. And schools especially need to recognize that living up to the guiding principles of the vision statement requires focused leadership, broad-based support, and time.

For more information about "First Amendment Schools: Educating for Freedom and Responsibility," visit the project Web site at www.firstamendmentschools.org.

Project Schools

Here's a brief look at the first 11 First Amendment project schools.

Elementary Schools

Edith Bowen Laboratory School is a public school in Logan, Utah, with 299 students in grades K–5. Named for a state educator mentored by John Dewey, Edith Bowen, located on the campus of Utah State University, has always worked to expose its students to world and national issues. Taking advantage of Utah State's many departments to enhance its own course offerings, Edith Bowen has also benefited culturally from the university's partnerships with schools in Africa, China, and South America. The students have their own weekly TV show, and the school's curriculum has been designed to teach students about other cultures, values, and belief systems.

As a First Amendment project school, the school community looks forward, in the words of Principal Kaye Rhees, to "addressing areas of the curriculum which we have long felt were very important but sadly neglected." More specifically, the school plans to develop, in conjunction with Utah State's Elementary Education Department, a First Amendment Curriculum Resource Guide of replicable activities and lessons "to enhance our ability to disseminate to other elementary schools in the state."

As a lab school, Edith Bowen is in a unique position to do just that. In fact, Rhees is most excited about "tapping into the energy, creativity and enthusiasm of the approximately 600 preservice teachers training and teaching at our school each year. During their time with us, these teachers will have many opportunities to learn about what it means to model and apply First Amendment principles in classrooms. They would then be able to use this material as they begin their careers throughout the state and the nation."

"Not only will this project provide essential resources to make this vision a reality," said 5th grade teacher Dorothy Dobson, "but it will also provide the framework and the structures—planning, development, implementation and evaluation—to ensure it is done right."

Fairview Elementary School is a public school in Modesto, California, with 1,070 students in grades K–6. Imagine elementary school students dressed up as famous U.S. patriots and reading the Preamble to the Constitution on a late spring Friday morning, and you'll begin to gauge the mood at Fairview.

The occasion was a kickoff rally for the school's announcement as a First Amendment project school; in addition to the symbolic readings, the community planted a tree and held a rocket launch. Graduates came back to speak about their experiences, and everyone spoke about how they could live up to the spirit of the First Amendment.

The school's ideas range from the quaint to the controversial. For example, the administration will ask the students to identify a better way to distribute balls during recess. Yet the administration will also let the student body vote on the school uniform policy and inaugurate a Youth Court, where the kids themselves can take responsibility for settling their disputes.

"We want them to realize that they're part of a bigger picture," said Chano Flores, a 6th grade teacher at the school and the coordinator of the project on campus.

But the project isn't just about the students. "Just the other day," said Principal Rob Williams, "a parent came up to me and said, 'I've got a great idea. Every student that leaves Fairview must sign a contract pledging that they understand what it means to live up to the spirit of the First Amendment, and that they'll identify ways in which they can build on their experiences in middle school.'" Williams paused and commented, "That's what taking the First Amendment more seriously has done for my school."

Nursery Road Elementary School is a public school in Columbia, South Carolina, with 696 students in grades K–5. In the past 10 years, Nursery Road, like many schools across the nation, has experienced dramatic demographic changes in its school community. According to Principal Mary Kennerly, "Our free and reduced lunch population, our minority population, and our disabled population have more than doubled. We have also added tremendous diversity to our faith communities."

At some schools, these changes could provoke confusion about how to create a sense of community among an increasingly diverse student body. For Kennerly and the rest of the Nursery Road community, however, "These changes have enriched our schools in many ways and have contributed to our ability to teach and practice tolerance, to appreciate differences, and to examine our values."

The ways Nursery Road will continue to expand its practice of tolerance are myriad: A flag display will be hung in the school cafeteria, representing each country of origin that is represented in the student body; each class (grades 1–5) will produce a class newspaper at least once a year, featuring opposing viewpoints and stories selected by the students; and, in addition to ongoing staff development for the faculty, First Amendment–related materials and resources will be distributed to the parents through the school's newsletter and Parent Center.

Most important, though, the Nursery Road community can continue in its work to emphasize, in the words of Principal Kennerly, "the need to understand the power of the five freedoms of the First Amendment, the ways to use them to become powerful, and the responsibility to each other those powers bring. When we demonstrate that this is possible for my school community, for all of us in the First Amendment Schools project, and for everyone in education, I believe we are on the verge of something truly big."

Middle School Consortium

The First Amendment Schools project will fund a consortium of middle schools in Salt Lake City, Utah. Through their shared commitment to democratic education, the middle school consortium will work collaboratively to develop a First Amendment Schools reform model that can inform similar work in middle schools across the country. The consortium is composed of the following schools.

Butler Middle School is a public school with 1,158 students in grades 7–9. Beginning with the first day of the school year, Butler students learn about their school's "strong commitment to teach, preserve, and protect First Amendment freedoms." Teachers accomplish this by providing their classes with the central principles of the 3Rs (Rights, Responsibilities, Respect) project, a statewide initiative in Utah that prepares educators to teach religious liberty and religion in ways that are constitutionally permissible and educationally sound.[1]

What are the results of this work? A school community with a shared understanding of civic duty, and classrooms with a conflict management tool in place that the kids themselves can use and regulate.

Butler students begin this process by developing and voting on a class code at the start of the school year. "What they discover," said

Martha Ball, a lifelong educator and the Utah coordinator for the 3Rs project, "is that everyone is interested in one central principle: respect. Once that is established, I show them that our list of rules means nothing unless we understand the *responsibility* we each have to guard those rights for one another."

To strengthen its emphasis on the 3Rs, BMS created the Roger Williams Award, given annually to someone within the school community who exemplifies a commitment to civic responsibility. And as a First Amendment project school, Butler hopes to create a student senate. As a first step in that direction, the school assembled a diverse committee of community stakeholders over the summer to decide how the senate should operate.

"What we teach our students about all day," said Ball, "is how societies are formed and what people have historically held to be most important. But our students also need to understand what it means to *live* in a democracy, and what our ideals look like and feel like when they are applied throughout a community."

Ball continues, "After all, if our children aren't taught in schools how to exercise these rights with responsibility, then who will teach them, and where will they learn this valuable lesson?"

Northwest Middle School is a public school with 805 students in grades 7–8. Those who visit Northwest will forget any preconceived notions they may have had about Salt Lake City. The largest and most culturally diverse student population of all the middle schools in Salt Lake City's school district, Northwest has more than 39 different countries represented in its student body. Because of its diversity, Northwest has always stressed the message that "each student brings vitality to our culture."

The school's four pillars—school, peers, family, and community—reinforce this emphasis. Recognizing that nearly half their students speak Spanish at home, three Northwest teachers and the assistant principal studied for a month in Oaxaca, Mexico, to improve their language skills. More than a third of the school's teachers are studying to obtain the English as a Second Language endorsement.

Translators are available in six different languages to assist in parent-teacher conferences, and registration materials are available in 11 languages. "Each of these efforts on the part of the school," said Principal Rosemary Baron, "sends the message to [members of] the community that they are not just valued members of the community, but . . . potentially valuable participants in the active life of the school."

To help the students understand this crucial message, Northwest also supports *The Warrior Times*, a monthly publication of work written, edited, and published by the students. "Through their involvement with the paper," Baron said, "students learn to balance the rights of a free press and the responsibility of supporting a sound and safe learning environment.

"The Northwest staff has long held the belief that it takes an entire community to educate our children, and so we are dedicated to linking the school with the community patrons and neighborhood resources so we can make Northwest the most inviting place in town."

Center City School is a public charter school with 107 students in grades 7–10. Like its partners in the FAS consortium, the Center City School (CCS) provides a caring faculty, a diverse student body, and a fully democratic learning community. Like the other schools, Center City's staff has also had extensive training in the 3Rs project, and all three school communities hope to one day serve as reform models for middle schools and high schools across the country.

Unlike its counterparts, however, Center City School has not been around for a long time. In just three years, CCS experienced both the best and the worst features associated with beginning a school from scratch. Teacher Michelle Biery adds, "Although all stakeholders support our charter to create a student-centered democratic learning community, we find that all too often we fall short and the overall principles break down in individual classrooms."

That's why, as a First Amendment project school, the CCS community will focus on "learning how to establish First Amendment classrooms in order to apply the general principles of our school democracy more consistently in each and every classroom," according to Biery.

In addition, the staff at CCS will continue to work at fine-tuning curriculum, which executive director Sonia Woodbury describes as "integrated, project-based academic service-learning." To do so, CCS will look to provide its students with meaningful choices and tasks, consistent challenges, and active learning opportunities.

"The goal at CCS," said Woodbury, "is to create standards that promote intrinsic values in order to get out of the often ineffective rewards and punishments system. All CCS standards are measured in terms of personal bests.

"We believe that being equal does not mean being the same; rather, it means being valued the same regardless of differences. As a First Amendment project school, we will continue striving to create standards that value the individual and promote the common good of all students and adults in our learning community."

High Schools

Cesar Chavez Public Charter High School for Public Policy is a public charter school in Washington, D.C., with 231 students in grades 9–12. On May 30, 2002, the school honored its first 24 graduates. Some of the young men and women are the first in their families to graduate from high school. All of them are planning to attend college.

Amid the school's celebration, student Monique Jackson remembered its opening, four years earlier, in the basement of a Safeway supermarket. "I kind of felt like we were guinea pigs," she said. "Going in, I'm like, 'Are we [really] going to meet in this school?' "[2]

The school eventually moved out of the basement and is now housed in an old laundry building in northwest Washington. It is far from an ideal learning space. But part of what makes the Chavez community special is its refusal to be limited by what it doesn't have. As Shirley Monastra, executive director of the D.C. Public Charter School Resource Center, put it, "The accomplishment [here] is pretty incredible. There is a message here for all charter schools: You can do it."[3]

Chavez's success begins with its principal, Irasema Salcido. A veteran of the public school system, Ms. Salcido founded Chavez with a special focus on public policy. "It just seemed so obvious to me," she said, "to make sure kids in the District would have a way of being involved in the decision making of what's happening in the city. . . . Congress is here, think tanks are here—everything is here."[4]

To facilitate that activist spirit, the Chavez curriculum is infused with public policy standards to "help the students see themselves as members of the school, community, country, and world." According to Salcido, "Our curriculum teaches students to be critical thinkers, writers and public speakers. They are encouraged to question, debate, and express themselves."

Despite their successes so far, Salcido envisions Chavez's selection as an inaugural First Amendment project school as an opportunity to "develop a more student-centered disciplinary model that honors due process and reflects First Amendment principles.

"We've already come so far, but now it is time that we strengthen our culture so that we not only teach but reflect these rights in every aspect of the school."

Federal Hocking High School is a public school in Stewart, Ohio, with 429 students in grades 9–12. Federal Hocking, a small high school in rural Appalachia, has known for a decade what being a First Amendment School is all about.

Beginning in 1992, the school, under the leadership of principal George Wood, began a radical restructuring. For over a year, a wide range of community members met, trying to develop a model that would allow Federal Hocking to become a more democratic community.

As a result of that work, the school adopted a new mission statement, schedule, internship program, and senior graduation portfolios. And for the longer term, the school has had a greater number of its students go on to college, fewer disciplinary referrals, a higher graduation rate, and higher test scores.

Teachers were trained in Socratic seminars; students were given more free time during the day—and the responsibility to decide how to use it wisely; and the staff was entrusted with all major decisions regarding the curriculum.

Hocking's evolution reflects its community's support for the idea that the purpose of education is to serve—in Wood's words—as "democracy's finishing school, the last shared experience for citizens in our republic and the place where we can inculcate the virtues of civic life."

"The problem," Wood said, "is that students often find themselves preached to about such values instead of practicing them. That's why our efforts have been to focus on practice rather than exhortation. Everything we do—classroom teaching practices, school governance, student experiences both inside and out of school, assessment, even the organization of the school day—is done with an eye toward developing democratic community.

"Becoming a First Amendment project school, however, allows our community to review its efforts, examine additional ways to engage the school community, and push forward on our work to ensure that democracy is not just a slogan, but a way of life."

Harmony High School is an independent, nonsectarian school in Bloomington, Indiana, with 60 students in grades 9–12. For nearly 30 years, Harmony has worked to "sensitize young people to the delicate balance between individual growth and community responsibility."

Harmony's emphasis on building community is reflected in the school's schedule, which provides time for two-hour family meetings on Fridays. Chaired and scribed by the students themselves, the family meetings allow the entire Harmony community to discuss a wide range of issues, from developing new school policies, to reviewing achievements (both academic and social-emotional), to interviewing and selecting new teachers. Harmony is also one of 14 schools in Indiana and Vermont participating in the VISTA Service-Learning Democracy Project, a program that encourages schools to help students become more engaged in antipoverty activism by linking the work to the school's curriculum.[5]

Striving to inculcate the moral courage of individuals like Martin Luther King Jr., the Harmony community is especially excited to begin working more directly to extend the promise of freedom more fairly and fully to every citizen. As Principal Steve Bonchek said, "One of Dr. King's favorite expressions was 'A child shall lead them.' At Harmony, we recognize young people's ability to make significant contributions to society, and to inspire adults to do the same."

Hudson High School is a public school in Hudson, Massachusetts, with 893 students in grades 8–12. Hudson is a large, suburban public school that began its work as a First Amendment project school in the midst of an innovative experiment in school governance. "In the first year," says Principal John Stapelfeld, "the entire Hudson High School community implemented a governance model based on democratic town meetings."

To facilitate the meetings, Hudson unveiled a new school building, the design of which reflects the school community's belief in two concepts: First, that a cluster model of organization (approximately 125–150 students per cluster) engenders closer connections among the students and the staff; and, second, that the cluster model provides an ideal democratic governance structure and involves more students in the daily life of the school's operation.

How does it work? The clusters are organized thematically around broad areas of student academic interest. Clusters do not restrict students academically, and students still have full access to the school's curriculum. Weekly cluster meetings, however, provide time for students to develop service projects, hear from guest speakers, attend workshops relative to their cluster themes, and participate in schoolwide governance meetings. At the same time, the clusters are places where a real democratic community can be built, one that affirms First Amendment rights within the context of a larger, expanding school population.

As Sheldon Berman, Hudson's superintendent, characterizes his district's work, "Our goal at Hudson is to build a sense of community and to educate knowledgeable, ethical, and active citizens who care about others.

"Through character education, community service learning, and student engagement in democratic governance, we are supporting the active goal of helping young people become effective citizens who appreciate the importance of our First Amendment rights in sustaining our democracy," says Berman.

Lanier High School is a public school in Jackson, Mississippi, with 911 students in grades 9–12. Serving a largely African American population in the city of Jackson, Lanier aspires to be one of the best high schools in the nation. It has a "nucleus of students, parents, teachers, administrators and community leaders who have laid a foundation for Lanier's full potential in training young people to lead the nation," according to Principal Johnny Hughes. The school is already home to award-winning programs in music and athletics.

A team of students, faculty, administrators and community members is working hard to make Lanier a model of the First Amendment in action. "To help make this happen," says Hughes, "a committee of community stakeholders will begin with a needs assessment." All students will be asked to identify their wishes for the school, and an advisory group will make recommendations about school policies and governance to give students a greater voice in shaping the life of the school.

The essence of Lanier's work as a First Amendment project school is a multiyear process to organize the local community. Volunteers conduct meetings in parents' homes, informing them about the potential for change and identifying ways to encourage greater parental involvement.

The school also plans to expand its elective offerings with the help of local colleges. With the help of community partners, Lanier has launched a student newspaper and now offers students education in the rights and responsibilities of a free press.

"What makes Lanier special," says Susan Glisson, a community aide and the director of the Center for Racial Reconciliation at the University of Mississippi, "is its dedication to preparing students for leadership in the community and our nation. If America is to realize its own promises, all students must have the opportunity to realize their potential."

Ouida Atkins, a teacher at Lanier, describes the school's hopes for the First Amendment Schools project: "The revitalization of the school will spur the renewal of the community, which will in turn reinvigorate the school's wellbeing. If we can do this, then the school and the community will help to restore each other, and teach each other about the freedoms which make us all Americans—and which make such renewal possible."

Although the First Amendment Schools project works closely with its eleven project schools, it is dedicated to providing assistance and resources for *all* schools. To find out more about *First Amendment Schools: Educating for Freedom and Responsibility*, visit www.firstamendmentschools.org.

Notes

[1]For more information about the 3Rs project, visit the First Amendment Center's Web site at www.firstamendmentcenter.org.

[2]Blum, J. (2002, May 31). D.C. charter school learns and grows. *Washington Post.*

[3]Ibid.

[4]Abell, A. (1999, October). Against the odds. *Washingtonian*, p. 72.

[5]For more information on the VISTA service-learning democracy project, visit www.americorps.org.

➤ PART II ➤

CORE ISSUES FOR ALL SCHOOLS
TO CONSIDER

1. **Does the First Amendment apply to public schools?**
Yes. The First Amendment applies to all levels of government, including public schools. Although the courts have permitted school officials to limit the rights of students under some circumstances, the courts have also recognized that students—like all citizens—are guaranteed the rights protected by the First Amendment.

Earlier in our history, however, the First Amendment did not apply to the states—and thus not to public schools. When adopted in 1791, the First Amendment applied only to Congress and the federal government ("Congress shall make no law . . ."). This meant that when public schools were founded in the mid-19th century, students could not make First Amendment claims against the actions of school officials.

The restrictions on student speech lasted into the 20th century. In 1908, for example, the Wisconsin Supreme Court ruled that school officials could suspend two students for writing a poem ridiculing their teachers that was published in a local newspaper.[1] The Wisconsin court reasoned, "such power is essential to the preservation of order, decency, decorum, and good government in the public schools." And in 1915, the California Court of Appeals ruled that school officials could suspend a student for criticizing and "slamming" school officials in a student assembly speech.[2]

In fact, despite the passage of the 14th Amendment in 1868, which provides that "no state shall . . . deprive any person of life, liberty or property without due process of law . . . ", it was not until 1925, by way of the Supreme Court case of *Gitlow v. New York*, that the Supreme Court held that the freedom of speech guaranteed by the First Amendment is one of the "liberties" incorporated by the Due Process Clause of the 14th Amendment.

In subsequent cases, the Court has applied all of the freedoms of the First Amendment to the states—and thus to public schools—through the 14th Amendment. But not until 1943, in the flag-salute case of *West Virginia v. Barnette*,[3] did the U.S. Supreme Court explicitly extend First Amendment protection to students attending public schools.

The *Barnette* case began when several students who were Jehovah's Witnesses refused to salute the flag for religious reasons. School officials punished the students and their parents. The students then sued, claiming a violation of their First Amendment rights.

At the time that the students sued, Supreme Court precedent painted a bleak picture for their chances. Just a few years earlier, the Court had ruled in favor of a similar compulsory flag-salute law in *Minersville School District v. Gobitis*.[4] As the Court stated in that ruling, "national unity is the basis of national security."

However, the high court reversed itself in *Barnette*, holding that the free speech and free exercise of religion provisions of the First Amendment guarantee the right of students to be excused from the flag salute on grounds of conscience.

Writing for the majority, Justice Robert Jackson said that the Supreme Court must ensure "scrupulous protection of constitutional freedoms of the individual, if we are not to strangle the free mind at its source and teach youth to discount important principles of our government as mere platitudes."[5] The Court then warned of the dangers of coercion by government in oft-cited, eloquent language:

> If there is any fixed star in our Constitutional constellation, it is that no official, high or petty, can prescribe what shall be orthodox in politics, nationalism, religion, or other matters of opinion or force citizens to confess by word or act their faith therein.[6]

Religious Liberty: The Establishment Clause

2. The First Amendment says that the government may not "establish" religion. What does that mean in a public school?

The meaning of the Establishment Clause, often referred to as the "separation of church and state," has been much debated throughout our history. Does it require, as described in Thomas Jefferson's famous 1801 letter to the Danbury Baptists, a high "wall of separation"? Or may government support religion as long as no one religion is favored over others? How can school officials determine when they are violating the Establishment Clause?

In the last several decades, the Supreme Court has crafted several tests to determine when state action becomes "establishment" of religion. No one test is currently favored by a majority of the Court. Nevertheless, no matter what test is used, it is fair to say that the Court has been stricter about applying the Establishment Clause in public schools than in other government settings. For example, the Court has upheld legislative prayer, but struck down teacher-led prayer in public schools.[7] The Court applies the Establishment Clause more rigorously in public schools, mostly for two reasons: (1) students are impressionable young people, and (2) they are a "captive audience" required by the state to attend school.

When applying the Establishment Clause to public schools, the Court often emphasizes the importance of "neutrality" by school officials toward religion. This means that public schools may neither inculcate nor inhibit religion. They also may not prefer one religion over another—or religion over nonreligion.

3. If school officials are supposed to be "neutral" toward religion under the Establishment Clause, does that mean they should keep religion out of public schools?

No. By "neutrality" the Supreme Court does not mean hostility to religion. Nor does it mean ignoring religion. Neutrality means protecting the religious liberty rights of all students while simultaneously rejecting school endorsement or promotion of religion.

In 1995, 24 major religious and educational organizations defined religious liberty in public schools this way:

> Public schools may not inculcate nor inhibit religion. They must be places where religion and religious conviction are treated with fairness and respect.
>
> Public schools uphold the First Amendment when they protect the religious liberty rights of students of all faiths or none. Schools demonstrate fairness when they ensure that the curriculum includes study *about* religion as an important part of a complete education.[8]

4. Does the Establishment Clause apply to students in a public school?

The Establishment Clause speaks to what *government* may or may not do. It does not apply to the private speech of students. School officials should keep in mind the distinction between government (in this case "school") speech endorsing religion—which the Establishment Clause prohibits—and private (in this case "student") speech endorsing religion, which the free speech and free exercise clauses protect.[9]

Student religious expression may, however, raise Establishment Clause concerns when such expression takes place before a captive audience in a classroom or at a school-sponsored event. Students have the right to pray alone or in groups or to discuss their faith with classmates, as long as they aren't disruptive or coercive. And they may express their religious views in class assignments or discussions, as long as it is relevant to the subject under consideration and meets the requirements of the assignment.[10] But students don't have a right to force a captive audience to participate in religious exercises.

It isn't entirely clear under current law where teachers and administrators may draw a line limiting student religious expression before a captive audience in a classroom or school-sponsored event. In several recent cases, lower courts have deferred to the judgment of educators about when to limit the religious expression of students in a classroom or school setting. A general guide might be to allow students to express their religious views in a classroom or at a school event as long as they don't ask the audience to participate in a religious activity, use the opportunity to deliver a proselytizing sermon, or give the impression that their views are supported by or endorsed by the school.[11]

5. How can school officials tell when a planned school action or activity might violate the Establishment Clause?

Here are some questions that teachers and administrators should ask themselves when planning activities that may involve religious content (e.g., a holiday assembly in December):

- Do I have a distinct *educational* or civic purpose in mind? If so, what is it? (It may not be the purpose of the public school to promote or denigrate religion.)

- Have I done what I can to ensure that this activity is not designed in any way to either promote or inhibit religion?
- Does this activity serve the educational mission of the school or the academic goals of the course?
- Have I done what I can to ensure that no student or parent may be made to feel like an outsider, and not a full member of the community, by this activity?
- If I am teaching about religion, am I balanced, accurate, and academic in my approach?

Religious Liberty: The Free Exercise Clause

6. What does "free exercise" of religion mean under the First Amendment?

The Free Exercise Clause of the First Amendment states that the government "shall make no law . . . prohibiting the free exercise of religion." Although the text sounds absolute, "no law" does not always mean "no law." The Supreme Court has had to place some limits on the freedom to practice religion. To take an easy example cited by the Court in one of its landmark "free exercise" cases, the First Amendment would not protect the practice of human sacrifice even if some religion required it.[12] In other words, while the freedom to believe is absolute, the freedom to act on those beliefs is not.

But where may government draw the line on the practice of religion? The courts have struggled with the answer to that question for much of our history. Over time, the Supreme Court developed a test to help judges determine the limits of free exercise. First fully articulated in the 1963 case of *Sherbert v. Verner,* this test is sometimes referred to as the *Sherbert* or "compelling interest" test. The test has four parts: two that apply to any person who claims that his freedom of religion has been violated, and two that apply to the government agency accused of violating those rights.

For the individual, the court must determine

- whether the person has a claim involving a sincere religious belief, and
- whether the government action is a substantial burden on the person's ability to act on that belief.

If these two elements are established, then the government must prove

- that it is acting in furtherance of a "compelling state interest," and
- that it has pursued that interest in the manner least restrictive, or least burdensome, to religion.[13]

The Supreme Court, however, curtailed the application of the *Sherbert* test in the 1990 case of *Employment Division v. Smith*. In that case, the Court held that a burden on free exercise no longer had to be justified by a compelling state interest if the burden was an unintended result of laws that are generally applicable.[14]

After *Smith*, only laws (or government actions) that (1) were intended to prohibit the free exercise of religion, or (2) violated other constitutional rights, such as freedom of speech, were subject to the compelling interest test. For example, a state could not pass a law stating that Native Americans are prohibited from using peyote, but it could accomplish the same result by prohibiting the use of peyote by everyone.

In the wake of *Smith*, many religious and civil liberties groups have worked to restore the *Sherbert* test—or compelling interest test—through legislation. These efforts have been successful in some states. In other states, the courts have ruled that the compelling interest test is applicable to religious claims by virtue of the state's own constitution. In many states, however, the level of protection for free exercise claims is uncertain.

Accommodating the Religious Needs and Requirements of Students

7. How should school officials determine when they must accommodate a religious liberty claim under the Free Exercise Clause?

As noted previously, the application of the *Sherbert* or compelling interest test was sharply curtailed by the 1990 Supreme Court decision, *Employment Division v. Smith*. But some states—such as Florida, Texas, and Connecticut—have passed laws requiring the use of a "compelling interest test" in free exercise cases. Moreover, since most cases involving public schools involve more than one constitutional right (e.g., the religion claim can be linked with a parental right or free speech claim), some might argue that the compelling interest test must be used even under *Smith*.

Regardless of how this is eventually settled in the courts, public schools fulfill the *spirit* of the First Amendment when they use the *Sherbert* test to accommodate the religious claims of students and parents where feasible.

8. May students be excused from parts of the curriculum for religious reasons?

As good educational policy, school officials, whenever possible, should try to accommodate the requests of parents and students for excusal for religious reasons from specific classroom discussions or activities.

In "A Parent's Guide to Religion in the Public Schools," the National PTA and the First Amendment Center give the following advice concerning excusal requests:

> If focused on a specific discussion, assignment, or activity, such
> requests should be routinely granted to strike a balance between
> the student's religious freedom and the school's interest in provid-
> ing a well-rounded education. If it is proved that particular lessons
> substantially burden a student's free exercise of religion and if the
> school cannot prove a compelling interest in requiring attendance,
> some courts may require the school to excuse the student.[15]

It is important for teachers and administrators to ask themselves the questions posed in the *Sherbert* test as they make decisions about how to accommodate excusal requests.

Let's look at one example of how the *Sherbert* test might be used in a public school: If parents ask for their child to be excused from reading a particular book for religious reasons, the teacher and administrator should first ask if the request is based on a sincere religious belief. Note that the religious belief need not be rational or even sensible to the school official. It need only be sincere. When parents and students take the time to object to a particular reading or activity, they are usually sincere.

Next, school officials must determine whether or not reading the assigned book would constitute a "substantial burden" on the student's religious liberty rights. This is more difficult to determine, but in most cases, if the parent and student find the book deeply offensive to their religious beliefs, then making the student read the book would likely be a substantial burden on her religious freedom.

The inquiry then shifts to the school, which needs to demonstrate it has a "compelling state interest"—described by the Supreme Court as "an interest of the highest order."[16] Clearly, public schools have a compelling interest in the education and welfare of children. In this instance, for example, the school clearly has a compelling interest in teaching the student to read. But the last part of the test requires that the school pursue that interest in a manner *least restrictive* of a complaining family's religion. Thus the school may have an interest in teaching the student to read, but can that interest be accomplished without making the student read that particular book? In other words, the school should choose a course of action that does not violate the student's religion if such a course of action is available and feasible for the school.

This may be easy to do if a student and parent object to a particular reading assignment on religious grounds. When this happens, the teacher may simply assign an alternate selection. If, however, requests for exemption become too frequent or too burdensome for the school, a court will probably find the school's refusal to offer additional alternatives to be justified.

9. How should school officials respond to requests for accommodation of religious practices during the school day?

Enforcing adherence to religious requirements, such as special diet or dress, is the responsibility of parents and students, not of the public school.

However, some religious requirements or practices may conflict with school practices or schedules. In those cases, school officials should try to accommodate these needs if feasible. Let's look at a few examples.

Jehovah's Witnesses may ask that their children be excused from birthday or holiday activities. Teachers should honor these requests by planning alternate activities or time in the library for affected students.

The school may have a "no caps" policy because of concerns about gang activity. But exemptions should be made for Orthodox Jews and other students who must wear head coverings for religious reasons.

Muslim students may request permission to pray in a designated area during the school day. If space is available, and if the educational process isn't disrupted, schools should try to grant this request. Schools may not set up "prayer rooms," but they may find ways to allow students to meet their religious obligations.

Students of various faiths may have dietary restrictions. Under the Establishment Clause, schools may not prepare special foods to fulfill a student's particular religious requirements. But schools may help their religious students and others by labeling foods and offering a variety of choices at every meal.

As noted in the answer to Question 6, it is not entirely clear under current law how much accommodation schools must make for "free exercise" claims. And the legal requirement to accommodate requests may vary from state to state, depending on state law and state constitutional provisions. Nevertheless, schools uphold the principles of religious liberty and the spirit of the First Amendment when they make every effort to accommodate religious requests for exemption from school policies or practices.

10. May students be absent for religious holidays?

Schools should have policies concerning absences that take into account the religious needs and requirements of students. Students should be allowed a reasonable number of excused absences, without penalties, to observe religious holidays within their traditions. Students may be asked to complete makeup assignments or tests in conjunction with such absences.

School Prayer and Student Religious Expression

11. Is it legal for students to pray in public schools?

Yes. Contrary to popular myth, the Supreme Court has never outlawed "prayer in schools." Students are free to pray alone or in groups, as long as such prayers are not disruptive and do not infringe upon the rights of others. But this right "to engage in voluntary prayer does not include the right to have a captive audience listen or to compel other students to participate."[17]

What the Supreme Court has repeatedly struck down are state-sponsored or state-organized prayers in public schools.

The Supreme Court has made clear that prayers organized or sponsored by a public school—even when delivered by a student—violate the First Amendment, whether in a classroom, over the public address system, at a graduation exercise, or even at a high school football game.[18]

12. May students share their religious faith in public schools?

Yes. Students are free to share their faith with their peers, as long as the activity is not disruptive and does not infringe upon the rights of others.

School officials possess substantial discretion to impose rules of order and other pedagogical restrictions on student activities. But they may not structure or administer such rules to discriminate against religious activity or speech.

This means that students have the same right to engage in individual or group prayer and religious discussion during the school day as they do to engage in other comparable activities.[19] For example, students may read their Bibles or other scriptures, say grace before meals, and pray before tests.

Generally, students may share their faith or pray in a nondisruptive manner when not engaged in school activities or instruction, subject to the rules that normally pertain in the applicable setting. Specifically, students in informal settings, such as cafeterias and hallways, may pray and discuss their religious views with each other, subject to the same rules of order as applied to other student activities and speech.[20]

Students may also speak to and attempt to persuade their peers about religious topics just as they do with regard to political topics. School officials, however, should intercede if a student's speech begins to constitute harassment of a student or group of students.

Students may also participate in before- or after-school events with religious content, such as "See You at the Pole" gatherings, on the same terms as they may participate in other noncurriculum activities on school premises. School officials may neither discourage nor encourage participation in such an event.

Keep in mind, however, that the right to engage in voluntary prayer or religious discussion free from discrimination does not necessarily include the right to preach to a "captive audience," like an assembly, or to compel other students to participate. To that end, teachers and school administrators should work to ensure that no student is in any way coerced—either psychologically or physically—to participate in a religious activity.[21]

13. May students express their beliefs about religion in classroom assignments or at school-sponsored events?

Yes, within limits. Generally, if it is relevant to the subject under consideration and meets the requirements of the assignment, students should be allowed to express their religious or nonreligious views during a class discussion, as part of a written assignment, or as part of an art activity.

This does not mean, however, that students have the right to compel a captive audience to participate in prayer or listen to a proselytizing sermon. School officials should allow students to express their views about religion, but should draw the line when students wish to invite others to participate in religious practices or want to give a speech that is primarily proselytizing. There is no bright legal line that can be drawn between permissible and impermissible student religious expression in a classroom assignment or at a school-sponsored event. In recent lower court decisions, judges have deferred to the judgment of educators to determine where to draw the line.[22]

14. Is it constitutional for a public school to require a "moment of silence?"

Yes, if, and only if, the moment of silence is genuinely neutral. A neutral moment of silence that does not encourage prayer over any other quiet, contemplative activity will not be struck down, even though some students may choose to use the time for prayer.[23]

If a moment of silence is used to promote prayer, it will be struck down by the courts. In *Wallace v. Jaffree* the Supreme Court struck down an Alabama "moment of silence" law because it was enacted for the express purpose of promoting prayer in public schools.[24] At the same time, however, the Court indicated that a moment of silence would be constitutional if it is genuinely neutral. Many states and local school districts currently have moment-of-silence policies in place.

15. May a student pray at graduation exercises or at other school-sponsored events?

This is one of the most confusing and controversial areas of the current school prayer debate. While the courts have not clarified all of the issues, some are clearer than others.

For instance, inviting outside adults to lead prayers at graduation ceremonies is clearly unconstitutional. The Supreme Court resolved this issue in the 1992 case *Lee v. Weisman*, which began when prayers were delivered by clergy at a middle school's commencement exercises in Providence, Rhode Island.[25] The school designed the program, provided for the invocation, selected the clergy, and even supplied guidelines for the prayer.

Therefore, the Supreme Court held that the practice violated the First Amendment's prohibition against laws "respecting an establishment of religion." The majority based its decision on the fact that (1) it is not the business of schools to sponsor or organize religious activities, and (2) students who might have objected to the prayer were subtly coerced to participate. This psychological coercion was not resolved by the fact that attendance at the graduation was "voluntary." In the Court's view, few students would want to miss the culminating event of their academic career.

A murkier issue is student-initiated, student-led prayer at school-sponsored events. On one side of the debate are those who believe that student religious speech at graduation ceremonies or other school-sponsored events violates the Establishment Clause. They are bolstered by the 2000 Supreme Court case of *Santa Fe v. Doe*,[26] which involved the traditional practice of student-led prayers over the public address system before high school football games.

According to the district, students would vote each year on whether they would have prayers at home football games. If they decided to do so, they would then select a student to deliver the prayers. To ensure fairness, the school district said it required these prayers to be "non-sectarian [and] non-proselytizing."

A 6 to 3 majority of the Supreme Court still found the Santa Fe policy to be unconstitutional. The majority opinion first pointed out that constitutional rights are not subject to a vote. To the contrary, the judges said the purpose of the Bill of Rights was to place some rights beyond the reach of political majorities. Thus, the Constitution protects a person's right to freedom of speech, press, or religion even if no one else agrees with the ideas a person professes.[27]

In addition, the Court found that having a student, as opposed to an adult, lead the prayer did not solve the constitutional dilemma. A football game is still a school-sponsored event, they held, and the school was still coercing the students, however subtly, to participate in a religious exercise.[28]

Finally, the Court ruled that the requirement that the prayer be "non-sectarian" and "non-proselytizing" not only failed to solve the problems addressed in *Lee v. Weisman*, it may have aggravated them.[29] In other words, while some might like the idea of an inclusive, nonsectarian "civil" religion, others might not. To some people, the idea of nonsectarian prayer is offensive, as though a prayer were being addressed "to whom it may concern." Moreover, the Supreme Court made clear in *Lee v. Weisman* that even nondenominational prayers or generic religiosity may not be established by the government at graduation exercises.[30]

Another thorny part of this issue is determining whether a particular prayer tends to proselytize. Such determinations entangle school officials in religious matters in unconstitutional ways. In fact, one Texas school district was sued for discriminating against those who wished to offer more sectarian prayers at graduation exercises.

On the other side of this debate are those who contend that not allowing students to express themselves religiously at school events violates the students' free exercise of religion and free speech rights.

Case law indicates, however, that this may be true only in instances involving strictly student speech, and not when a student is conveying a message controlled or endorsed by the school. As the 11th Circuit case of *Adler v. Duval County* suggests, it would seem possible for a school to provide a forum for student speech within a graduation ceremony when prayer or religious speech might occur.[31]

For example, a school might allow the valedictorian or class president an opportunity to speak during the ceremony. If such a student chose to express a religious viewpoint, it seems unlikely it would be found unconstitutional unless the school had suggested or otherwise encouraged the religious speech.[32] In effect, this means that in order to distance itself from the student's remarks, the school must create a limited open forum for student speech in the graduation program.

Again, there is a risk for school officials in this approach. By creating a limited open forum for student speech, the school may have to accept almost anything the student wishes to say. Although the school would not be required to allow speech that was profane, sexually explicit, defamatory, or disruptive, the speech could include political or religious views offensive to many, as well as speech critical of school officials.

If school officials feel a solemnizing event needs to occur at a graduation exercise, a neutral moment of silence might be the best option. This way, everyone could pray, meditate, or silently reflect on the previous year's efforts in her own way.

16. Are baccalaureate services constitutional?

Yes, if they are privately sponsored. Public schools may not sponsor religious baccalaureate ceremonies. But parents, faith groups, and other community organizations are free to hold such services for students who wish to attend. The school may announce the baccalaureate in the same way it announces other community events. If the school allows community groups to rent or otherwise use its facilities after hours, then a privately sponsored baccalaureate may be held on campus under the same terms offered to any private group.

Student Extracurricular Clubs and Activities

17. May students form religious or political clubs in secondary public schools?

Yes, if the school allows other extracurricular (noncurriculum-related) groups. Although schools do not have to open or maintain a limited open forum, once they do, they may not discriminate against a student group because of the content of its speech.

The Equal Access Act (EAA), passed by Congress in 1984 and upheld as constitutional by the Supreme Court in 1990, makes it "unlawful for any public secondary school that receives federal funds and which has a limited open forum to deny equal access or a fair opportunity to, or discriminate against, any students who wish to conduct a meeting within that limited open forum on the basis of the religious, political, philosophical, or other content of the speech at such meetings."

The EAA covers student-initiated and student-led clubs in secondary schools with a limited open forum. According to the act, "non-school persons may not direct, conduct, or regularly attend activities of student groups."

A "limited open forum" is created whenever a public secondary school provides an opportunity for one or more "noncurriculum related groups" to meet on school premises during noninstructional time. The forum created is said to be "limited" because only the school's students can take advantage of it.

18. What is a "noncurriculum related student group" under the Equal Access Act?

In the 1990 Supreme Court case of *Westside Community Schools v. Mergens*,[33] the Court interpreted a "noncurriculum related student group" to mean "any student group [or club] that does not directly relate to the body of courses offered by the school."

According to the Court, a student group directly relates to a school's curriculum only if (1) the subject matter of the group is actually taught, or will soon be taught, in a regularly offered course; (2) the subject matter of the group concerns the body of courses as a whole; or (3) participation in the group is required for a particular course or results in academic credit.

As examples, the Court identified three groups that were noncurriculum related at the Westside schools: (1) a scuba club, (2) a chess club, and (3) a service club. The Court found these groups to be noncurriculum related because they did not meet the criteria set forth above. Conversely, the French club was found to be curriculum related since the school regularly offered French classes.

Subject to review by the courts, local school authorities must determine whether a student group is curriculum related or not. Schools may not, however, substitute their own definition of "noncurriculum related" for the definition provided by the Court.

If the school violates the EAA, an aggrieved person may bring suit in U.S. district court to compel the school to observe the law. Although violations of equal access will not result in the loss of federal funds, the school could be liable for damages and the attorney's fees of a student group that successfully challenges a denial to meet under the act.

19. What control does the school retain over student meetings in a limited open forum?

The EAA does not take away a school's authority to establish reasonable time, place, and manner regulations for a limited open forum. For example, a school may establish for its student clubs a reasonable meeting time on any one school day, a combination of days, or all school days. It may assign the rooms in which student groups can meet. It may enforce order and discipline during the meetings. The key, however, is that the school's time, place, and manner regulations must be uniform, nondiscriminatory, and neutral in viewpoint.

20. May teachers or other school employees participate in student religious clubs?

No. The EAA states that "employees or agents of the school or government are present at religious meetings only in a nonparticipatory capacity."

For insurance purposes, or because of state law or local school policy, teachers or other school employees are commonly required to be present during student meetings. But if the student club is religious in nature, school employees may be present as monitors only. Such custodial supervision does not constitute sponsorship or endorsement of the group by the school.

21. May religious leaders or other outside adults attend the meetings of student clubs?

Yes, if the students invite these visitors and if the school does not have a policy barring all guest speakers or outside adults from extracurricular club meetings. However, the EAA states that the nonschool persons "may not direct, conduct, control, or regularly attend activities of student groups."[34]

22. May noncurriculum-related student groups use school media to advertise their meetings?

Yes. A student group may use school media—such as the public address system, school paper, and school bulletin board—as long as other noncurriculum-related student groups are allowed to do so. Any policy concerning the use of school media must be applied to all noncurriculum-related student groups in a nondiscriminatory manner. Schools, however, may issue disclaimers indicating that extracurricular student groups are not school sponsored or endorsed.

23. May the school exclude any student extracurricular group?

Yes. According to guidelines endorsed by a broad coalition of educational and religious liberty organizations, "student groups that are unlawful, or that materially and substantially interfere with the orderly conduct of educational activities, may be excluded. However, a student group cannot be denied equal access simply because its ideas are unpopular. Freedom of speech includes the ideas the majority may find repugnant."[35]

Most schools require students to submit a statement outlining the purpose and nature of the proposed club. School officials do not have to allow meetings of groups that advocate violence or hate or engage in illegal activity. This does not mean, however, that schools may bar students from forming clubs to discuss controversial social and legal issues such as abortion or sexual orientation. Again, student-initiated clubs in a limited open forum may not be barred on the basis of the viewpoint of their speech.

Some schools require parental permission for students to join an extracurricular club. Although this step is not required by the EAA, it has enabled schools to keep the forum open in communities where student clubs have sparked controversy.

24. Do students have the right to form religious or political clubs below the secondary level?

Probably not, but current law is unclear on this point. Although the EAA does not apply to public schools below the secondary level, some have argued that the Free Speech Clause protects the right of middle school students to form religious or political clubs on an equal footing with other student-initiated clubs. When the EAA was debated in Congress, many lawmakers expressed doubt that young children could form religious clubs that would be truly initiated and led by students. In addition, younger students are more likely to view religious clubs meeting at the school as "school sponsored." For these and other reasons, Congress declined to apply equal access below the secondary level.

May administrators permit students to form religious or political clubs in middle schools, even if the law does not require that such clubs be allowed? Again, current law is unclear on this point. If school officials decide to allow middle school students to form religious or political clubs, then at the very least the school should have in place a clear policy and ground rules for the clubs, consistent with the EAA, and explain that the student clubs are not school sponsored.

25. May students solicit funds at school?

Yes, a school may allow students to solicit funds, but students have no independent right to do so. Although courts have seldom addressed this question, the few cases that are available make clear that schools may prohibit students from soliciting funds while at school.

In the seminal case on this issue, the Second Circuit Court of Appeals ruled in *Katz v. McAulay* that the Union Free School District's policy prohibiting solicitation on school grounds did not violate the First Amendment rights of students. The court found that students were a captive audience during the school day, and to allow them to be solicited, by outside adults or even other students, would be intrusive to students and act as a distraction from the educational mission of the school.[36]

26. What First Amendment rights do students retain at school-sponsored social events?

At school-sponsored social events, the conduct and regulation of students have constitutional implications.

In particular, issues involving gay and lesbian students wishing to bring a date of the same sex to school social events have raised controversy. In one case, for example, a senior male student wanted to bring a male date to the senior banquet. The school rejected the student's request, citing fears of violence against the couple.

The school's rationale, however, did not convince the court, which found that a same-sex couple attending a school function was an expressive act, and as such was protected by the First Amendment. As to claims of possible violence, the judge stated:

> I have concluded that even a legitimate interest in school discipline does not outweigh a student's right to peacefully express his views in an appropriate time, place, and manner. To rule otherwise would completely subvert free speech in the schools by granting other students a "heckler's veto," allowing them to decide through prohibited and violent methods what speech will be heard. The First Amendment does not tolerate mob rule by unruly school children.[37]

Teaching About Religion

27. Is it constitutional to teach about religion in a public school?

Yes. In the 1960s-school-prayer cases that prompted rulings against state-sponsored school prayer and devotional Bible reading, the U.S. Supreme Court indicated that public school education may include teaching about religion. In *Abington v. Shempp*, Associate Justice Tom Clark wrote for the Court:

> [I]t might well be said that one's education is not complete without a study of comparative religion or the history of religion and its relationship to the advancement of civilization. It certainly may be said that the Bible is worthy of study for its literary and historic qualities. Nothing we have said here indicates that such study of the Bible or of religion, when presented objectively as part of a secular program of education may not be effected consistently with the First Amendment.[38]

28. What does it mean to teach "about" religion under the First Amendment?

The key is to understand the difference between the teaching *of* religion—that is, religious indoctrination or faith formation—and teaching *about* religion—that is, the academic study of religion. The distinction may be summarized this way:

- The school's approach to religion is *academic*, not *devotional*.
- The school strives for student *awareness* of religions, but does not press for student *acceptance* of any religion.
- The school sponsors study *about* religion, not the *practice* of religion.
- The school may *expose* students to a diversity of religious views, but may not *impose* any particular view.
- The school *educates* about all religions; it does not *promote* or *denigrate* religion.
- The school *informs* students about various beliefs; it does not seek to make students *conform* to any particular belief.[39]

Classroom discussions concerning religion must be conducted in an environment that is free of advocacy on the part of the teacher. Students may express their own religious views, as long as such expression is germane to the discussion. But public school teachers are required by the First Amendment to teach about religion fairly and objectively, neither promoting nor denigrating religion in general or specific religious groups in particular. When discussing religion, many teachers must guard against injecting personal religious beliefs by teaching through attribution (e.g., by using such phrases as "most Buddhists believe . . . " or "according to the Hebrew scriptures . . .").

29. Why should study about religion be included in the curriculum?

Growing numbers of educators throughout the United States recognize that study about religion in social studies, literature, art, music, and other subjects is an important part of a well-rounded education. "Religion in the Public School Curriculum: Questions and Answers," issued by a coalition of seventeen major religious and educational organizations, describes the importance of religion in the curriculum this way:

> Because religion plays a significant role in history and society, study about religion is essential to understanding both the nation and the

world. Omission of facts about religion can give students the false impression that the religious life of humankind is insignificant or unimportant. Failure to understand even the basic symbols, practices, and concepts of the various religions makes much of history, literature, art, and contemporary life unintelligible.

Study about religion is also important if students are to value religious liberty, the first freedom guaranteed in the Bill of Rights. Moreover, knowledge of the roles of religion in the past and present promotes cross-cultural understanding essential to democracy and world peace.[40]

The following principles should be kept in mind as public schools address teaching about religion:

- The Supreme Court has made clear that study *about* religion in public schools is constitutional.
- Inclusion of study about religion is important for students to be broadly educated about some of the major ways in which people understand the world.
- Religion must be taught objectively and neutrally. The purpose of public schools is to educate students about a variety of religious traditions, not to promote or indoctrinate them into any tradition.[41]

30. Does the First Amendment require that "equal time" be given to all faiths in the public school curriculum?

No. The grade level of the students and the academic requirements of the course should determine which religions to study and how much to discuss about religion.

In the elementary grades, the study of family, community, culture, history, literature, the nation, and other themes and topics should naturally involve some discussion of religion. Elementary students are introduced to the basic ideas and practices of the world's major religions by focusing on the generally agreed-upon meanings of religious faiths—the core beliefs and symbols as well as important figures and events. Stories drawn from various faiths may be included among the wide variety of stories read by students, but the material selected must always be presented in the context of learning about religion.

On the secondary level, the social studies, literature, and the arts offer opportunities for the inclusion of study about religions, their ideas, and practices. The academic needs of the course should determine which religions are studied and how much time is required to provide an adequate understanding of the concepts and practices under consideration.

In a U.S. history course, for example, some faith communities may be given more time than others simply because of their predominant influence on the development of the nation. In world history, a variety of faiths must be studied, based on the regions of the world, in order to understand the various civilizations and cultures that have shaped history and society.

Fair and balanced study about religion on the secondary level includes critical thinking about historical events involving religious traditions. Religious beliefs have been at the heart of some of the best and worst developments in human history. The full historical record, and various interpretations of it, should be available for analysis and discussion. Using primary sources whenever possible allows students to work directly with the historical record.

Of course, fairness and balance in U.S. or world history and literature is difficult to achieve, given the brief treatment of religious ideas and events in most textbooks and the limited time available in the course syllabus. Teachers will need scholarly supplemental resources that enable them to cover the required material within the allotted time, while enriching the discussion with study of religion. In fact, some schools now offer electives in religious studies to provide additional opportunities for students to study about the major faith communities in greater depth.

Overall, the curriculum should include all major voices, and many minor ones, in an effort to provide the best possible education.

31. Is it legal to invite guest speakers to help teach about religion?

Yes, if the school district policy allows guest speakers in the classroom.

If a guest speaker is invited, care should be taken to find someone with the academic background necessary for an objective and scholarly discussion of the historical period and the religion under consideration. Faculty from local colleges and universities often make excellent guest speakers, or they can recommend others who might be appropriate for working with students in a public school setting.

Religious leaders in the community may also be a resource. Remember, however, that they have commitments to their own faith. Above all else, be certain that any guest speaker understands the First Amendment guidelines for teaching about religion in public education and is clear about the academic nature of the assignment.

32. What is the relationship between teaching about religion and character education?

The First Amendment requires that public schools be neutral toward religion—and that means teaching about religions in ways that are objective. But this does not mean that schools should be neutral about the moral values widely shared in our society. Teachers can and should teach the personal and civic virtues, such as honesty, caring, fairness, and integrity, that are widely held in our society.

Public school teachers should teach good character and citizenship—but they must do so without either invoking religious authority or denigrating the religious or philosophical commitments of students and parents. Character education cannot use religious exercises or teachings to nurture the development of character. At the same time, however, character education should not implicitly convey the idea that religion is irrelevant to morality. In teaching core moral values, teachers should make clear that people's moral convictions are often grounded in religious traditions.

Parents are the first and most important moral educators of their children. Thus public schools should develop character education programs only in close partnership with parents and the community. Local communities need to work together to identify the core moral and civic virtues that they wish to be taught and modeled in all aspects of school life. For guidance on how to develop and implement a comprehensive, quality character education program, contact the Character Education Partnership in Washington, D.C.[42]

Religious Holidays

33. How should religious holidays be treated in the classroom?

Teachers must be alert to the distinction between teaching about religious holidays, which is permissible, and celebrating religious holidays, which is not. Recognition of and information about holidays may focus on how and when they are celebrated, their origins, histories, and generally agreed-upon meanings. If the approach is objective and sensitive, neither promoting nor inhibiting religion, this study can foster understanding and mutual respect for differences in belief. Teachers may not, however, use the study of religious holidays as an opportunity to proselytize or otherwise inject their personal religious beliefs into the discussion.

The use of religious symbols is permissible as a teaching aid or resource, provided they are used only as examples of cultural or religious heritage. Religious symbols may be displayed only on a temporary basis as part of the academic lesson being studied. Students may choose to create artwork with religious symbols, but teachers should not assign or suggest such creations.

The use of art, drama, music, or literature with religious themes is permissible if it serves a sound educational goal in the curriculum. Such themes should be included on the basis of their academic or aesthetic value, and not as a vehicle for promoting religious beliefs. For example, sacred music may be sung or played as part of the academic study of music. School concerts that present a variety of selections may include religious music. Concerts should, however, avoid programs dominated by religious music, especially when these coincide with a particular religious holiday.

34. What should schools do in December?

Decisions about what to do in December should begin with the understanding that public schools may not sponsor religious devotions or celebrations; study about religious holidays does not extend to religious worship or practice.

Does this mean that all seasonal activities must be banned from the schools? Probably not, and in any event, such an effort would be unrealistic. The resolution would seem to lie in devising holiday programs that serve an educational purpose for all students—programs that make no students feel excluded or forcibly identified with a religion not their own.

Holiday concerts in December may appropriately include music related to Christmas, Hanukkah, and other religious traditions, but religious music should not dominate. Any dramatic productions should emphasize the cultural aspects of the holidays. Conversely, nativity pageants or plays portraying the Hanukkah miracle would not be appropriate in the public school setting.

In short, while recognizing the holiday season, none of the school activities in December should have the purpose, or effect, of promoting or inhibiting religion.

35. How should religious objections to holidays be handled?

Students from certain religious traditions may ask to be excused from classroom discussions or activities related to particular holidays. For example, holidays such as Halloween and Valentine's Day, which are considered by many people to be secular, are viewed by others as having religious overtones.

Excusal requests may be especially common in the elementary grades, where holidays are often marked by parties and similar nonacademic activities. Such requests should be routinely granted in the interest of creating good policy and upholding the religious liberty principles of the First Amendment.

In addition, some parents and students may make requests for excusals from discussions of certain holidays, even when these holidays are treated from an academic perspective. If these requests are focused on a limited, specific discussion, administrators should grant such requests, in order to strike a balance between the student's religious freedom and the school's interest in providing a well-rounded education.

Administrators and teachers should understand, however, that a policy or practice of excusing students from a specific activity or discussion may not be used as a rationale for school sponsorship of religious celebration or worship for the remaining students.

Use of School Facilities by Outside Groups

36. Do outside groups have the right to distribute material on campus?

No. Adults from outside the school do not have the right to distribute materials to students in a public school. May school officials allow them to do so? Although this area of the law is somewhat unclear, it is fair to say that schools should exercise great caution before giving an outside group access to students during the school day. Giving some groups access opens the door to others. Moreover, if a religious group is allowed to actively distribute religious literature to students on campus, that activity is likely to violate the Establishment Clause.

At least one lower court has upheld "passive" distribution of materials by religious and other community groups. Note that in this case the group left materials for students to browse through and take only if they wished. Also, a wide variety of community groups were given similar privileges, and the school posted a disclaimer explaining that the school did not endorse these materials. Under those conditions, this court allowed passive distribution, but only in a secondary school setting.[43]

Schools may announce community events or meetings of groups—including religious groups—that work with students. All of these groups should be treated in the same way. The school should make clear that it does not sponsor these community groups.

37. May public school facilities be used by outside community groups during nonschool hours?

Generally, yes. Although schools are not required to open their facilities to any community group, when they do, all groups—including those with a religious viewpoint—must be treated the same.[44] In fact, the Supreme Court has ruled unanimously that schools may not discriminate on the basis of religious viewpoint when making their facilities available to community groups during nonschool hours.[45]

Schools may, of course, impose reasonable, content-neutral restrictions on the use of their facilities. For example, schools may decide when meetings may be held, how long they may last, whether they may continue during weeks or months when school is not in session, what maintenance fee must be paid, and what insurance might be required.

Some content-based restrictions may also be allowed. For example, schools may probably exclude for-profit, commercial businesses even though community nonprofits are allowed to use school facilities after hours. They may also limit the use of the facilities to such things as "educational purposes," but such distinctions may prove difficult to administer, as many groups may claim to meet the stipulated purpose.

Schools should be aware that the imposition of content-based restrictions could raise difficult constitutional questions. For example, the Supreme Court has held in *Good News v. Milford* that in the case of the Good News Club, a content-based restriction excluding religious worship and instruction amounted to impermissible viewpoint discrimination.[46] School districts should be especially mindful to consult with legal counsel if they decide to draft content-based restrictions.

Cooperative Agreements Between Public Schools and Religious Communities

38. May public schools and religious communities enter into cooperative agreements to help students with such programs as tutoring?

Yes, but only if appropriate constitutional safeguards are in place. Remember, public schools must remain neutral among religions and between religion and nonreligion. For that reason, religious groups must refrain from proselytizing students during any cooperative programs with public schools. Participation or nonparticipation by students in such cooperative programs should not affect the student's academic ranking or ability to participate in other school activities. In addition, cooperative programs may not be limited to religious groups, but must be open to all responsible community groups.[47]

Released-Time Programs

39. May students be released for off-campus religious instruction during the school day?

Yes. Subject to applicable state laws, public schools have the discretion to release students who have parental permission to attend off-campus religious instruction during the school day. The Supreme Court in the 1952 case *Zorach v. Clausen* ruled "released-time" programs constitutional.[48]

If a public school decides to allow released time, the program must take place off campus and must be wholly organized and run by religious or community groups and not by the school. Schools may not encourage or discourage participation by students or in any way penalize students who do not attend.

Free Expression Rights of Students

40. What are the free expression rights of students in public schools under the First Amendment?

The freedoms of speech, press, assembly, and petition are often collectively referred to as the freedom of expression, and the U.S. Supreme Court has developed a separate body of case law regarding the free expression rights of students. In defining the free expression rights of students in a public school, the Court has developed three tests from the following landmark cases.[49]

I. The *Tinker* Standard (*Tinker v. Des Moines Independent School District*, 1969)

When 15-year-old John Tinker, his sister Mary Beth, 13, and Christopher Eckhardt, 16, wore black armbands to their Iowa public schools in

December 1965 to protest the Vietnam conflict, they never imagined that their actions would lead to a landmark First Amendment decision. Nonetheless, their protests eventually culminated in the leading First Amendment free speech case for public school students.[50]

The case arose when a group of parents and students in Des Moines, Iowa, met at the Eckhardt home and decided to protest U.S. involvement in Vietnam. The group agreed that one way to protest would be to have the students wear black armbands to public schools.

School officials learned of this planned protest and quickly enacted a no-armband policy. The school then enforced its no-armband rule while allowing the wearing of other symbols, including the Iron Cross.

The students sued in federal court and lost before a federal trial court. The trial court sided with the school officials' argument that they had enacted the policy out of a reasonable fear that the wearing of the armbands would create disturbances at school.

The case eventually made its way to the U.S. Supreme Court, which overturned the previous decision and ruled in favor of the students. In oft-cited language, the Supreme Court wrote, "it can hardly be argued that either students or teachers shed their constitutional rights to freedom of speech and expression at the schoolhouse gate."[51]

Writing for the majority, Justice Abe Fortas noted that the school officials could point to no evidence that the wearing of armbands would disrupt the school environment. As a result, the Court ruled that "undifferentiated fear or apprehension of disturbance is not enough to overcome the right to freedom of expression."[52]

In this decision, the Supreme Court established what has become known as the *Tinker* standard, considered to be the high watermark of students' First Amendment rights. In its ruling, the Court wrote: "the record does not demonstrate any facts which might reasonably lead school authorities to forecast substantial disruption of or material interference with school activities, and no disturbances or disorders on the school premises in fact occurred."[53]

Simply put, this ruling means school officials may not silence student expression just because they dislike it. They must reasonably forecast, based on evidence and not on an "undifferentiated fear or apprehension of disturbance," that the student expression would lead to either (a) a substantial disruption of the school environment, or (b) an invasion of the rights of others.

The *Tinker* standard governed student expression for years until the Supreme Court decided two other cases in the 1980s. The first of those rulings came in 1986.

II. The *Fraser* Standard (*Bethel School District. No. 403 v. Fraser,* 1986)

In the case of *Bethel v. Fraser*, the Supreme Court ruled that school officials could punish high school senior Matthew Fraser for giving a speech before the student assembly that contained lewd references.[54] In his speech, Fraser nominated classmate Jeff Kuhlman for a student government office. The speech contained numerous sexual references. In court, Fraser argued that a speech nominating another classmate for a student elective office was entitled to as much protection as the black armbands in *Tinker*. The high court disagreed, distinguishing his "vulgar" speech during a school-sponsored event from the pure "political" speech in the *Tinker* decision.

In its opinion, the court majority stated that "the constitutional rights of students in public school are not automatically coextensive with the rights of adults in other settings."[55] Instead, the high court set up a balancing test: "the freedom to advocate unpopular and controversial views in schools and classrooms must be balanced against society's countervailing interest in teaching students the boundaries of socially appropriate behavior."[56]

The high court added: "Surely, it is a highly appropriate function of public school education to prohibit the use of vulgar and offensive terms in public discourse."[57]

Despite the ruling in the case, courts are still divided in how they apply the *Fraser* standard. Some courts apply *Fraser* to all vulgar or lewd student speech even if the speech is student-initiated. Other courts only apply *Fraser* to vulgar student speech that is in some way school sponsored.

The question is significant because school officials consider a large amount of student speech offensive or vulgar even if the expression also contains a political message. For example, what standard applies if a student wears a T-shirt with a vulgar, political message? One court confronted this issue when a junior high school student wore a T-shirt to class bearing the words "Drugs Suck!"[58]

The student argued that the shirt conveyed an important, "anti-drug message" and did not cause a disruption of the school environment. The school responded that the shirt was inappropriate for the school environment because the word *sucks* has a vulgar connotation.

The court, siding with the school based on a broad application of the *Fraser* standard, wrote:

> Teachers and administrators must have the authority to do what they reasonably believe is in the best interest of their educational responsibilities, as we cannot abandon our schools to the whims or proclivities of children. The Court finds that . . . School Officials had an interest in protecting their young students from exposure to vulgar and offensive language.[59]

III. The *Hazelwood* Standard (*Hazelwood School District v. Kuhlmeier*, 1988)

Many First Amendment experts believe that the Supreme Court went too far in limiting the *Tinker* standard by its ruling in *Bethel v. Fraser*. The Court went even further, however, in its 1988 opinion in *Hazelwood School District v. Kuhlmeier*. In *Hazelwood*, the Court ruled that students' First Amendment rights were not violated when a school principal censored two student articles on controversial topics—pregnancy and divorce—in the school newspaper, *The Spectrum*.

The principal had ordered the stories removed from the paper because he believed the story about teen pregnancy was inappropriate for some of the younger students at the school, based on its discussion of sexual activity and birth control. In addition, he decided to censor the divorce article because the writers did not afford the parent of one of the students mentioned in the article a chance to respond to certain comments.

Several staff members of the paper, however, challenged the principal's action in federal court, claiming a violation of their First Amendment rights. The district court sided with the school, finding that the principal's concerns were reasonable and legitimate.

However, a federal appeals court reversed, finding that under the *Tinker* standard, the principal could not show a reasonable fear of disruption.

The case eventually reached the U.S. Supreme Court. The Court first discussed the First Amendment concept of a public forum—places such as a public park or street where the government has less leeway to regulate speech than in others—and asked whether the school officials had by policy or practice opened up a "public forum" or "forum for student expression" by allowing students to make content decisions.

The Court ruled that it had not, finding that school officials had always retained some control in the content decisions regarding the school paper, which was produced as part of the school curriculum—a journalism class.

By this ruling, the Court created the *Hazelwood* standard, which states that "educators do not offend the First Amendment by exercising editorial control over the style and content of student speech in school-sponsored expressive activities so long as their actions are reasonably related to legitimate pedagogical concerns."[60]

The Court ruled that "a school must be able to set high standards for the student speech that is disseminated under its auspices—standards that may be higher than those demanded by some newspaper publishers or theatrical producers in the 'real world.' " In addition, the ruling contains broad language on what type of speech school officials may censor, including any speech that might "associate the school with any position other than neutrality on matters of political controversy."

The Court then defined school-sponsored expression equally broadly, including "school-sponsored publications, theatrical productions, and other expressive activities that students, parents and members of the public might reasonably perceive to bear the imprimatur of the school . . . whether or not they occur in a traditional classroom setting, so long as they are supervised by faculty members and designed to impart particular knowledge or skills to student participants and audiences."

Since the ruling, courts have applied the *Hazelwood* standard not only to school-sponsored newspapers, but also to the selection of school band songs, school assignments, and even student campaign speeches.[61]

However, even if *Hazelwood* applies, it does not end the inquiry. A reviewing court must still review whether the school officials' actions were "reasonably related to a legitimate pedagogical interest."

In one decision, for example, a New Jersey appeals court determined that a school principal acted unreasonably when he ordered the removal of two reviews of R-rated movies from a junior high school newspaper.[62] As the court wrote, "when censorship of a school-sponsored publication has no valid educational purpose, the First Amendment is directly implicated and requires judicial intervention."

41. How do school officials and the courts apply these three standards?

Generally speaking, most courts have divided student speech into these three categories:

I. Vulgar, lewd, obscene, and plainly offensive speech (*Fraser* standard)[63]
II. School-sponsored speech (*Hazelwood* standard)
III. All other student speech (*Tinker* standard)[64]

To help clarify how courts review the actions of students and school officials, let's take an example involving the controversial symbol of the Confederate flag.

If a student were disciplined for wearing a piece of Confederate flag clothing to school, a reviewing court would likely begin by applying the *Tinker* "substantial disruption" standard. Why? Because the speech is student initiated (not school sponsored) and is not lewd.

Under *Tinker*, the court would have to determine whether the school officials could have reasonably forecasted a "substantial disruption" of the school environment, perhaps based on past incidents of racial tension, or if the school officials overreacted out of an "undifferentiated fear or apprehension."

School officials, however, might argue that the expression should be banned based on the more deferential *Fraser* standard. In one recent case, in fact, a federal appeals court agreed with this logic, reasoning that "the more flexible *Fraser* standard applies where the speech involved intrudes upon the function of the school to inculcate manners and habits of civility."[65]

More recently, a federal appeals court ruled that students could not be ordered to remove clothing adorned with Confederate flags absent a reasonable fear of disruption based on past experience. Even then, the court indicated that school officials must be willing to apply the ban evenhandedly to other racially divisive symbols, such as a Malcolm X T-shirt.[66]

To use a slightly different example, imagine if a principal decides to change her school's "Johnny Reb" mascot because she has received complaints from members of the community, who believe the symbol to be racially insensitive. Now which standard should apply?

A reviewing court would likely apply the *Hazelwood* standard because the mascot is a form of school-sponsored speech. In fact, in a decision based on these details, a federal appeals court reasoned that "a school mascot or symbol bears the stamp of approval of the school itself" and concluded that the principal "eliminated the symbol based on legitimate concerns."[67]

Finally, imagine that a group of students published a story about the Confederate flag and how students viewed the symbol in a privately published, underground student newspaper. Which standard would apply here?

In this case, the *Tinker* standard would apply, because the newspaper is student initiated, rather than school sponsored.

42. May schools limit the time, place, and manner of student expression?

Yes, as long as the time, place, and manner regulations are reasonable and nondiscriminatory.

The U.S. Supreme Court has said that "laws regulating the time, place or manner of speech stand on a different footing than laws prohibiting speech altogether."[68] First Amendment jurisprudence provides that time, place, and manner restrictions on speech are constitutional if (1) they are content neutral (i.e., they do not treat speech differently based on content); (2) they are narrowly tailored to serve a governmental interest; and (3) they leave open ample alternative means of expression.

Courts will generally grant even more deference to time, place, and manner restrictions in public schools because students do not possess the same level of rights as adults in a public forum. However, the time, place, and manner regulations must still be reasonable. This means that school officials could limit student distribution of material to certain locations and at certain times, but those regulations would need to be both reasonable and nondiscriminatory.

43. May schools prohibit students from wearing armbands or buttons that contain a political or religious message?

Probably not. In the *Tinker* case, the U.S. Supreme Court ruled that school officials violated the First Amendment rights of several students when they suspended them for wearing black armbands to school to protest U.S. involvement in Vietnam. The high court in *Tinker* even distinguished the wearing of the armbands from student dress.

More recently, a federal judge in Tennessee ruled that students had a First Amendment right to wear buttons protesting the adoption of a school uniform policy, finding that "the wearing of the protest logos in this case embodies exactly the kind of speech that is entitled to First Amendment protection."[69] Other recent cases have upheld the right of students to wear armbands to protest certain school policies.[70]

This does not mean school officials have no authority to regulate buttons or armbands if they are disruptive or vulgar. In fact, if an armband or button could be shown to have created a substantial disruption, then school officials could prohibit such material under the *Tinker* standard. Likewise, if the buttons were pervasively vulgar, then the school officials could prohibit them under the *Fraser* standard.

44. Must a public school student salute the flag during a recitation of the Pledge of Allegiance?

No. In a 1943 decision, *West Virginia Board of Education v. Barnette*, the Supreme Court determined that a group of Jehovah's Witnesses who objected to the flag salute and mandatory pledge recitation for religious reasons could not be forced to participate.[71] This means that public school students who choose not to join in the flag salute for reasons of conscience may not be compelled to recite the Pledge of Allegiance.

The Court's decision in *Barnette* was highly unusual, given that just three years earlier the Court ruled that students *could* be compelled to recite the Pledge in school. Writing for the Court in the 1940 decision of *Minersville School District v. Gobitis*, Justice Felix Frankfurter said:

> Even if it were assumed that freedom of speech . . . includes freedom from conveying what may be deemed an implied but rejected affirmation, the question remains whether school children . . . must be excused from conduct required of all the other children in the promotion of national cohesion.[72]

In the *Barnette* decision, however, the Court reversed course, declaring:

> If there is any fixed star in our constitutional constellation, it is that no official, high or petty, can prescribe what shall be orthodox in politics, nationalism, religion, or other matters of opinion or force citizens to confess by word or act their faith therein.[73]

The Pledge of Allegiance has been a source of controversy for other reasons as well. Some students and parents view the words "under God" in the Pledge as government endorsement of religion under the Establishment Clause.[74] This argument had failed in the courts until 2002 when a panel of the Ninth Circuit Court of Appeals ruled that state-mandated recitations of the pledge in public schools were unconstitutional because of the words "under God."[75] Most legal experts agree that this ruling will be overruled—either by the full circuit court or by the U.S. Supreme Court. In a number of past decisions, the Court has viewed references to God in patriotic exercises and on our money as "ceremonial deism" that does not rise to the level of government establishment of religion prohibited by the First Amendment.

45. How far may schools go in restricting student speech in the interest of school safety?

School safety is arguably the single most compelling interest of any community—and certainly the foremost issue in the minds of many parents. Therefore, courts have become increasingly deferential to school safety concerns.

This is especially true since the school shootings in Littleton, Colorado; Springfield, Oregon; and other communities, which have caused school administrators to focus more attention on ensuring safe school environments. As a result, many public schools across the country have adopted a variety of restrictions on students' free expression rights.[76]

However, some restrictions of student speech rights have been excessive, and many students have been punished for artwork, class essays, and poems. Two commentators neatly illustrate the problem:

> In this evolving area of the law, the goal of creating safe and orderly school environments and the potential for school district liability demand that schools carefully assess threats of violence and determine appropriate responses. Yet, in marshalling resources to curb aggression and violence in our nation's schools, policy makers, administrators, and teachers must balance the often competing demands for safer schools with the constitutional rights of their students. The goal of school safety cannot be achieved by compromising the constitutional guarantees of those who comprise our school communities.[77]

From a legal perspective, schools can restrict student speech in the name of safety if (1) they can reasonably forecast substantial disruption under *Tinker*, or (2) the student expression is a true threat.

However, though school safety is a compelling governmental interest that may justify various kinds of restrictions on student speech, those restrictions must still be reasonable. For example, the Ninth Circuit Court of Appeals applied the reasonableness standard in a case where a student was expelled for writing a poem filled with violent imagery. In *Lavine v. Blaine School District*, the court wrote: "We review . . . with deference, schools' decisions in connection with the safety of their students even when freedom of expression is involved."[78]

The case originated when James Lavine wrote a poem entitled "Last Words" that examined the feelings of a student who murdered his classmates. Lavine said he wrote the poem to "understand the phenomenon" of school shootings. However, his English teacher, a school counselor, and the school's administrators were concerned Lavine might harm himself or others.

Lavine and his father sued the school, contending that the emergency expulsion based on the content of Lavine's poem violated his First Amendment rights. School officials countered that they were justified under *Tinker* and the true-threat line of cases.

A district court sided with Lavine.[79] However, a federal appeals panel reversed, finding that under the totality of the circumstances, the school district was justified in believing that the expulsion was necessary for safety reasons.

"Even in its most mild interpretation, the poem appears to be a 'cry for help' from a troubled teenager contemplating suicide," the Ninth Circuit wrote. "Taken together and given the backdrop of actual school shootings, we hold that these circumstances were sufficient to have led school authorities to forecast substantial disruption of or material interference with school activities—specifically, that James was intending to inflict injury upon himself or others."[80]

In other cases involving student expression, however, courts have determined that school officials violated the First Amendment by punishing students for their writing or artwork. For example, in *Boman v. Bluestem Unified School District*, a federal court in Kansas ruled that school officials overreacted by expelling a student for posting a poem on a classroom door.[81] The court noted that the evidence "simply fails to show that the poster caused or was likely to cause a substantial disruption in the operation of the school."[82]

Speech Codes

46. May schools enforce speech codes on school grounds?

Yes. Within limits, public schools have discretion in implementing speech codes, especially those involving harassment. Such codes are usually part of an effort by school officials to create a nondiscriminatory, safe environment where all students are comfortable and free to learn.

Despite the best of intentions, however, speech codes often collide with the free speech rights of students. Problems tend to arise when these codes extend beyond their intended goal and restrict areas of protected First Amendment speech, such as an individual's right to express religious or political views or to discuss values and morality.[83]

Many recent speech codes use antibullying approaches to harassment and craft their speech codes accordingly. For example, in June 2001 Governor Bill Owens of Colorado signed into law a bill designed to prevent bullying in school. The law, which requires school districts to adopt "a specific policy concerning bullying prevention and education," also mandates that "each school district board of education shall adopt a mission statement for the school district, which statement shall include making safety a priority in each public school of the school district."[84]

However, as discussed in the questions and answers that follow, many attempts at promoting more thoughtful behavior, though well meaning, may violate students' constitutional rights.

47. When does student speech become "harassment?"

There is no bright legal line that determines when student speech becomes harassment. Generally, however, when a student or a group of students repeatedly intimidate or threaten another student, the behavior rises to the level of harassment. Harassment may also be written, oral, or physical acts that harm a student, damage the student's property, interfere with the student's education, or disrupt the orderly operation of a school.

School officials must restrict certain kinds of harassing language and actions they know about or they can be held civilly liable.[85] Categories of harassment are found in several federal statutes and prohibit discrimination based on gender;[86] disability;[87] and religion, race, color, or national origin.[88] The Supreme Court recognizes that students may even bring suit against the school for a "hostile environment" based on student-to-student sexual harassment. In such cases, the student must prove (1) the sexual harassment is "severe, pervasive, and objectively offensive"; and (2) that it "undermines and detracts from the victim's education experience" to the point that the harassed student is denied equal access to resources and opportunities.[89] In order to be held liable for student-to-student harassment, the school must have actual knowledge of the misconduct, the harassment must be severe and pervasive, and the school must be willfully indifferent.

For example, a mother seeking monetary and injunctive relief under Title IX of the Education Amendments of 1972, alleged that her 5th grade daughter had been the victim of sexual harassment by another student in her class. The case made its way to the Supreme Court, which considered whether a private damages action may lie against the school board in cases of student-to-student harassment.

In its ruling, the Court wrote the following conclusion:

> We conclude that [a private damages action] may [be brought against a school], but only where the funding recipient acts with deliberate indifference to known acts of harassment in its programs or activities. Moreover, we conclude that such an action will lie only for harassment that is so severe, pervasive, and objectively offensive that it effectively bars the victim's access to an educational opportunity or benefit.[90]

Using these parameters, schools can, and in some cases must, craft speech codes restricting harassing language and conduct. Concern about harassment, however, should not lead to the hasty adoption of speech codes that would censor protected forms of student speech. Under the First Amendment, schools may not implement speech codes that are overly broad or vague.

Some recent "anti-bullying codes" fall into this category. As the Pennsylvania case of *Saxe v. State College Area School District* demonstrates, schools may not create speech codes that forbid all offensive or hurtful language.[91] As the Supreme Court has pointed out, one of the foundational principles of the First Amendment is that "the government may not prohibit the expression of an idea simply because society finds the idea offensive or disagreeable."[92]

In essence, this means student speech that expresses ideas about values, morality, religion, or politics may not be restricted without some clear evidence that such speech interferes with the rights of another.

48. How do courts determine whether speech is a true threat?

The Supreme Court has ruled that true threats receive no First Amendment protection.[93] Unfortunately, the Court has not clearly defined a test for determining what types of speech constitute a true threat.[94] As a result, the lower courts have adopted a variety of tests to determine whether speech constitutes a true threat.

Some courts have determined that "if a reasonable person would foresee that an objective rational recipient of the statement would interpret its language to constitute a serious expression . . . [then] the message conveys a 'true threat.' "[95]

Other courts consider a series of factors in determining whether speech constitutes a true threat, including (1) the reaction of the recipient of the speech; (2) whether the threat was conditional; (3) whether the speaker communicated the speech directly to the recipient; (4) whether the speaker had made similar statements in the past; and (5) whether the recipient had reason to believe the speaker could engage in violence.[96]

The Louisiana Supreme Court, for example, ruled that a student could face criminal charges for saying that it would be easy to shoot students he didn't like and that he was going to blow up the school.[97] The state high court noted that the student made the comments only five days after the Columbine tragedy, and emphasized "the climate of fear already surrounding the school."[98]

However, a California appeals court recently ruled that a student could not be criminally charged under an antithreat law for turning in a painting depicting extreme violence against a peace officer who, a month earlier, had cited the student for drug possession.[99]

The state appeals court noted that "a painting—even a graphically violent painting—is necessarily ambiguous."[100] The appeals court also noted that the student never showed the painting to the peace officer, but simply turned in the painting as a class project.

Many cases regarding true threats made by students are just now circulating through the state and federal courts. Consequently, school officials are advised to seek legal counsel in this evolving area of the law.

49. What limits, if any, may school officials place on student expression that occurs off school grounds?

Traditionally, courts have been reluctant to permit restrictions on student speech that occurs entirely off school grounds, finding that the connection to the school is "too attenuated."[101] Yet the courts are also quick to point out that if the student speech has a closer connection to the school, such as the distribution on school grounds of newspapers that were created off campus, school officials may be able to provide the connection needed to bring this situation under their control.[102]

In addition, if there is a connection between off-campus speech and on-campus disruption, the off-campus speech and behavior may be subject to reasonable regulation. For example, a student's off-campus drug dealing provides a sufficient basis for an expulsion because of the likelihood that the student will also sell drugs on campus. Similarly, off-campus threats to do harm on campus may also give rise to disciplinary measures.[103]

With the advent of the Internet, however, the traditional view of off-campus speech has changed. Although most courts continue to view off-campus speech as beyond the jurisdiction and responsibility of the school, some courts have taken the view that, if a student's off-campus expression is sufficiently disruptive to the learning environment, the school may discipline the student. In one case, this rationale allowed the court to uphold the suspension of a student for offensive material posted on his home Web site that disrupted the school environment.[104]

50. Is profanity a form of expression protected by the First Amendment?

It can be, depending upon the circumstances and context. There is no general exception for profanity under the First Amendment unless the profanity qualifies as "fighting words." Fighting words are defined as words that by their very nature incite an immediate breach of the peace.

One case worth noting is the 1971 case of *Cohen v. California*, in which the U. S. Supreme Court reversed the conviction of a man who had been arrested for wearing a jacket in a courthouse bearing the words "F*** the Draft."[105] The court noted that the profane word on the jacket was not directed at a particular individual and aroused no violent reaction.

However, public school students have greater restrictions placed on their First Amendment rights than adults. In fact, school officials generally can prohibit vulgar and offensive student language under the Supreme Court's 1986 decision in *Bethel Sch. Dist. No. 403 v. Fraser*.[106] In that decision, the Supreme Court wrote that "it is a highly appropriate function of public school education to prohibit the use of vulgar and offensive terms in public discourse."[107]

In sum, one federal appeals court judge clarified the distinction between free speech and profanity quite well: "the First Amendment gives a high school student the classroom right to wear Tinker's armband, but not Cohen's jacket."[108]

Student Distribution of Literature

51. May students distribute religious or political literature at school?

Yes. Generally, students have a right to distribute religious or political literature on public school campuses, subject to reasonable time, place, and manner restrictions. This means that the school may specify at what times the distribution may occur (e.g., during lunch hour, or before or after classes begin), where it may occur (e.g., outside the school office), and how it may occur (e.g., from fixed locations as opposed to roving distribution). These restrictions should be reasonable and must apply evenly to all nonschool student literature.[109]

Public school officials may insist on screening all student materials prior to distribution to ensure the appropriateness for a public school. Any such screening policy should provide for a speedy decision, a statement of reasons for rejecting the literature, and a prompt appeals process.

Because the speech rights of students are not coextensive with those of adults, schools may prohibit the distribution of some types of student literature altogether. Included in this category would be materials that

- would likely cause substantial disruption of the operation of the school. Literature that uses fighting words or other inflammatory language about students or groups of students would be an example of this type of material.
- violate the rights of others. Included in this category would be literature that is libelous, that invades the privacy of others, or infringes on a copyright.
- are obscene, lewd, or sexually explicit.
- advertise products that are illegal for minors, such as alcohol.
- students would reasonably believe to be sponsored or endorsed by the school. One recent example of this category was a religious newspaper that was formatted to look like the school newspaper.

Although school officials have considerable latitude in prohibiting the distribution of materials that conflict with their educational mission, schools may not generally ban materials based solely on content. Similarly, schools should not allow a "heckler's veto" by prohibiting the distribution of materials simply because they are unpopular or controversial. If Christian students are allowed to distribute their newsletters, for example, Buddhists, Muslims, and others must be given the same privilege.[110]

Student Dress and School Uniforms

52. Is a student's choice of dress protected by the First Amendment?

Yes, in some cases. Courts have recognized that students' choice of clothing can communicate certain messages and ideas, ranging from their stance on political and social issues to their social standing or religious beliefs.

This protection is largely the result of the *Tinker* case, in which the Court said that the decision of several students to wear black armbands to protest U.S. involvement in Vietnam was "akin to pure speech" and entitled them to constitutional protection. However, the high court also made the following statement with regard to student dress: "The problem posed by the present case does not relate to regulation of the length of skirts or the type of clothing, to hair style or deportment."[111]

Proponents and opponents of dress codes cite different parts of the *Tinker* opinion to support their respective positions. Most lower courts, however, recognize that student clothing, at the very least, implicates the First Amendment. In other words, student clothing may be a form of expression that leads to a balancing of student free expression rights with the interests of the school, if by wearing the clothing the student intends to convey a message that could be understood by an observer.

Although student dress may implicate the First Amendment, more and more school districts are turning to dress codes and uniforms as a way to increase discipline and school safety. And federal judges in several states have upheld school uniform policies in the face of constitutional challenges brought by students and parents.

The courts have recognized, however, that students have the right to protest school policies as long as they do so in a nondisruptive fashion. For example, a federal judge in Louisiana ruled that a student had a

First Amendment right to wear black armbands protesting the adoption of uniforms.[112]

Generally, this means that a student has more First Amendment protection to wear a protest button or logo than to wear certain types of clothing. Keep in mind, however, that the Supreme Court has never decided a student dress code case.

53. What are the policy arguments for and against uniforms and school dress codes?

Many school districts are adopting various restrictions on student dress for a variety of reasons. Uniform and dress code proponents argue that they increase student attendance, promote discipline, and reinforce positive attitudes toward authority.

As Carl A. Cohn, superintendent of Long Beach Unified School District—one of the first school districts to require uniforms—puts it, school uniforms work because they "help to improve the learning climate, eliminate gang attire, encourage students to take school seriously as their place of business, reduce friction between students from different backgrounds and level the playing field so that students are judged by what they learn and can do, not by the price of what they wear."

Conversely, those opposed to uniforms contend that they threaten students' free expression rights. They also argue that dress codes, and especially uniforms, could discourage individuality and critical thinking. As one commentator put it, "uniform policies too broadly sweep students' First Amendment rights and, therefore, cannot withstand constitutional scrutiny. . . . The United States is not a 'nation bent on turning out robots'; allowing uniform regulations is certainly a step in the wrong direction."[113]

Because each side argues so passionately about the merits of school uniform policies, the issue could ultimately find its way to the Supreme Court. Until then, we are likely to continue to see challenges to various school uniform policies around the country.

54. What are the constitutional objections to mandatory dress codes and uniform policies?

Generally, the most common constitutional claims alleged are (1) violations of students' First Amendment rights to freedom of expression; (2) violations of students' First Amendment rights to freely practice their religion; or (3) violations of parents' 14th Amendment liberty interests in rearing their children.

Many students claim that requiring them to wear particular clothing deprives them of the ability to freely express themselves through their choice of dress. In one case, students from a Kentucky high school claimed that their school's dress code policy that prohibited clothing with any logos other than the official school logo was a violation of their free expression rights. The federal court, however, sided with the school district, finding that it had "struck a reasonable balance" between preventing potential disruptions and protecting students' First Amendment rights.[114]

In another case, a high school student brought a lawsuit challenging the constitutionality of a school board policy prohibiting male students from wearing earrings. The school, which had enacted the ban as part of an effort to curb the presence and influence of gangs on campus, provided substantial evidence of gang presence and activity—and the resulting violence—in its schools. Ultimately the court upheld the district's dress code policy, concluding that the board's concern for the safety and well-being of its students and the curtailment of gang activities was rational and did not violate the First Amendment.[115]

Some students have also argued that a particular dress code or uniform policy conflicts with their religious beliefs, in violation of the Free Exercise Clause. For example, two high school students in Texas sued after school officials prohibited them from wearing rosaries to school, based on the belief that the rosaries were considered "gang-related" apparel. The students claimed that the application of the rule to them violated both their free speech and free exercise rights.[116]

This time, the federal court ruled that the school *had* violated the First Amendment rights of the two students. Although the court did "not doubt that a dress code can be one means of restricting gang activity on campus," it also concluded that "the regulation places an undue burden on Plaintiffs, who seek to display the rosary not to identify themselves with a gang, but as a sincere expression of their religious beliefs."

Yet another objection, this one raised by parents, has been that forcing students to wear particular clothing infringes on a parent's 14th Amendment liberty interest in rearing their child, in violation of the Due Process Clause. In fact, many parents around the country have formed groups devoted to challenging school uniforms.[117] These groups have argued that the implementation of restrictive uniform and dress code policies violates the First Amendment and the principle of democratic self-choice.

So far, though, the courts are tending to side with school districts on parental and student challenges to uniform policies. Because the law is still rapidly developing in this area, school districts should consult with legal counsel before adopting a broad-based uniform policy. At the very least, any school policies requiring uniforms should have a provision that protects the right of parents and students to opt out on religious grounds.

55. How does a court determine if a student's choice of dress is constitutionally protected?

Courts will employ a variety of tests to determine whether restrictions on student dress violate First Amendment free expression rights. Some courts apply a two-part test taken from the Supreme Court's flag-burning cases.[118] Under this test, a court will ask two questions: (1) Did the student intend to convey a particularized message? (2) Is that particularized message one that a reasonable observer would understand?

As an example, a federal court in New Mexico applied this legal test to determine that a student did not have a First Amendment right to wear sagging pants. The student argued that his wearing of the sagging pants conveyed the particular message of African American heritage in the hip-hop fashion and lifestyle. The court rejected the student's First Amendment claim, finding that a reasonable observer would not find a particularized message in his conduct. "Sagging is not necessarily associated with a single racial or cultural group, and sagging is seen by some merely as a fashion trend followed by many adolescents all over the United States," the judge wrote.[119]

Other courts will apply the *Tinker* standard to student dress. Under the *Tinker* standard, school officials cannot regulate student expression unless they can reasonably forecast that the expression will cause a material interference or substantial disruption of the school environment.[120]

Still other courts will apply the more deferential standard from the Court's 1986 decision in *Bethel v. Fraser*. In *Fraser*, the court deemed that school officials had greater leeway to regulate student speech that was indecent and lewd. Though the case involved an actual student speech before a school assembly, lower courts have used the *Fraser* decision to uphold school restrictions on T-shirts and other clothing with messages deemed lewd or indecent.

For example, a federal court in Virginia upheld a middle school student's suspension for wearing a T-shirt with the message "Drugs Suck."

Rejecting the students' argument that the shirt was simply an antidrug shirt, the court focused instead on the fact that the word "suck" was vulgar.[121]

Finally, some courts will analyze student dress challenges under yet another legal analysis, the so-called *O'Brien* standard.[122] Under the *O'Brien* test, a dress code or uniform policy will be constitutional if

- the policy is authorized under state law;
- the policy furthers an important governmental interest;
- the policy is unrelated to the suppression of free expression; and
- the incidental restriction on First Amendment freedoms is no more than necessary to further the governmental interest.

56. May schools adopt mandatory uniform policies?

The Supreme Court has not decided a case on school uniforms. However, most lower courts are siding with school districts that adopt uniform policies.

The push for school uniforms gained momentum in 1996 when President Clinton stated: "If it means that teenagers will stop killing each other over designer jackets, then our public schools should be able to require school uniforms." The president ordered the U.S. Department of Education to issue manuals on the efficacy of school uniforms. The manual (available at www.ed.gov/updates/uniforms.html) states that school uniforms represent "one positive and creative way to reduce discipline problems and increase school safety."

One federal appeals court that recently upheld a school uniform policy in Louisiana gave the following explanation for its decision:

> The School Board's purpose for enacting the uniform policy is to increase test scores and reduce disciplinary problems throughout the school system. This purpose is in no way related to the suppression of student speech. Although students are restricted from wearing clothing of their choice at school, students remain free to wear what they want after school hours.[123]

The same federal appeals court upheld a mandatory uniform policy in a Texas school district and rejected students' First Amendment challenges to the policy. The court reasoned that the policy "was adopted for other legitimate reasons unrelated to the suppression of student expression."[124]

Though the trend among the courts seems to be in favor of uniforms, the policies will still face legal challenges. If a school district adopts a uniform policy, it would be wise to contain an exemption for those students with sincere religious objections. The district should also consider providing financial assistance to those students who cannot afford the uniforms.

57. May a school constitutionally punish students for wearing long hair or dying their hair an unusual color?

The courts are much divided on this issue. The First, Second, Fourth, Seventh, and Eighth Circuits seem receptive to students' claims regarding personal choice with respect to their hair.[125] However, the Third, Fifth, Sixth, Ninth, and Tenth Circuits seem unreceptive.[126]

Many of the student hair cases today deal not with length but color. For example, a high school student from Virginia sued his school district in federal court after school officials suspended him for having blue hair. A federal judge reinstated the student, finding a violation of his constitutional rights.[127]

Generally speaking, the courts that have found a constitutional issue have ruled along similar lines, claiming that a student's choice of hair color and style raises either a First Amendment free expression issue or a 14th Amendment liberty or equal protection interest. Some courts have even pointed out that regulating a student's choice of hairstyle impacts with greater permanence than regulating a student's dress because, unlike with hairstyle or color, the student can wear what he pleases outside school.

Conversely, the courts that have sided with school districts have generally ruled that the students' wearing of long hair "does not rise to the dignity of a protectable constitutional issue."[128]

Either way, different courts have simply come to different legal conclusions. As a result, students' rights in this regard largely depend on where they live.

58. May a school punish a student for wearing Confederate flag attire?

It depends on whether the school officials can reasonably forecast that the wearing of the Confederate flag will lead to a substantial disruption of the school environment. In one decision, a court rejected a student's First Amendment right to wear a Confederate flag jacket because the school officials had cited "several incidents of racial tension." According to the court, "school officials are not required to wait until disorder or invasion occurs" but only need "the existence of facts which might reasonably lead school officials to forecast substantial disruption."[129]

Another federal court, using the same criteria, recently reached the opposite conclusion, finding that a school district in Kentucky failed to satisfy the *Tinker* standard by showing any reasonable forecast of substantial disruption.[130] The appeals court determined that the school district's policy with respect to the Confederate flag appeared to be a "targeted ban" that was not applied evenhandedly to other racially divisive symbols.

Still another court applied the *Fraser* standard to a Confederate flag. This federal court ruled that the controlling legal standard does not come from *Tinker*. School officials' actions can be analyzed, they stated, under "the more flexible *Fraser* standard where the speech involved intrudes upon the function of the school to inculcate manners and habits of civility."[131]

59. What should a school do if a student has a sincere religious objection to a uniform policy?

In the spirit of the First Amendment and as a matter of good policy, schools should have opt-out provisions for those students who have a sincere religious objection to a uniform policy. Although the courts have not ruled directly on this point, schools may not be legally required to allow exemptions to their uniform policies under current law.[132] However, at least one court has indicated there was enough ambiguity in a case over religious objections to a dress code to have justified a trial. In that case, the family of an elementary school student in North Carolina obtained a settlement in a federal lawsuit that provided a religious exemption to the school's uniform policy.

Aaron Ganues had been suspended twice for not wearing a school uniform. His great-grandmother—Aaron's guardian and a local minister— argued that wearing the uniforms would conflict with the family's religious beliefs that uniforms teach students to obey authority mindlessly, making them vulnerable to the devil.[133] The school district fought the lawsuit but agreed to settle after a federal judge refused to dismiss the suit in December 1999. Consequently, the school district agreed to amend its policy to provide exemptions from its policy for sincere religious objections.[134]

Students and the Internet

60. What are the primary considerations to make when determining issues of student speech that occur in cyberspace?

Student speech and the Internet raise some important and complex issues for educators, students, and parents.

Until recently, there was little law governing what was and wasn't acceptable speech on the Internet. In fact, the U.S. Supreme Court didn't issue a ruling on Internet speech until 1997. In that year, the Court returned a verdict in the case of *Reno v. ACLU* that helped clarify how Internet speech should be treated in the future.

The Court had been asked to resolve a challenge to the constitutionality of the Communications Decency Act (CDA) of 1996. In particular, the American Civil Liberties Union (ACLU) took issue with two provisions of the CDA that prohibited the online communication of "patently offensive" and "indecent" speech.

The Court agreed that the disputed provisions of CDA were unconstitutional under the First Amendment because "the general undefined terms 'indecent' and 'patently offensive' cover large amounts of non-pornographic material with serious educational or other value." The Court then stressed that speech on the Internet should be entitled to the highest possible degree of protection, just as it would in print.

In light of this ruling, schools should consider the following factors before regulating student speech on the Internet:

- Was the content created as part of the school curriculum, such as a class project or the official school newspaper? If so, then the speech in question is considered school sponsored, and the *Hazelwood* standard of expression would apply. In that case, schools are granted greater leeway in regulating speech that "students, parents, and members of the public might reasonably perceive to bear the imprimatur [endorsement] of the school."
- Was the content created on school computers during the student's free time? If it was, the student will likely contend the *Tinker* standard governs. Under that standard, the speech in question is entitled to protection under the First Amendment as long as it does not (a) cause a material or substantial disruption to the school community, or (b) infringe on the rights of others. An attorney for the school, however, would

likely argue that the speech should be held to the *Hazelwood* standard of expression because school computers were being used.

- Was the content created during a structured class or lab time? If so, the *Hazelwood* standard should apply, because the content could be linked to the curriculum.

These factors, of course, relate to student speech on the Internet that occurs on the school grounds. If the speech in question occurs on a private Web site, a different set of issues is at stake.

61. What limits, if any, can be placed on the private Web sites of students?

Case law in this area is still developing, so a clear legal standard has yet to be defined.

School officials, however, should exercise caution before attempting to limit student expression on a private Web site maintained off school grounds.

On one hand, schools have a vital interest in keeping all members of their community safe; if a student produces speech that constitutes a "true threat," schools have a responsibility to act. However, in the majority of lawsuits between students and administrators so far, judges have been more likely to defend the free expression rights of the students, whose speech they usually determined did not constitute a "true threat."

As one judge put it, in a case where students had been punished for publishing an underground newspaper that was produced and sold off campus, "our willingness to defer to the schoolmaster's expertise in administering school discipline rests . . . upon the supposition that the arm of authority does not reach beyond the schoolhouse gate."[135]

To help understand the distinctions that educators should make when considering off-campus Internet speech, Edwin Darden, senior staff attorney for the National School Boards Association (NSBA), suggests that student Web sites be divided into three categories:

- Sites that are offensive, obnoxious, and insulting.
- Sites that are offensive, obnoxious, and insulting, and also contain some sort of veiled threat of violence or of destruction of property.
- Sites that contain an outright blatant threat.

Darden suggests that for the first category, under which most student sites fall, "my advice to schools is, you just need to develop a thick skin." For the second category, because the nature of the threat is unclear, educators should be sure to get further information on the subject before passing judgment too quickly.[136]

For the third category, however, if the speech in question represents an actual threat, the student could be punished, as long as schools can demonstrate that the speech could disrupt the school or that it seriously threatens harm to a member of the school community.

For example, in the case of *J.S. v. Bethlehem Area School District*, an 8th grader asked visitors of his Web site for $20 to "help pay for the hit man" to kill his math teacher. The student was expelled as a result, prompting the parents to sue the school district. Then the teacher followed by filing a defamation suit against the family. The family countersued.

When the Pennsylvania Commonwealth Court issued their ruling in July 2000, they ruled that the child's threat materially disrupted the educational process.[137] Then, a jury awarded the teacher $500,000 in damages.

Several other state and federal courts have determined that school officials exceeded their authority in regulating students' online speech created wholly off campus.[138] For example, one federal judge rejected school officials' actions in suspending a student for lampooning school officials on his private Web site. The judge wrote: "Disliking or being upset by the content of a student's speech is not an accepted justification for limiting student speech under *Tinker*."[139]

So what does this all mean?

Because the Supreme Court has granted cyberspeech the highest degree of protection under the First Amendment, school officials need to be aware that student speech that occurs off school grounds is private and not subject to the authority of school officials unless it causes a substantial disruption. If, however, a student's speech crosses the line and suggests actual physical harm—such as Eric Harris's Internet "hit list" prior to the Columbine massacre—then schools should immediately consult an attorney.

62. Must schools now use filtering software on school computers?

Yes, if your school receives federal money for its technology budget—although this mandate could change in the near future.

This requirement is the result of the Children's Internet Protection Act (CIPA), which was passed by Congress in December 2000. According to the act, any schools or libraries that receive federal E-rate funds—money from a federal program that subsidizes telecommunications expenses—must meet a series of filtering requirements.

As it stands, based on the Federal Communications Commission's (FCC's) rules for compliance, any school that wants to continue receiving E-rate funds must have certified that they have added the required policies and technology. All schools that do not comply will become ineligible for funding.

In response, the American Civil Liberties Union (ACLU) and the American Library Association (ALA) filed suit on March 20, 2001, claiming that the law is unconstitutional and a violation of the First Amendment rights of library patrons. On May 31, 2002, a panel of three federal judges ruled in *American Library Association v. United States* that the Children's Internet Protection Act violated the First Amendment.[140]

The judges determined that the CIPA law violated the First Amendment because it blocked access to "substantial amounts of constitutionally protected speech."[141] The government appealed the decision directly to the U.S. Supreme Court. The Court reversed the decision by a 6–3 vote and said the blocking requirement was valid—especially as a string attached to federal funds.

Though the focus of litigation thus far concerns public libraries, the ACLU has indicated that they may also challenge the application of CIPA to public schools. "The law presents serious First Amendment problems with respect to filtering at public schools for the same reasons that it does for public libraries," said Chris Hansen, senior national staff counsel for the ACLU. Hansen stated:

> Blocking software restricts students and others from accessing constitutionally protected material. There is no software product that purports to make decisions based on any legal category. These companies admit that they create their own categories of material that is not based on legally recognized categories.[142]

63. According to the most recent definition of the law, what material is considered "harmful to minors"?

According to the Children's Internet Protection Act (CIPA), the term "harmful to minors" means "any picture, image, graphic image file, or other visual depiction that

- taken as a whole and with respect to minors, appeals to a prurient interest in nudity, sex, or excretion;
- depicts, describes, or represents, in a patently offensive way with respect to what is suitable for minors, an actual or simulated sexual act or sexual contact, actual or simulated normal or perverted sexual acts, or a lewd exhibition of the genitals; and
- taken as a whole, lacks serious literary, artistic, political, or scientific value as to minors.[143]

The CIPA standard is a revision of a similar law that was twice ruled unconstitutional. However, the constitutionality of the Act was argued by the American Civil Liberties Union and the American Library Association. On June 23, 2003, the Supreme Court upheld the constitutionality of the law by a 6–3 vote in the case of *United States v. American Library Association*.[144]

64. Does the use of Internet filters raise First Amendment concerns?

The answer to that question depends on whom you ask. There is clearly significant congressional support for the use of filtering technology, as evidenced by the passage of the Children's Internet Protection Act (CIPA). In addition, local school districts have already begun incorporating the technology into their computer systems, demonstrating their belief that the technology serves a useful, even essential, purpose.

However, a 2001 review of filtering software by *Consumer Reports* suggests that filtering technology has a long way to go. According to the report, computer filters, on average, fail to block one out of every five sites deemed "objectionable." AOL's Young Teens setting, for example, did better than most of the sites surveyed, by blocking 86 percent of the targeted sites. At the same time, it prevented 63 percent of the "legitimate" sites from being seen as well.[145]

The question of whether filtering works is a highly subjective one. It undoubtedly eliminates a host of undesirable sites, but the limitations of the technology raise some compelling First Amendment rights issues, especially with regard to older students.

If your school is not bound by law to install filters, you may want to consult with counsel and solicit the input of a wide range of stakeholders in the community before making a decision. That way, whatever decision is reached will include the greatest possible variety of perspectives.

65. Is using filtering software the only way to encourage responsible use of the Internet by students?

No. Another approach is to offer instruction in the responsible use of the Internet. Many Catholic schools, for example, have adopted Ethical Internet Use Policies. A partnership of school community members works together to outline the ethical responsibilities of any person involved in Internet use in school. Students are then granted "Internet licenses" after signing contracts or taking a course in ethical behavior. If a student violates the terms of the contract, they are denied Internet privileges.

The appeal of this model is twofold. First, a clear case of cause and effect is established, which clarifies the rules and responsibilities for all students; second, each student is given an understanding of what constitutes proper and improper behavior. By addressing both areas, these types of policies help students to make good decisions about Internet use in school and at home.

Student Publications

66. Is it constitutional for school officials to censor a school-sponsored publication, such as a newspaper or a yearbook?

How much school officials may censor school-sponsored student publications depends on whether the school has created an open public forum.

For years, students were protected by a high standard of freedom of expression based on the Supreme Court's historic 1969 ruling in the *Tinker* case, in which the Court ruled that school officials couldn't prevent students from expressing their opinions on school grounds, as long as they didn't (a) cause a material or substantial disruption of the school environment, or (b) intrude on the rights of others.

For years, most courts supported the notion of granting students a high degree of protection under the First Amendment. That changed in 1988.

In January 1988 the Supreme Court, in a narrow 5–3 vote, ruled that the principal of Hazelwood East High School was justified in censoring a series of controversial articles in his school's newspaper, *The Spectrum*.[146]

In the ruling of *Hazelwood v. Kuhlmeier*, the Supreme Court established a new standard of protection for student expression, by ruling that schools may limit the personal expression of students if their speech can be perceived to bear the imprimatur of the school.[147] Writing for the majority, Justice Byron White said "censorship of school-sponsored student expression is permissible when school officials can show that it is reasonably related to legitimate pedagogical concerns" (see Figure 3).

As a result, administrators now have a great deal of leeway in determining what is and isn't acceptable material in school-sponsored publications and events, but *only if* their school has not established a public forum.

In other words, if the school has an official policy of prior review in place, or can clearly establish a history of prior review, the *Hazelwood* standard applies and a greater degree of censorship is allowed. If, however, the school declares itself an open forum for ideas, then the *Tinker* standard applies.

67. What is a public forum?

A public forum is a place that has, by tradition or practice, been held out for general use by the public for speech-related purposes.

To determine which of the standards of student expression applies in a given case, many courts first conduct a "public forum analysis." The public forum analysis determines whether individuals may have access to places for communicative purposes.[148]

There are three types of public forums:

I. A "traditional, or open, public forum" is a place with a long tradition of freedom of expression, such as a public park or a street corner. The government can normally impose only content-neutral time, place, and manner restrictions on speech in a public forum. Restrictions on speech in a public forum that are based on content will be struck down, unless the government can show the restriction is necessary to further a compelling governmental interest.

II. A "limited public forum" or "designated public forum" is a place with a more limited history of expressive activity, usually only for certain groups or topics. Examples of a limited public forum would include a university meeting hall or a city-owned theater. The government can limit access to certain types of speakers in a limited public forum, or limit the use of such facilities for certain subjects. Despite these more proscriptive guidelines, however, a governmental institution may still not restrict expression at a limited forum unless that restriction serves a "compelling interest."

FIGURE 3

This diagram explains the rights of high school student journalists following the U.S. Supreme Court's decision in *Hazelwood School District v. Kuhlmeier.*

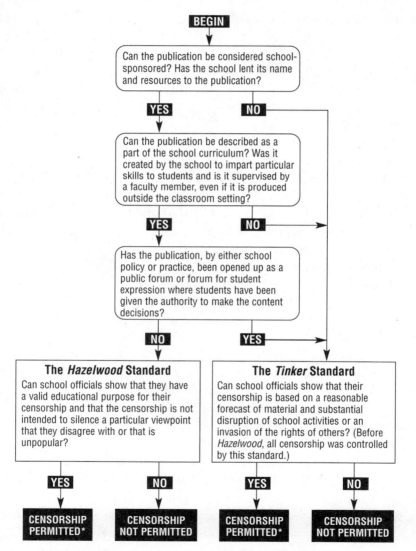

*If you live in Arkansas, California, Colorado, Iowa, Kansas, Massachusetts, Pennsylvania, or Washington, censorship may not be permitted under your state law or regulations.

© 2001 Student Press Law Center. Used with permission.

III. A "closed public forum" is a place that, traditionally, has not been open to public expression, such as a jail or a military base. Governmental restrictions on access to a nonpublic forum will be upheld as long as they are reasonable and not based on a desire to suppress a particular viewpoint. This standard is far more deferential to government officials.

With regard to public schools, the Supreme Court elaborated on the public forum doctrine in cases involving the use of teacher mailboxes, *Perry Education Association v. Perry Local Educators' Association*,[149] and student newspapers, *Hazelwood School District v. Kuhlmeier*.[150]

In *Perry*, the Court determined that in-school teacher mailboxes were not public forums, and that the school district could allow the official teacher union sole access to the mailboxes, even if it meant excluding a rival teacher union. "Implicit in the concept of the nonpublic forum is the right to make distinctions in access on the basis of subject matter and speaker identity," the Court wrote.[151]

The Court went on to say that the deferential access provided to the official teachers' union was a reasonable way to "prevent the District's schools from becoming a battlefield for inter-union squabbles."[152]

In *Hazelwood*, the Supreme Court determined that a high school newspaper produced as part of a journalism class was not a public forum. Citing *Perry*, the Court wrote: "Hence, school facilities may be deemed to be public forums only if school authorities have 'by policy or practice' opened those facilities for 'indiscriminate use by the general public,' or by some segment of the public, such as student organizations."[153] The majority in *Hazelwood* also reasoned that because the production of the newspaper was "part of the educational curriculum and a regular classroom activity," it was a nonpublic forum.

Since the *Hazelwood* decision, many courts have continued to defer to the judgment of school officials. As a result, many forms of censorship that had previously been unacceptable under the *Tinker* standard of expression have been upheld.

68. Since the *Hazelwood* ruling, how important is state law in determining the rights of student journalists?

It is very important. With the exception of California, which passed a state law in 1971 guaranteeing all students full protection under the First Amendment, every other state needed to make a decision after the ruling: Did they want to abide by the standard given in *Hazelwood v.*

Kuhlmeier, or did they want to pass a state law providing more protection for student expression?

Shortly after the ruling, in July 1988, Massachusetts became the first state since California to pass a law strengthening the First Amendment rights of students. This broadly worded law provides that "the right of students to freedom of expression in the public schools of the commonwealth shall not be abridged, provided that such right shall not cause any disruption or disorder within the school."[154]

Kansas, Colorado, Iowa, and Arkansas have since followed suit and passed so-called anti-Hazelwood laws, and similar legislation has been introduced in more than half the other states. In fact, the constitutions of most states have language that supports, to varying degrees, free expression. If you are unsure of what protections exist in your state, check the state and local laws as well as the state constitution.

69. May a school legally censor an off-campus, "underground" student publication?

Partly because of the *Hazelwood* standard, which allows administrators to censor school-sponsored publications as long as the decision is "reasonably related to legitimate pedagogical concerns," a greater number of students have resorted to their own independent newspapers. Because these publications are not school sponsored, they receive the same level of protection any other newspaper receives, and they are not bound by the *Hazelwood* standard of expression.

Consequently, if students don't distribute their paper on school grounds, a school is very limited in its ability to censor a privately produced student publication.[155] If, however, they do distribute on school grounds, a majority of the courts will apply the *Tinker* standard.[156] In addition, administrators may place reasonable restrictions on the time, place, and manner[157] of its distribution.

Courts have been divided on this issue, however, partly because there are differences of opinion when applying the public forum analysis, a legal method for determining to what extent someone should be protected by the First Amendment on government-owned property. Some courts have claimed that the hallways of schools are closed public forums, and therefore students' rights to distribute material should be limited. Others have been more receptive to the rights of students, so, as always, the interpretation of the law depends on the judge reviewing the case.

70. Do school publications have to accept advertisements that some may find offensive?

This debate was played out on a national stage in 2001, when activist David Horowitz submitted a controversial advertisement, entitled "Ten Reasons Why Reparations for Slavery Is a Bad Idea," to college newspapers across the country. Although college newspaper editors are not bound by the same rules as middle or high school newspaper editors, the scenario raises an interesting question for any journalist: Is it better, in the interest of free expression, to accept and run an ad that is likely to be found offensive by a significant part of the community, or to refuse to accept it?

The decisions of the college editors varied. In an article in the April 1, 2001, edition of *The Washington Post*, several editors discussed the choices they made. Alexander Conant, the editor for the University of Wisconsin's *Badger Herald*, ran the ad because, in his opinion, "A newspaper that refused the ad, or ran it followed by an apology, is censoring ideas and cannot possibly purport to be a forum for public discussion. Instead, it becomes a soapbox for only certain viewpoints."

Conversely, Jennifer Schaum, the editor of the University of Virginia's *Cavalier Daily*, refused to run the ad and said the decision was "just as easy" as Conant's. "This doesn't mean the *Cavalier Daily* is squelching unpopular viewpoints," she said. On the contrary, "the paper is willing to print all views on reparations on the opinion page. That's where opposing viewpoints should be expressed."

The Supreme Court addressed some of these issues in one of the most significant First Amendment cases of the last 50 years, *The New York Times Co. v. Sullivan*. In that 1964 case, an Alabama official sued *The New York Times* for libel in an editorial advertisement that had been placed in the paper by individuals and groups working on behalf of the civil rights movement. In its decision, the Court overturned the previous two judgments that had favored the official, and ruled for the *Times*. As Justice Arthur Goldberg wrote in his concurring opinion, "if newspapers, publishing advertisements dealing with public issues . . . risk liability, there can also be little doubt that the ability of minority groups to secure publication of their views on public affairs and to seek support for their causes will be greatly diminished."[158]

Based on the *Sullivan* decision, then, professional newspaper editors have the legal protection necessary to run ads that some may find controversial as a way to safeguard free expression in the press. It is not at all clear that a high school newspaper can engage in viewpoint discrimination when accepting advertising, absent an extremely compelling reason.

In a recent case from the First Circuit, however, the full panel of the court ruled that a high school newspaper's decision not to run a pro-abstinence ad from a member of the community did not violate the First Amendment. The court ruled there was no First Amendment violation because the rejection of the ad was a private decision by the student editors and the school was not involved.[159]

However, the standards established by the *Fraser* and *Hazelwood* cases seem to give schools the right to reject offensive ads. In the *Hazelwood* decision, for example, the Court said a school can censor material that "associate[s] the school with any position other than neutrality on matters of political controversy."

Based on that language, then, it would seem that a school newspaper could reject such advertisements. However, the application of the public forum doctrine might lead to a different result. If a public school paper rejected an ad based on viewpoint discrimination, for example, there could be a First Amendment problem.[160] For more information on this and other issues relating to the student press, contact the Student Press Law Center or visit their Web site at www.splc.org.

Teacher and Administrator Rights and Responsibilities

71. Do school officials forfeit their First Amendment protections once they become public employees?

No. The Supreme Court has ruled that public school teachers, like other public employees, do not forfeit all constitutional protections when they take a government job. In fact, the Court has stated that "it can hardly be argued that either teachers or students shed their constitutional rights to freedom of speech or expression at the schoolhouse gate."[161]

For the early part of the 20th century, courts ruled that public employees had no right to object to conditions placed upon public employment. The courts subscribed to the view given by Justice Oliver Wendell Holmes who, as a justice of the Supreme Judicial Court of Massachusetts, wrote: "A policeman may have a constitutional right to talk politics, but he has no constitutional right to be a policeman."[162]

The Supreme Court abandoned this view later in the 20th century with a series of decisions regarding loyalty oaths. Then, in 1968, the U.S. Supreme Court decided the seminal public employee First Amendment case, *Pickering v. Board of Education*. In that decision, the high court ruled that school district officials violated the First Amendment rights of high school science teacher Marvin Pickering when they fired him for writing a letter to the editor in his local paper criticizing the superintendent, the school board, and the board's allocation of monies between academics and athletics.

Justice Thurgood Marshall, writing for the court, noted that "the problem in any case is to arrive at a balance between the interests of the teacher, as a citizen, in commenting upon matters of public concern and the interest of the State, as an employer, in promoting the efficiency of the public services it performs through its employees."[163]

The Court first noted that Pickering's letter referred to important matters of public concern in the community. Pointing out that Pickering should not lose the rights he possessed as a citizen simply because he worked as a public school teacher, the court also minimized the board's argument that the letter disrupted the efficient operation of the schools.

Finally, the Court concluded that "the interest of the school administration in limiting teachers' opportunities to contribute to public debate is not significantly greater than its interest in limiting a similar contribution by any member of the general public."[164]

72. What types of laws protect teachers who believe they have been unfairly treated by a school board, school superintendent, or other school official?

Many types of laws provide some protection for teachers. Many states have teacher tenure laws that prohibit school officials from arbitrarily taking adverse employment actions. Many teachers are also protected by a contract between the local teachers union and the applicable school authorities. These contracts are called collective bargaining agreements, and they spell out the legal parameters of the employment relationship.

In addition, public school teachers have protections afforded by the U.S. Constitution. Both the Bill of Rights and the 14th Amendment protect individuals from unconstitutional infringements by governmental officials. School boards and school administrative officials qualify as such governmental actors.

The Due Process Clause of the 14th Amendment provides that teachers cannot be deprived of a "liberty" or "property" interest without notice and a hearing. The First Amendment also provides protection for teachers who speak out on matters of public concern.

73. How do courts balance a teacher's First Amendment rights against the interests of the public school system?

It depends on the context and the particular court reviewing the claim. Some courts apply the general line of public employee free-speech case law when evaluating a claim by a public school teacher. Under this test, a court first asks whether the teacher's speech touched on a matter of public concern.

If the teacher's speech does touch on a matter of public concern, the court balances the teacher's right to free expression against the school district's interests in an efficient workplace.[165] The general *Pickering-Connick* test applies to most teacher speech that occurs outside the classroom environment.

If the teacher speech involves the curriculum or occurs in the classroom, most courts apply the more deferential standard in *Hazelwood*. This standard asks whether there is a legitimate educational reason for the school board's policy. In fact, one federal appeals court even determined that the *Hazelwood* standard—where any form of censorship must be reasonably related to a legitimate educational reason—should apply to a teacher's in-class speech.[166] That court ruled as follows:

> We are convinced that if students' expression in a school newspaper bears the imprimatur of the school, then a teacher's expression in the "traditional classroom setting" also bears the imprimatur of the school. . . . Although the *Pickering* test accounts for the state's interests as an employer, it does not address the significant interests of the state as educator.[167]

As this case indicates, many courts are highly deferential to employer interests, especially public school officials. As a result, teachers should understand that the traditional First Amendment rights of academic freedom generally accorded to university professors are much more limited in public primary and secondary schools.

74. How do the courts determine whether a teacher's speech touches on a matter of public concern?

The Supreme Court has established that speech touches on a matter of public concern when the public employee's speech deals with matters of political, social, or other concerns to the community.

To determine whether public employee speech rises to the level of First Amendment protection, the lower courts have been instructed to look at the "content, form, and context of a given statement, as revealed by the whole record." In addition, "as a matter of good judgment . . . [courts have been advised to] be receptive to constructive criticism offered by their employees." They have also been reminded, however, that "the First Amendment does not require a public office to be run as a roundtable for employee complaints over internal office affairs."[168]

Some courts will apply the so-called *Pickering-Connick* analysis, or citizen-employee test, to determine the degree of First Amendment protection that should be assigned to a particular teacher's speech. If the court determines the public employee is speaking more as a citizen, the court considers the speech to be on a matter of public concern. If the court determines that the employee is speaking more as an employee, the court finds that the speech is a personal employment grievance or private speech.

Speech that deals with issues of significant importance to the public as a whole is more likely to satisfy a reviewing court. For example, one federal appeals court, ruling in favor of a teacher's speech about racial discrimination, wrote that "[s]ociety possesses a compelling interest in the unrestrained discussion of racial problems."[169]

Many courts, however, hold that speech relating to personal employment grievances does not rise to the level of public concern. In *Sanguigni v. Pittsburgh Board of Public Education*, for example, the Third Circuit ruled that a teacher's complaints about low teacher morale and retaliation against teachers who complained about school administration were not matters of public concern.[170] The court reasoned that the teacher's statements "did not comment on any broad social or policy issue" and "focused solely on employee morale."[171]

Many legal commentators, however, have pointed out that the public concern test has led to inconsistent results in the lower courts.[172] For more detailed information on laws affecting teachers' rights, teachers are advised to consult with their union official or seek legal counsel.[173]

75. Does a school violate the First Amendment if it disciplines a teacher for speech that touches on a matter of public concern?

It depends. It is important to remember that the test developed by the *Pickering-Connick* line of cases has two basic prongs. First, the court must determine whether the speech in question touches on a matter of public concern. If it does not, the teacher will not receive any First Amendment protection. If the speech *does* touch on a matter of public concern, the court proceeds to the balancing prong of the test. At that point, the court must balance the public school teacher's interest in commenting upon a matter of public concern against the school officials' interest in promoting an efficient workplace of public service.

Some balancing factors for a court to consider include

- whether the statement impairs discipline by superiors or harmony among coworkers,
- whether the statement has a detrimental impact on close working relationships for which personal loyalty and confidence are necessary, and
- whether the speech in question interferes with the normal operation of the employer's business.

Sometimes in considering these factors, the courts will side with school officials in a First Amendment lawsuit although the public school teachers' speech touches upon a matter of public concern. In one recent case, for example, the Eighth Circuit determined that a school principal did not violate the First Amendment rights of three teachers who were ordered to quit talking about the care and education of special needs students.[174]

Subsequent appeals in the case acknowledged that the teachers' complaints about the lack of care for special needs students touched on matters of public concern. Nonetheless, the appeals court noted that the teachers' speech "resulted in school factions and disharmony among their co-workers and negatively impacted [the principal's] interest in efficiently administering the middle school."[175]

Conversely, the Eleventh Circuit reached a different conclusion in the case of *Belyeu v. Coosa County Board of Education*.[176] In this decision, a teacher's aide alleged that school officials failed to rehire her because of a speech she made about racial issues at a PTA meeting. The aide said the school should adopt a program to commemorate Black History month. Immediately after the meeting, the principal asked to speak with her and told her he wished she had raised this issue privately rather than publicly. A lower court determined that the speech clearly touched on a matter of public concern, but that the school system's interest in avoiding racial tensions outweighed the aide's right to free speech. On appeal, however, the Eleventh Circuit reversed, writing that the aide's "remarks did not disrupt the School System's function by enhancing racial division, nor, based on the nature or context of her remarks, was her speech likely to do so."[177]

76. If a teacher is in part terminated for constitutionally protected speech, may a school board still avoid any constitutional violation?

Public employers, including school boards, do have the opportunity to make a so-called *Mt. Healthy* defense and claim they would have made the same decision to take adverse action against the employee, even if the employee had not engaged in any constitutionally protected speech.

The Supreme Court established this defense in the case of *Mt. Healthy City School District Board v. Doyle*.[178] In *Mt. Healthy*, a teacher alleged he was fired in retaliation for calling a radio station about the adoption of a teacher dress code.

The school board admitted it had fired the teacher in part for his action in contacting the radio station about school board policy. However, the school board also cited several other instances of the teacher's misconduct, including allegedly making an obscene gesture to two female students who would not obey his orders, insulting students with foul language, and arguing and engaging in physical contact with another teacher.

Lower courts determined that the teacher showed that his constitutionally protected conduct of contacting the radio station on a matter of public concern was a "substantial" or "motivating" factor in the decision to discharge him. And on appeal, the Supreme Court accepted the lower court's finding that the teacher's speech was constitutionally protected speech. However, the Court determined that the lower court "should have gone on to determine whether the Board had shown by a preponderance of the evidence that it would have reached the same decision as to respondent's reemployment even in the absence of the protected conduct."[179]

Thus, a court in a First Amendment retaliation case must ask two questions:

1. whether the employee's First Amendment–protected activity was a substantial or motivating factor in the adverse employment action; and
2. whether the employer would have reached the same decision even if the employee had not engaged in the constitutionally protected conduct.

77. Must a public school teacher salute the flag during a recitation of the Pledge of Allegiance?

Probably not. This answer stems from the landmark 1943 Supreme Court decision *West Virginia State Board of Education v. Barnette*, where the high court ruled that public school students had a First Amendment right not to salute the flag.[180]

Even though the *Barnette* decision speaks directly about public school students, the same principles have been extended to teachers in subsequent decisions. In one case, a federal appeals court ruled that school officials violated the First Amendment rights of a public school arts teacher when they fired her for refusing to salute the flag.[181] "We take guidance, instead," they ruled, "from the Supreme Court's instruction in *Tinker*, whose lesson is that neither students nor teachers 'shed their constitutional rights to freedom of speech or expression at the schoolhouse gate.' "[182] The court noted that the teacher did not "proselytize" her students but stood in respectful silence and that another teacher led the students in the pledge.

A teacher's right not to salute the flag, however, may not extend to all other exercises related to the school. In a case from the Seventh Circuit, for example, a Jehovah's Witness kindergarten teacher was fired when she informed the principal she could not teach any part of the curriculum that involved patriotic activities. Although one of these activities included saluting the flag, the teacher felt she must also not engage in prescribed elements of the curriculum involving patriotism, in any secular or religious holiday, or in the celebration of student birthdays. As the court ruled, "[t]here is a compelling state interest in the choice and adherence to a suitable curriculum. . . . It cannot be left to individual teachers to teach what they please."[183]

78. May a teacher wear clothing not approved by a teacher dress code?

Probably not. The few published court decisions dealing with teacher dress codes have sided with school officials.

The 1970s case of Richard Brimley is instructive. Brimley, an English teacher in a Connecticut high school, challenged a reprimand he received for violating the teacher dress code by refusing to wear a necktie. The school board argued that its tie code supported its interest in maintaining a professional image for its teachers, and for engendering respect and discipline from the students. Brimley, through the teachers union, argued that his failure to wear a necktie implicated his First Amendment free expression rights in several ways, including (1) presenting himself as someone not tied to "establishment conformity"; and (2) showing his students that he rejected many of the values associated with the older generation.

A panel of three federal judges in the Second Circuit struck the balance in favor of Brimley, finding that the case implicated both a 14th Amendment liberty interest and a First Amendment free speech interest.

However, the full panel of the Second Circuit reversed in *East Hartford Education Association v. Board of Education*.[184] "The very notion of public education implies substantial public control," the full appeals court wrote. "Educational decisions must be made by someone; there is no reason to create a constitutional preference for the views of individual teachers over those of their employers."[185] The appeals court concluded: "If Mr. Brimley has any protected interest in his neckwear, it does not weigh very heavily on the constitutional scales."[186]

Other courts have reached similar results in teacher dress code cases. For example, a federal court in Mississippi upheld the discharge of a teacher's aide for refusing to abide by the dress code of the school.[187] The aide asserted she had a constitutional right to wear berets to show her African American heritage and her religious beliefs. The school district countered that the berets were "inappropriate attire." Ultimately, the court sided with the school board, finding that the teacher failed to communicate to school district officials that she had a religious basis for her conduct. However, the court noted that the "[d]istrict is required, under the First Amendment and Title VII, to make some accommodation for the practice of religious beliefs when it pursues an end which incidentally burdens religious practices."[188]

Despite this statement in the *McGlothlin* case, other courts have rejected claims that state statutes restricting teachers from wearing religious clothing are unconstitutional. In *United States v. Board of Education*, for example, the Third Circuit rejected a Title VII[189] religious discrimination claim against a school board for prohibiting a Muslim substitute teacher from wearing her religious clothing.[190]

The case originated with a Pennsylvania statute, called the "Garb Statute," which provided that "no teacher in any public school shall wear . . . or while engaged in the performance of his duty as such teacher any dress, mark, emblem or insignia indicating the fact that such teacher is a member or adherent of any religious order, sect or denomination." In its ruling, the Third Circuit determined it would impose an "undue hardship" on the school to require it to accommodate the Muslim teacher's request to wear her religious clothing. Such an accommodation, according to the court, would represent a "significant threat to the maintenance of religious neutrality in the public school system."[191]

Similarly, the Oregon Supreme Court rejected a free exercise challenge— under the First Amendment and a provision of the state constitution— to an Oregon statute prohibiting teachers from wearing religious clothing.[192] The teacher, who was an adherent to the Sikh religion, argued against the constitutionality of a state law that provided: "No teacher in any public school shall wear any religious dress while engaged in the performance of duties as a teacher."

The Oregon high court upheld the statute, writing that "the aim of maintaining the religious neutrality of the public schools furthers a constitutional obligation beyond an ordinary policy preference for the legislature."[193]

It should be noted that although these decisions permit states and school districts to restrict the wearing of religious garb, they do not require such restrictions. Two states, Arkansas and Tennessee, have statutes explicitly allowing teachers to wear religious garb in public schools. In states without such laws, the vast majority of state courts have held that public schools may allow teachers to wear religious clothing.[194]

79. May teachers wear religious jewelry in the classroom?

Most experts agree that teachers are permitted to wear unobtrusive jewelry, such as a cross or a Star of David. But they should not wear clothing with a proselytizing message (e.g., a "Jesus Saves" T-shirt).

80. Is a teacher's classroom a public forum?

According to many courts, a teacher's classroom is *not* a public forum.

Recently, for example, a high school English teacher in Pennsylvania asserted that school classrooms were designated public forums and that she had a constitutional right to post Learn ball literature, symbols, and paraphernalia in her classroom.

A federal district court, however, rejected her claim in the case of *Murray v. Pittsburgh Board of Public Education*.[195] The court noted that the teacher failed "to direct the court to a single case in which a public high school classroom was determined to be a designated open public forum," and added:

> This is not surprising as it is simply not the law. A public high school classroom is a nonpublic forum. As such, a school may restrict the use of its classrooms to serve the school's intended educational purposes as long as the restrictions are reasonable and are not an effort to suppress a teacher's expression merely because the school opposes his particular views.[196]

In another case, a federal court in Virginia implied that school officials *could* create a designated public forum on teachers' classroom doors by allowing speech about certain topics. However, the court in that case also ruled that the school principal could prohibit a teacher from posting a pamphlet advertising banned books on his classroom door. "It would be ludicrous to insist that teachers could post anything they want on their doorways," the judge wrote.[197]

81. May a teacher be punished for teaching subjects school officials or parents deem unsuitable?

Probably. Teachers must remember that most courts consistently rule that teachers do not have a First Amendment right to trump the curriculum mandated by the school board. Furthermore, some courts take a narrow view of what constitutes "communicative conduct" that implicates the First Amendment.

For example, the Sixth Circuit ruled that school officials did not violate the First Amendment rights of a teacher when they fired her for showing the R-rated movie *Pink Floyd—The Wall* in her classroom. Even though the Supreme Court has determined since the 1950s that movies are a form of expression protected by the First Amendment, the Sixth Circuit determined that the teacher's conduct in showing the R-rated movie was not "expressive or communicative, under the circumstances presented."[198]

However, the same Sixth Circuit reinstated a former elementary school teacher who had claimed she was fired for inviting actor Woody Harrelson to come speak to her class about the environmental benefits of hemp. A lower court had dismissed her suit, ruling that the teacher's choice of classroom speaker "was neither expressive nor intended to con-vey a particularized message." On appeal, the Sixth Circuit reversed, find-ing that a teacher's choice of an in-class speaker was a form of expression entitled to at least some First Amendment protection.[199]

82. May a teacher refuse to teach certain materials in class if she feels the curriculum infringes on her personal beliefs?

Generally, teachers must instruct their students in accordance with the established curriculum. For example, the Ninth Circuit ruled in 1994 against a high school biology teacher who had challenged his school dis-trict's requirement that he teach evolution, as well as its order barring him from discussing his religious beliefs with students. In the words of the court, "[a] school district's restriction on [a] teacher's right of free speech in prohibiting [the] teacher from talking with students about religion dur-ing the school day, including times when he was not actually teaching class, [is] justified by the school district's interest in avoiding [an] Estab-lishment Clause violation."[200]

More recently, a state appeals court ruled again that a high school teacher did not have a First Amendment right to refuse to teach evolution in a high school biology class.[201] The teacher had argued that the school district had reassigned him to another school and another course because it wanted to silence his criticism of evolution as a viable scientific theory. The state appeals court rejected that argument, pointing out that the teacher could not override the established curriculum.

Other courts have similarly found that teachers do not have a First Amendment right to trump school district decisions regarding the cur-riculum.[202] One court wrote: "the First Amendment has never required school districts to abdicate control over public school curricula to the unfettered discretion of individual teachers."[203] More recently, the Fourth Circuit ruled that a teacher had "no First Amendment right to insist on the makeup of the curriculum."[204]

83. May a teacher censor a student's artistic expression?

Teachers possess a great deal of control over classroom assignments and other matters related to teaching the curriculum. In the context of an assigned art project, for example, teachers have the right to make sure that students are meeting the requirements of their assigned work. In art class, this may mean that a student's work receives poor marks if it fails to meet the standards and requirements of the assignment.

One federal appeals court, for example, rejected a student's First Amendment claim in the context of a research topic. The court wrote: "[F]ederal courts should exercise particular restraint in classroom conflicts between student and teacher over matters falling within the ordinary authority over curriculum and course content."[205]

Of course, this does not mean that a teacher may mark a student down simply because the teacher disagrees with the message the work intends to convey, especially if other aspects of the work meet the requirements of the assignment.

Teachers are sometimes unsure about whether they may allow students to include religious images or ideas in their assignments. Generally, students may express their beliefs about religion if such expression is relevant to the subject under consideration and meets the requirements of the assignment.[206] To censor such forms of expression may violate a student's free exercise rights.

However, some recent lower court decisions have upheld the decision by school officials to prohibit religious expression by primary students, if the teacher has a concern that the expression might be seen as school promotion of religion.[207]

If a student's artistic expression is *not* part of her schoolwork, then the work should be examined by the tests set out in the *Tinker* and *Fraser* standards. Under *Fraser*, if it is vulgar, profane, or obscene, then a teacher has the authority to remove the work or restrict its presence on school grounds. If the expression does not violate those restrictions, then the school, under *Tinker*, must prove they have evidence that the expressive work will substantially interfere with the working of the school or will interfere with the rights of others.

84. May teachers and administrators pray or otherwise express their faith while at school?

As employees of the government, public school teachers and administrators are subject to the Establishment Clause and thus required to be neutral concerning religion while carrying out their duties. That means, for example, that school officials do not have the right to pray with or in the presence of students during the school day.

Of course, teachers and administrators—like students—bring their faith with them through the schoolhouse door each morning. Because of the First Amendment, however, school officials who wish to pray or engage in other religious activities—unless they are silent—should do so outside the presence of students.

If a group of teachers wishes to meet for prayer or scriptural study in the faculty lounge during free time in the school day, most legal experts see no constitutional reason why they should not be permitted to do so, as long as the activity is outside the presence of students and does not interfere with their duties or the rights of other teachers.[208]

As noted in an earlier question, teachers are permitted to wear unobtrusive jewelry, such as a cross or the Star of David. But teachers should not wear clothing with a proselytizing message (e.g., a "Jesus Saves" T-shirt).

When not on duty, of course, educators are free like all other citizens to practice their faith. But school officials must refrain from using their position in the public school to promote their outside religious activities.

85. How should teachers respond if students ask them about their religious beliefs?

Some teachers prefer not to answer the question, believing that it is inappropriate for a teacher to inject personal beliefs into the classroom. Other teachers may choose to answer the question directly and succinctly in the interest of an open and honest classroom environment.

Before answering the question, however, teachers should consider the age of the students. Middle and high school students may be able to distinguish between a personal conviction and the official position of the school; very young children may not. In any case, the teacher may answer at most with a brief statement of personal belief—but may not turn the question into an opportunity to proselytize for or against religion. Teachers may neither reward nor punish students because they agree or disagree with the religious views of the teacher.

Book Selection and Other Decisions About the Curriculum

86. Do students have a First Amendment right to receive information in books?

Yes, the First Amendment protects the right to receive information and ideas. In 1982, the Supreme Court determined in *Board of Education, Island Trees v. Pico* that "the First Amendment rights of students may be directly and sharply implicated by the removal of books from the shelves of a school library."[209]

In the *Pico* case, the school district argued that decisions by school officials about library books did not raise a First Amendment issue, and that they should have *carte blanche* to remove a library book for any reason. The Court disagreed, ruling that school officials had violated the First Amendment when they removed library books simply because they disagreed with the ideas and information contained therein.

It is important to note that the Court's decision applies only to the removal of books from library shelves, and not to either the acquisition of books or to matters related to the curriculum. In those circumstances, school officials have more leeway when selecting books for a school reading list than in removing books from library shelves.

87. May school officials remove library books for reasons other than objections to the ideas contained in the books?

Yes. According to the Supreme Court in *Pico*, although school officials may not remove books simply because they disagree with the ideas expressed therein, they can remove books from the library if they deem them to be "pervasively vulgar" or educationally unsuitable.

The issue centers on the motivation of school officials. In Louisiana, for example, a school board removed the book *Voodoo & Hoodoo* after a parent complained that the book caused children to become infatuated with the supernatural. The school board eventually voted 12 to 2 to remove the book, even though a school-level committee had voted unanimously to retain it. In response, one parent sued on behalf of her child, claiming the removal of the book violated the First Amendment. A federal trial court ruled in favor of the parent. On appeal, however, the Fifth Circuit reversed, finding there were genuine factual disputes as to the school board's motivation for removing the book.

The appeals court, in ruling there would need to be further fact finding in the lower court to determine the true motivation for the removal of the book, wrote: "Further development of the record is necessary to determine whether the School Board exercised its discretion over educational matters in a manner that comports with the First Amendment."[210]

88. Do school officials possess greater authority in removing books from the curriculum than in the school library?

Yes, school officials possess greater authority to regulate matters pertaining to the curriculum. In fact, using the *Hazelwood* standard of student expression, several lower courts have determined that school officials can remove books from the curriculum as long as they have a reasonable educational basis for doing so.

For example, one federal appeals court determined that school officials could remove a humanities textbook because two selections in the book, Aristophanes' *Lysistrata* and Geoffrey Chaucer's *The Miller's Tale*, were deemed too sexually explicit and vulgar. A group of students and parents protested, pointing out that the two challenged pieces were "acclaimed masterpieces of Western literature."[211] The court acknowledged this, but determined that the school board's actions were, under *Hazelwood*, reasonably related "to its legitimate concerns regarding the appropriateness (for this high school audience) of the sexuality and vulgarity in these works."

89. What types of books are most subject to censorship?

Many different types of books have been subject to censorship, although most are censored for (a) vulgar or sexually explicit language; (b) "racist" language; (c) gay and lesbian themes; or (d) discussions of witchcraft and the occult.

Two of the biggest targets in recent years, as identified by a report from the American Library Association, are Maya Angelou's *I Know Why the Caged Bird Sings* and Mark Twain's *The Adventures of Huckleberry Finn* (see Figure 4).

Many school districts have received complaints about Angelou's work because it contains a rape scene and because some perceive it as "anti-white." Mark Twain's *Huck Finn* has been subject to censorship for language deemed demeaning to African Americans.

These examples demonstrate that *any* book, if it contains any ideas that could be deemed controversial, may be questioned. As a result, school districts should develop policies on how to handle challenges to certain books, and how to ensure that decisions regarding removal of books from the library comport with the First Amendment.

90. Is it constitutional for public schools to post "In God We Trust" in classrooms?

The courts have not directly answered this question about the use of the national motto in public schools.[212] Now that several states have passed laws requiring public schools to post "In God We Trust" in classrooms, we are likely to see legal challenges to the practice.

FIGURE 4

The 10 Most Frequently Challenged Books of 1990–1999

1. *Scary Stories* (Series) by Alvin Schwartz
2. *Daddy's Roommate* by Michael Willhoite
3. *I Know Why the Caged Bird* Sings by Maya Angelou
4. *The Chocolate War* by Robert Cormier
5. *The Adventures of Huckleberry Finn* by Mark Twain
6. *Of Mice and Men* by John Steinbeck
7. *Forever* by Judy Blume
8. *Bridge to Terabithia* by Katherine Paterson
9. *Heather Has Two Mommies* by Leslea Newman
10. *The Catcher in the Rye* by J.D. Salinger

Adapted from the American Library Association's list of the 100 Most Frequently Challenged Books of 1990–1999. For more information, visit http://ala.org. Used with permission.

Some Supreme Court observers argue that the Court is unlikely to strike down posting "In God We Trust" in classrooms. They point out that in several past cases involving school prayer and holiday displays, the justices have sometimes described references to God in the Pledge of Allegiance and the national motto as mere "ceremonial deism" that do not rise to the level of government establishment of religion.

Others contend that the courts are generally stricter when applying the Establishment Clause in public schools because impressionable young people at school are a "captive audience." It's possible, therefore, that a judge might view posting "In God We Trust" in public schools as state endorsement of religion, especially if it could be shown that the primary purpose of the posting is to promote religion.

In light of previous Supreme Court cases involving holiday displays, a display of the national motto placed in historical context (e.g., a history of how the motto came to be adopted, or discussion of E Pluribus Unum, our other national motto) might be more likely to be upheld as constitutional. Some schools in states that require the posting of the motto have decided to create an educational display about the history and meaning of both national mottos. In this way, the display serves an academic purpose and is less likely to be perceived as school endorsement of religion.

Notes

[1]State ex rel. Dresser v. Dist. Bd. of Sch. Dist. No. 1, 135 Wis. 619, 116 N.W. 232 (Wis. 1908).

[2]Wooster v. Sunderland, 27 Cal. App. 51, 148 P. 959 (Cal. App. 1915).

[3]West Virginia Sch. Bd. v. Barnette, 319 U.S. 624 (1943).

[4]Minersville Sch. Dist. v. Gobitis, 310 U.S. 586 (1940).

[5]Barnette, 319 U.S. at 637.

[6]Id. at 642.

[7]Marsh v. Chambers, 463 U.S. 783 (1983) (legislative prayer); Engel v. Vitale, 370 U.S. 421 (1962) (teacher-led prayer).

[8]From Religious liberty, public education, and the future of American democracy, a statement of principles found in Haynes & Thomas (2001). *Finding common ground: A guide to religious liberty in public schools*. Nashville, TN: First Amendment Center.

[9]See Bd. of Education v. Mergens, 496 U.S. 226 (1990).

[10]Settle v. Dickson County Sch. Bd., 53 F.3d 152 (6th Cir. 1995), *cert. denied*, 516 U.S. 989 (1995).

[11]DeNooyer v. Livonia Public Schools, 799 F. Supp. 744 (E.D. Mich. 1992); Guidry v. Broussard, 897 F.2d 181 (5th Cir. 1989); Cole v. Oroville Union High Sch., 229 F.3d 1092 (9th Cir. 2000).

[12]Reynolds v. U.S., 98 U.S. 145 (1878).

[13]Sherbert v. Verner, 374 U.S. 398 (1963).

[14]Employment Div. v. Smith, 494 U.S. 872 (1990).

[15]Twenty-two national educational and religious organizations agreed to this language in "A teacher's guide to religion in the public schools," found in Haynes & Thomas (2001).

[16]Wisconsin v. Yoder, 406 U.S. 205 (1972).

[17]This is the language supported by a broad range of civil liberties and religious groups in a joint statement of current law. For more information, go to http://www.ed.gov/Speeches/04–1995/prayer.html.

[18]Engel v. Vitale, 370 U.S. 421 (1962); Sch. Dist. of Abington Township v. Shempp, 374 U.S. 203 (1963); Lee v. Weisman, 505 U.S. 577 (1992); Santa Fe Independent Sch. Dist. v. Doe, 530 U.S. 290 (2000).

[19]See generally, Tinker v. Des Moines Independent Sch. Dist., 393 U.S. 503 (1969).

[20]Id.

[21]Lee v. Weisman, 505 U.S. 577 (1992).

[22]C.H. v. Olivia, 226 F.3d 198 (2nd Cir. 2000), *cert. denied*, 533 U.S. 915 (2001).

[23]See Bown v. Gwinnett County Sch. Dist., 112 F.3d 1464 (11th Cir. 1997).

[24]Wallace v. Jaffree, 472 U.S. 38 (1985).

[25]Lee v. Weisman, 505 U.S. 577 (1992).

[26]Santa Fe Independent Sch. Dist. v. Doe, 530 U.S. 290 (2000).

[27]Id. at 305–306.

[28]Id. at 306.

[29]Id.

[30]Id.

[31]Adler v. Duval County, 250 F.3d 1330 (11th Cir. 2001), *cert. denied*, 122 S. Ct. 664 (2001).

[32]See Doe v. Madison Sch. Dist., 177 F.3d 789 (9th Cir. 1998, vacated on other grounds); Adler v. Duval County, 250 F.3d 1330 (11th Cir. 2001), *cert. denied*, 122 S. Ct. 664 (2001).

[33]Bd. of Education v. Mergens, 496 U.S. 226 (1990).

[34]20 U.S.C. 4071(c)(3).

[35]The Equal Access Act: Questions and answers, found in Haynes & Thomas (2001).

[36]Katz v. McAulay, 438 F.2d 1058 (2nd Cir. N.Y. 1971), *cert. denied*, 405 U.S. 933 (1972).

[37]Fricke v. Lynch, 491 F. Supp. 381 (D.R.I. 1980). It is important to note that this case was appealed to the First Circuit where it was dismissed as moot.

[38]Abington Sch. Dist. v. Shempp, 374 U.S. 203 (1963).

[39]Based on guidelines originally published by the Public Education Religious Studies Center at Wright State University and subsequently agreed to by 17 national religious and educational organizations in "Religion in the public school curriculum: Questions and answers." The full guidelines may be found in Haynes & Thomas (2001).

[40]*Finding Common Ground*, pp. 89–102.

[41]For a full discussion of teaching about religion in public schools, see Nord & Haynes (1998). *Taking religion seriously across the curriculum*. Alexandria, VA: Association for Supervision and Curriculum Development; and Nashville, TN: First Amendment Center.

[42]The Character Education Partnership provides complete information on how to start a character education program and provides a clearinghouse of character education resources. Contact the Character Education Partnership at 1025 Connecticut Ave. NW, Suite 1011, Washington, DC 20036, or visit the CEP Web site at www.character.org.

[43]Peck v. Upshur County, 155 F.3d 274 (4th Cir. 1998).

[44]Good News Club v. Milford, 533 U.S. 98 (2001).

[45]Lamb's Chapel v. Center Moriches Union Free Sch. Dist., 508 U.S. 384 (1993); Good News Club v. Milford, 533 U.S. 98 (2001).

[46]Good News Club v. Milford, 533 U.S. 98 (2001).

[47]For more detailed guidelines, see *Public schools and religious communities: A First Amendment guide* (1999) published by the American Jewish Congress, Christian Legal Society, and First Amendment Center and co-signed by 12 additional educational and religious organizations.

[48]Zorach v. Clauson, 343 U.S. 306 (1952).

[49]This is different from the religious liberty tests, which are general rules applicable to society at large.

[50]Hudson, D. On 30-year anniversary, Tinker participants look back on landmark case. [Online] Available: http://www.firstamendmentcenter.org/analysis.aspx?id=5582&SearchString=david.

[51]Tinker v. Des Moines Independent Sch. Dist., 393 U.S. 503, 506 (1969).

[52]Id. at 508.

[53]Id. at 514.

[54]Bethel Sch. Dist. v. Fraser, 478 U.S. 675 (1986).

[55]Id. at 683.

[56]Id. at 681.

[57]Id. at 683.

[58]Broussard v. School Board of the City of Norfolk, 801 F. Supp. 1526 (E.D. Virg. 1992).

[59]Id. at 1537.

[60]It is interesting to note that the Hazelwood standard closely approximates the standard from the 1987 prison case of Turner v. Safley, 482 U.S. 78 (1987), one year before Hazelwood. In that ruling, the U.S. Supreme Court established the following standard for prisoner constitutional rights: "[W]hen a prison regulation impinges on inmates' constitutional rights, the regulation is valid if it is reasonably related to legitimate penological interests."

[61]See Henerey v. City of St. Charles Sch. Dist., 200 F.3d 1128 (8th Cir. 1999).

[62]Desilets v. Clearview Bd. of Education, 630 A.2d 333, (S. Ct. N.J. 1993), *aff'd*, 137 N.J. 585 (1994).

[63]A few courts have determined that the Fraser case only applies to vulgar student speech that is school sponsored. See D.G. v. Independent Sch. Dist. No. 11, 2000 U.S. Dist. LEXIS 12197 (N.D. Okl.)(8/21/2000).

[64]See Chandler v. McMinnville Sch. Dist., 978 F.2d 524 (9th Cir. 1992).

[65]Denno v. Sch. Bd. of Volusia County, 218 F.3d 1267 (11th Cir. 2000).

[66]Castorina v. Madison County Sch. Bd., 246 F.3d 536 (6th Cir. 2001).

[67]Crosby v. Holsinger, 852 F.2d 801, 802 (4th Cir. 1988).

[68]Linmark Associates, Inc. v. Township of Willingboro, 431 U.S. 85 (1977).

[69]Vinson v. Wilson County Sch. Bd., No. 3:00–0287 (M.D. Tenn.)(9/1/2000).

[70]See ACLU victorious in student armband case. [Online] Available: http://www.aclu.org/news/1999/n083099c.html.

[71]The West Virginia Board of Education had passed a resolution requiring public school students to salute the flag and recite the Pledge of Allegiance. Students who failed to comply were deemed insubordinate and subject to expulsion. The students' parents were subject to fines and 30 days in jail.

[72]Minersville Sch. Dist. v. Gobitis, 310 U.S. 586 (1940).

[73]West Virginia Bd. of Education v. Barnette, 319 U.S. 624 (1943).

[74]The words "under God" were added to the pledge by Congress in 1954 at the height of the Cold War.

[75]Newdow v. U.S. Congress, No. 00-16423 (9th Cir. 2002).

[76]Calvert, C. (2000). Free speech and public schools in a post-Columbine world: Check your speech rights at the schoolhouse metal detector, *Denv. L. Rev.*, 77, 739; Hudson, D. L., Jr. (2000). Censorship of student Internet speech: The effect of diminishing student rights, fear of the Internet and Columbine. *L. Rev. M.S.U.-D.C.L*, 199, 209–210.

[77]Watkins, W. D., & Hooks, J. S. (1999). The legal aspects of school violence: Balancing school safety with students' rights, *Miss. L.J.*, *69* 641, 642–643.

[78]Lavine v. Blaine School District, 257 F.3d 981 (9th Cir. 2001) *cert. denied*, 122 S. Ct. 2663 (2002).

[79]Hudson, D. (2000, February 28). School violence poem was protected speech, not true threat, judge rules. [Online] Available: http://www.firstamendmentcenter.org/news.aspx?id=8305&SearchString=david.

[80]Lavine, 257 F.3d at 990.

[81]Boman v. Bluestem Unified Sch. Dist. No. 205, 2000 U.S. Dist. LEXIS 5297, Case No. 00-1034-WEB, (Dist. Kan.) (Feb. 14, 2000).

[82]Id. at *6.

[83]See Saxe v. State College Area Sch. Dist., 240 F.3d 200 (3rd Cir. 2001).

[84]Colo. Rev. Stat. δ 22-32-109.1 (2001).

[85]Franklin v. Gwinnett County Public Sch., 503 U.S. 60 (1992); Davis v. Monroe County Bd. of Education, 526 U.S. 629 (1999).

[86]Title IX of the Education Amendment of 1972, 20 U.S.C. § 1681(a).

[87]Rehabilitation Act of 1973, 29 U.S.C. § 794.

[88]Title VI of the Civil Rights Act of 1964, 42 U.S.C. § 2000d. Age has also been a protected category, though age is not a factor in the public primary or secondary school discussion.

[89]Davis v. Monroe County Bd. of Education, 526 U.S. 629 (1999).

[90]Id.

[91]Saxe v. State College Area Sch. Dist., 240 F.3d 200 (3rd Cir. 2001).

[92]Texas v. Johnson, 491 U.S. 397, 414 (1989).

[93]Watts v. U.S., 394 U.S. 705 (1969).

[94]Rothman, J. E. (2001). Freedom of speech and true threats. *Harv. J. L. & P.P.*, *25*, 283, 288 ("Even though the Supreme Court has made clear that true threats are punishable, it has not clearly defined what speech constitutes a true threat.").

[95]U.S. v. Miller, 115 F.3d 361 (6th Cir. 1997), *cert. denied*, 522 U.S. 883 (1997).

[96]See Jones v. State of Arkansas, 64 S.W.3d 728, 735 (Ark. 2002) (determining that a student giving his rap song threatening violence to another student was a true threat).

[97]State ex rel. *R.T.*, 781 So.2d 1239 (La. 2001).

[98]Id. at 1247.

[99]In re Ryan D., Case No. C035092, 2002 Cal. App. LEXIS 4453 (Cal. App. 3rd Dist., July 30, 2002).

[100]Id. at *16.

[101]Thomas v. Granville, 607 F.2d 1043 (2nd Cir. 1979), *cert. denied*, 444 U.S. 1081 (1980); Klein v. Smith, 635 F. Supp. 1440 (Dist. Me. 1986).

[102]Boucher v. Sch. Bd. of the Sch. Dist. of Greenfield, 134 F.3d 821 (7th Cir. 1998).

[103]See Lavine v. Blaine Sch. Dist., 257 F.3d 981 (9th Cir. 2001), *cert. denied*, 122 S. Ct. 2663 (2002).

[104]J. S. v. Bethlehem Area Sch. Dist., 757 A.2d 412 (Pa. Cmwlth. 2000).

[105]403 U.S. 15 (1971).

[106]478 U.S. 675 (1986).

[107]Id. at 683.

[108]Thomas v. Bd. Of Educ., Granville Cent. Sch. Dist., 607 F.2d 1043, 1057 (J. Newman, concurring).

[109]Hedges v. Wauconda Community Sch. Dist., 9 F.3d 1295 (7th Cir. 1993).

[110]Id.

[111]Tinker v. Des Moines Independent Sch. Dist., 393 U.S. 503, 507–508 (1969).

[112]Hudson, D. (2000, September 14). Students can wear logos protesting school dress code, said federal judge. [Online]. Visit www.firstamendmentcenter.org for the full article.

[113]Ray, A. (1995). A nation of robots? The unconstitutionality of public school uniform codes, *J. Marshall L. Rev.*, *28*, 645, 682.

[114]Long v. Bd. of Education of Jefferson County, Kentucky, 121 F. Supp. 2d. 621 (W.D. Kent. 2000), *aff'd*, 2001 U.S. App. LEXIS 18103 (2001).

[115]Oleson v. Bd. of Education of Sch. Dist., No. 228, 676 F. Supp. 820 (N.D. Ill. 1987).

[116]Chalifoux v. New Caney Independent Sch. Dist., 976 F. Supp. 659 (S.D. Tex. 1997).

[117]Hudson, D. (1999, August 17). Parents across the South battle mandatory school dress codes. [Online] Available: http://www.firstamendmentcenter.org/news.aspx?id=7810&SearchString=david.

[118]Texas v. Johnson, 491 U.S. 397 (1989); Spence v. Washington, 418 U.S. 405 (1974).

[119]Bivens v. Albuquerque Public Schools, 899 F. Supp. 556 (D. N.M. 1995), *aff'd*, 1997 U.S. App. LEXIS 34008 (1997).

[120]A court will most likely apply the *Tinker* standard to student clothing that conveys a political or religious message.

[121]Broussard v. Sch. Bd. of the City of Norfolk, 801 F. Supp. 1526 (E.D. Va. 1992).

[122]U.S. v. O'Brien, 391 U.S. 367 (1968).

[123]Canady v. Bossier, 240 F.3d 437, 443 (5th Cir. 2001); see also Littlefield v. Forney Independent Sch. Dist., 268 F.3d 275 (5th Cir. 2001).

[124]Littlefield, 268 F.3d at 287.

[125]Richards v. Thurston, 424 F.2d 1281 (1st Cir. 1970); Dwen v. Barry, 483 F.2d 1126 (2nd Cir. 1973); Massie v. Henry, 455 F.2d 779 (4th Cir. 1972); Arnold v. Carpenter, 459 F.2d 939 (7th Cir. 1972); Bishop v. Colaw, 450 F.2d 1069 (8th Cir. 1971).

[126]Zeller v. Donegal Sch. Dist., 517 F.2d 600 (3rd Cir. 1975); Karr v. Schmidt, 460 F.2d 609 (5th Cir. 1972); Gfell v. Rickelman, 441 F.2d 444 (6th Cir. 1971); King v. Saddleback Jr. College Dist., 445 F.2d 932 (9th Cir. 1971), *cert. denied*, 404 U.S. 979 (1971); Hatch v. Goerke, 502 F.2d 1189 (10th Cir. 1974).

[127]See Federal court reinstates high school student suspended for blue hair. (1999, June 4). American Civil Liberties Union. [Online] Available: http://www.aclu.org/news/1999/n060499a.html.

[128]Zeller, 517 F.2d. at 605–606.

[129]Phillips v. Anderson County Sch. Dist., 987 F. Supp. 488 (D.S.C. 1997).

[130]Castorina v. Madison County Sch. Bd., 246 F.3d 536 (6th Cir. 2001).

[131]Denno v. Sch. Bd. of Volusia County, 218 F.3d 1267 (11th Cir. 2000), *cert. denied*, 531 U.S. 958 (2000).

[132]See Employment Div. v. Smith, 494 U.S. 872 (2000).

[133]Haynes, C. (2000, January 16). School officials ease up on uniform enforcement [Online] http://www.firstamendmentcenter.org//commentary.aspx?id=2433&SearchString=charles.

[134]Id.

[135]See Thomas v. Bd. of Education Granville Central Sch. Dist., 607 F.2d 1043 (2nd Cir. 1979), *cert. denied*, 444 U.S. 1081 (1980).

[136]http://www.ojr.org/ojr/ethics/1017961581.php.

[137]J.S. v. Bethlehem Area Sch. Dist., 757 A.2d 412 (Pa. Cmwlth. 2000).

[138]See generally Hudson (2000).

[139]Beussink v. Woodland R-IV Sch. Dist., 30 F. Supp. 2d 1175, 1180 (E.D. Mo. 1998).

[140]ALA v. U.S., 201 F. Supp.2d 401, 2002 U.S. Dist. LEXIS 9537 (E.D. Pa. 2002).

[141]Id. at *18.

[142]Chris Hansen, senior national staff counsel for the American Civil Liberties Union (personal communication, August 19, 2002).

[143]Pub. L. No. 106-554.

[144]CIPA's predecessor, the Child Online Protection Act (COPA), was ruled unconstitutional in November of 1998. On appeal, the U.S. Supreme Court sent the case back for further review, but the Third Circuit Court of Appeals ruled again, in March 2003, that COPA was unconstitutional because it was still not "narrowly tailored" enough to avoid infringing on the free speech rights of adults.

[145]*Consumer Reports*, March 2001.

[146]The students had prepared a two-page center spread that featured stories on teenage pregnancy, divorce, and runaways. They learned that the pages had been omitted when the paper returned from the printers. Almost immediately, three of the student journalists filed suit.

[147]With regard to school newspapers, the Supreme Court suggested that any publication that is supervised by a faculty member and created by the school to offer a particular set of skills is curricular, and would bear the school's imprimatur. By extension, that also means that the *Hazelwood* ruling can apply to school yearbooks, school plays, literary magazines, or any other form of school-sponsored speech that fulfills the given criteria.

[148]See generally O'Neill, K. F. (2000). A First Amendment compass: Navigating the speech clause with a five-step analytical framework, *SW Univ. L. Rev.*, *29* 223, 284–289.

[149]460 U.S. 37 (1983).

[150]484 U.S. 260 (1988).

[151]460 U.S. at 49.

[152]Id. at 51.

[153]484 U.S. at 267.

[154]Mass. Ann. Laws ch. 71, § 82 (2001).

[155]See Thomas v. Bd. of Education, 607 F.2d 1043, 1051 (2nd Cir. 1979), *cert. denied*, 444 U.S. 1081 (1980).

[156]Some courts, however, have granted school officials greater authority to regulate the distribution of underground newspapers that are pervasively vulgar. See Bystrom v. Fridley High Sch., 822 F.2d 747 (8th Cir. 1987).

[157]The key word here is "reasonable." School officials may not place restrictions on the distribution of materials that are intended to stifle the dissemination of viewpoints the school may dislike.

[158]New York Times v. Sullivan, 376 U.S. 254 (1964). It is important to note, however, that the decision in *Sullivan* only applies to public figures, who can still sue if the inaccurate statement has been published with "actual malice"—namely, actual knowledge of its falsity or reckless disregard for the truth. For private figures, such as students, the standard is still simple negligence as per Gertz v. Robert Welch, Inc., 418 U.S. 323 (1974).

[159]Yeo v. Town of Lexington, 131 F.3d 241 (1st Cir. 1997), *cert. denied*, 524 U.S. 904 (1998).

[160]See Nisbet, M. (1998). Public access to student publications: Does the rejection of a political advertisement violate the right to free speech? *J.L. & Educ.* 27 323.

[161]Tinker, 393 U.S. at 506.

[162]McAuliffe v. Mayor of New Bedford, 155 Mass. 216, 29 N.E. 517 (1892).

[163]Pickering v. Bd. of Education, 391 U.S. 563 (1968).

[164]Hudson, D. (2001, July 20). Teacher looks back on letter that led to firing—and Supreme Court victory. [Online] Available: http://www.firstamendmentcenter.org//analysis.aspx?id=4828& SearchString=david.

[165]Pickering v. Bd. of Education, 391 U.S. 563 (1968); Connick v. Myers, 461 U.S. 138 (1983).

[166]Miles v. Denver Public Schools, 944 F.2d 773 (10th Cir. 1991).

[167]Id. at 776–777.

[168]Connick v. Myers, 461 U.S. 138, 147–148 (1983).

[169]Belyeu v. Coosa County Bd. of Education, 998 F.2d 925, 929 (11th Cir. 1993).

[170]Sanguigni v. Pittsburgh Bd. of Public Education., 968 F.2d 393 (3rd Cir. 1992).

[171]Id. at 399.

[172]Ma, P. (1996). Public employee speech and public concern: A critique of the U.S. Supreme Court's threshold approach to public employee speech cases, *John Marshall L. Rev.*, *30*, 121, 125; Schoen, R. B. (1999). Pickering plus thirty years: Public employees and free speech, *Tex. Tech L. Rev. 30*, 5; Hoppman, K. B. (1997). Concern with public concern: Toward a better definition of the Pickering/ Connick Threshold Test, *V & L. Rev.*, *50*, 993.

[173]Fischer, L., Schimmel, D., & Stellman, L. (2002). *Teachers and the law* (Boston: Allyn & Bacon) is a helpful book that examines the rights of teachers in greater detail.

[174]Fales v. Garst, 235 F.3d 1122 (8th Cir. 2001).

[175]Id. at 1124.

[176]Belyeu v. Coosa County Bd. of Education, 998 F.2d 925 (11th Cir. 1993).

[177]Id. at 929.

[178]Mt. Healthy City Sch. Dist. Bd. of Education v. Doyle, 429 U.S. 274 (1977).

[179]Id. at 287.

[180]West Virginia State Bd. of Education v. Barnette, 319 U.S. 624 (1943).

[181]Russo v. Central Sch. Dist. No. 1, 469 F.2d 623 (2nd Cir. 1972), *cert. denied*, 411 U.S. 932 (1973).

[182]Id. at 632.

[183]Palmer v. Board of Education, 603 F.2d 1271 (7th Cir. 1979), *cert. denied*, 444 U.S. 1026 (1980).

[184]East Hartford Ed. Asso. v. Bd. of Education, 562 F.2d 838 (2nd Cir. 1977).

[185]Id. at 858.

[186]Id. at 861.

[187]McGlothin v. Jackson Municipal Separate Sch. Dist., 829 F. Supp. 853 (S.D. Miss. 1992).

[188]Id. at 866.

[189]Title VII of the Civil Rights Act of 1964 forbids public and private employers from discriminating against employees based on several factors, including religion.

[190]U.S. v. Bd. of Education, 911 F.2d 882 (3rd Cir. 1990).

[191]Id. at 894.

[192]Cooper v. Eugene Sch. Dist. No. 41, 301 Ore. 358 (1986), *app. dismissed*, 480 U.S. 942 (1987).

[193]Id. at 375.

[194]See Moore v. Bd. of Education, 212 N.E. 2d 833 (Ohio 1965); Rawlings v. Butler, 290 S.W.2d 801 (Ky. 1956); Zellers v. Huff, 236 P.2d 949 (N.M. 1951); City of New Haven v. Town of Torrington, 43 A.2d 455 (Conn. 1945); Johnson v. Boyd, 28 N.E.2d 256 (Ind. 1940); Gerhardt v. Heid, 267 N.W. 127 (N.D. 1936).

[195]Murray v. Pittsburgh Bd. of Public Education, 919 F. Supp. 838 (W.D. Penn. 1996), *aff'd*, 107 F.3d 862 (1997).

[196]Id. at 844.

[197]Newton v. Slye, 116 F. Supp.2d 677 (W.D. Virg. 2000).

[198]Fowler v. Bd. of Education of Lincoln County, Ky., 819 F.2d 657 (6th Cir. 1987), *cert. denied*, 484 U.S. 986 (1987).

[199]Cockrel v. Shelby County Sch. Dist., 270 F.3d 1036 (6th Cir. 2001).

[200]Peloza v. Capistrano Unified Sch. Dist., 37 F. 3rd 517 (9th Cir. 1994), *cert. denied*, 515 U.S. 1173 (1995).

[201]LeVake v. Independent Sch. Dist. No. 656, 625 N.W.2d 502 (Minn. App. 2001), *cert. denied*, 122 S. Ct. 814 (2002).

[202]Clark v. Holmes, 474 F.2d 928 (7th Cir. 1972), *cert. denied*, 411 U.S. 972 (1973); Webster v. New Lenox Sch. Dist. No. 122, 917 F.2d 1004 (7th Cir. 1990).

[203]Kirkland v. Northside Independent Sch. Dist., 890 F.2d 794 (5th Cir. 1989), *cert. denied*, 496 U.S. 926 (1990).

[204]Boring v. Buncombe County Bd. of Education, 136 F.3d 364 (4th Cir. 1998), *cert. denied*, 525 U.S. 813 (1998) (teacher had no First Amendment right to select particular play for students to perform).

[205]Settle v. Dickson County School Bd., 53 F.3d 152 (6th Cir. 1995), *cert. denied*, 516 U.S. 989 (1995).

[206]This answer is drawn from the advice given in *Religious expression in public schools*, guidelines published by the U.S. Department of Education: "Students may express their beliefs about religion in the form of homework, artwork, and other written and oral assignments free of discrimination based on the religious content of their submissions. Such home and classroom work should be judged by ordinary academic standards of substance and relevance, and against other legitimate pedagogical concerns identified by the school."

[207]C.H. v. Olivia, 226 F.3d 198 (2nd Cir. 2000), *cert. denied*, 533 U.S. 915 (2001).

[208]See generally, McFarland, S. T. (1996). A religious equality amendment? The necessity and impact of the proposed religious equality amendment, *B.Y.U.L. Rev*, 627; (2001). *A teacher's guide to religion in the public schools*. Nashville, TN. The teacher's guide was endorsed by 21 organizations,

from the Anti-Defamation League to the Christian Legal Society to the Council on Islamic Education. For more information on the guide, visit the First Amendment Center Web site at www.firstamendmentcenter.org.

[209]Bd. of Education v. Pico, 457 U.S. 853, 866 (1982).

[210]Campbell v. St. Tammany Parish Sch. Bd., 64 F.3d 184, 191 (5th Cir. 1995).

[211]Virgil v. Sch. Bd. of Columbia County, Florida, 862 F.2d 1517 (11th Cir. 1989).

[212]The phrase "In God We Trust" first appeared on coins in 1864, in the aftermath of the Civil War. It was not until 1956, during the Cold War, that Congress established "In God We Trust" as a national motto. Note that Congress adopted the first national motto, "E Pluribus Unum," in 1782.

⇀ PART III ↽

50 KEY LEGAL CASES

In Part II, you read about many different court cases that have shaped First Amendment law in a school setting. In this section, that information will be presented to you in a different way.

Each of the 50 cases that follow is presented as a *brief*—or an outline of the specifics of a case—to help the reader digest the most important facts. To brief a case, the following categories have been used:

Case: What is the name of the case? Where can the full case record be found? In what year was the case decided?

Facts: What are the key issues between the central parties of the case? What happened that is of legal significance?

Issue: What are the central legal issues the court must decide to arrive at a decision?

Holding: What did the court decide?

Reasoning: Why does the court decide the way it does? What is its logic and analysis of the facts?

For every case, a quote from the *majority* opinion has been provided. Wherever it seems helpful or noteworthy, an excerpt from a *dissenting* opinion has also been given. These quotes have been provided to allow the reader to hear directly from the judges and to better understand how a legal argument is framed.

The cases that follow are not meant to be the definitive list of First Amendment school cases. Rather, they were chosen to help readers understand how the courts apply the First Amendment in a school setting.

Although the list is not exhaustive—especially in the lower courts—these 50 cases are essential for understanding how First Amendment law has evolved in public schools. In both the Supreme Court and lower courts sections, the cases are listed chronologically.

Finally, remember that lower court decisions have *limited precedent*. That means the ruling of one lower court does not necessarily bind other lower courts. A court is bound only by the decisions of higher courts that have direct jurisdiction over it. Because it is the highest court in the country, however, all courts must follow precedent established by the U.S. Supreme Court.

Case Directory

Supreme Court Case Summaries

1. *West Virginia State Board of Education v. Barnette*, 319 U.S. 624 (1943)
2. *Everson v. Board of Education of Ewing Township*, 330 U.S. 1 (1947)
3. *McCollum v. Board of Education*, 333 U.S. 203 (1948)
4. *Zorach v. Clausen*, 343 U.S. 306 (1952)
5. *Engel v. Vitale*, 370 U.S. 421 (1962)
6. *Abington School District v. Schempp*, 374 U.S. 203 (1963)
7. *Epperson v. Arkansas*, 393 U.S. 97 (1968)
8. *Pickering v. Board of Education*, 391 U.S. 563 (1968)
9. *Tinker v. Des Moines Independent Community School District*, 393 U.S. 503 (1969)
10. *Lemon v. Kurtzman*, 403 U.S. 602 (1971)
11. *Wisconsin v. Yoder*, 406 U.S. 205 (1972)
12. *Mt. Healthy City School District Board of Education v. Doyle*, 429 U.S. 274 (1977)
13. *Stone v. Graham*, 449 U.S. 39 (1980)
14. *Board of Education, Island Trees Union Free School District No. 26 v. Pico*, 457 U.S. 853 (1982)
15. *Wallace v. Jaffree*, 472 U.S. 38 (1985)
16. *Bethel School District No. 403 v. Fraser*, 478 U.S. 675 (1986)
17. *Edwards v. Aguillard*, 482 U.S. 578 (1987)
18. *Hazelwood School District v. Kuhlmeier*, 484 U.S. 260 (1988)
19. *Board of Education of Westside Community Schools v. Mergens*, 496 U.S. 226 (1990)

20. *Lee v. Weisman*, 505 U.S. 577 (1992)
21. *Reno v. American Civil Liberties Union*, 521 U.S. 844 (1997)
22. *Santa Fe Independent School District v. Doe*, 530 U.S. 290 (2000)
23. *Good News Club, et al. v. Milford Central School*, 533 U.S. 98 (2001)
24. *Zelman v. Simmons-Harris*, 536 U.S. 639 (2002)

Lower Court Case Summaries

25. *Burnside v. Byars*, 363 F.2d 744 (5th Cir. 1966)
26. *Scoville v. Board of Education of Joliet Township High School District 204*, 425 F.2d 10 (7th Cir. 1970)
27. *Karr v. Schmidt*, 460 F.2d 609 (5th Cir. 1972)
28. *Melton v. Young*, 465 F.2d 1332 (6th Cir. 1972)
29. *Thomas v. Board of Education Granville Central School District*, 607 F.2d 1043 (2nd Cir. 1979)
30. *Klein v. Smith*, 635 F.Supp. 1440 (Dist. Me. 1986)
31. *Virgil v. School Board of Columbia County*, 862 F.2d 1517 (11th Cir. 1989)
32. *Chandler v. McMinnville School Dis*trict, 978 F.2d 524 (9th Cir. 1992)
33. *DeNooyer v. Livonia Public Schools*, U.S. App. LEXIS 30084 (6th Cir. 1993)
34. *Settle v. Dickson County School Board*, 53 F.3d 152 (6th Cir. 1995)
35. *Hsu v. Roslyn School District*, 85 F.3d 839 (2nd Cir. 1996)
36. *Pyle v. School Committee of South Hadley*, 423 Mass. 283, 667 N.E.2d 869 (1996)
37. *Beussink v. Woodland R-IV School District*, 30 F.Supp. 2d 1175 (E.D. Mo. 1998)
38. *Boring v. Buncombe Board of Education*, 136 F.3d 364 (4th Cir. 1998)
39. *Lacks v. Ferguson Reorganized School District R-2*, 147 F.3d 718 (8th Cir. 1998)
40. *Henerey v. City of St. Charles*, 200 F.3d 1128 (8th Cir. 1999)
41. *Boroff v. Van Wert City Board of Education*, 240 F.3d 465 (6th Cir. 2000)
42. *Cole v. Oroville Union High School District*, 228 F.3d 1092 (9th Cir. 2000)
43. *J.S. v. Bethlehem Area School District*, 757 A.2d 412 (Pa.Cmwlth. 2000)
44. *West v. Derby Unified School District No. 260*, 206 F.3d 1358 (10th Cir. 2000)
45. *Adler v. Duval*, 250 F.3d 1330 (11th Cir. 2001)
46. *Canady v. Bossier Parish School Board*, 240 F.3d 437 (5th Cir. 2001)

47. *Chambers v. Babbitt*, 145 F. Supp. 2d 1068 (District of Minn. 2001)
48. *Lavine v. Blaine School District*, 257 F.3d 981 (9th Cir. 2001)
49. *Littlefield v. Forney Independent School District*, 268 F.3d 275 (5th Cir. 2001)
50. *Saxe v. State College Area School District*, 240 F.3d 200 (3rd Cir. 2001)

◆ ◆ ◆ ◆ ◆

Supreme Court Case Summaries

Case 1: *West Virginia State Board of Education v. Barnette*, 319 U.S. 624 (1943)

Facts: The West Virginia Board of Education adopted a measure requiring that all public school students salute the flag and recite the Pledge of Allegiance. Students who did not participate could be expelled; their parents could even lose custody of them. A group of Jehovah's Witnesses challenged the law on First Amendment grounds. They argued that the forced flag salute conflicted with their religious beliefs against idol worship and graven images and, therefore, violated their free exercise of religion and freedom of speech rights under the First Amendment.

Issue: Whether school officials violate the First Amendment by forcing students to salute the flag and recite the Pledge of Allegiance.

Holding: By a 6–3 vote, the Court held that school officials do violate the First Amendment by compelling students to salute the flag and recite the Pledge of Allegiance.

Reasoning: The First Amendment prohibits government officials from compelling individuals to speak or espouse orthodox beliefs that are at odds with their conscience and values. "There is no doubt that, in connection with the pledges, the flag salute is a form of utterance." The purpose of the First Amendment is to ensure that individuals have an individual sphere of freedom of thought and belief that the government cannot invade. "Authority here is to be controlled by public opinion, not public opinion by authority."

Majority: "If there is any fixed star in our constitutional constellation, it is that no official, high or petty, can prescribe what shall be orthodox in politics, nationalism, religion, or other matters of opinion or force citizens to confess by word or act their faith therein." (Justice Robert Jackson)

Dissent: "An act compelling profession of allegiance to a religion, no matter how subtly or tenuously promoted, is bad. But an act promoting good citizenship and national allegiance is within the domain of governmental authority and is therefore to be judged by the same considerations of power and of constitutionality as those involved in the many claims of immunity from civil obedience because of religious scruples." (Justice Felix Frankfurter)

◆   ◆   ◆   ◆   ◆

Case 2: *Everson v. Board of Education of Ewing Township*, 330 U.S. 1 (1947)

Facts: A New Jersey statute authorized local school districts to make rules and contracts for the transportation of children to and from public and private schools. The Board of Education of Ewing Township authorized reimbursement to parents of money spent by them for the bus transportation of their children on regular buses operated by the public transportation system. A taxpayer brought suit claiming that reimbursement to the parents of parochial school students violated the Establishment Clause of the First Amendment.

Issue: Whether reimbursing parents for their children's transportation to and from religious schools violates the Establishment Clause when it is part of a general transportation reimbursement scheme.

Holding: By a 5–4 vote, the Court held that the state does not violate the Establishment clause when it reimburses parents, as the money flows to the parents as part of a general secular policy designed to keep children safe while en route to and from school.

Reasoning: The Court found that while the Establishment Clause requires that the state remain neutral among religions and between religion and nonreligion, the New Jersey plan merely provided money to parents as part of a general government service that was not inherently religious in character, similar to providing sewer and police services to churches.

Majority: "The 'establishment of religion' clause of the First Amendment means at least this: Neither a state nor the Federal Government can set up a church. Neither can pass laws which aid one religion, aid all religions, or prefer one religion over another. Neither can force nor influence a person to go to or to remain away from church against his will or force him to profess a belief or disbelief in any religion.

No person can be punished for entertaining or professing religious beliefs or disbeliefs, for church attendance or non-attendance. No tax in any amount, large or small, can be levied to support any religious activities or institutions, whatever they may be called, or whatever form they may adopt to teach or practice religion. Neither a state nor the Federal Government can, openly or secretly, participate in the affairs of any religious organizations or groups and *vice versa*. In the words of Jefferson, the clause against establishment of religion by law was intended to erect 'a wall of separation between church and State.' " (Justice Hugo Black)

Dissent: Although the Court was unanimous in affirming the principle of "neutrality" by the government toward religion, four justices disagreed with the majority's view that allowing reimbursement for bus transportation to parents of students in parochial schools was not a breach of church-state separation. In a dissenting opinion, Justice Wiley B. Rutledge defined "no establishment" this way: "The prohibition broadly forbids state support, financial or other, of religion in any guise, form or degree. It outlaws all use of public funds for religious purposes."

❖   ❖   ❖   ❖   ❖

Case 3: *McCollum v. Board of Education*, 333 U.S. 203 (1948)

Facts: The Champaign (Illinois) County Board of Education authorized a program of religious instruction in which outside religious teachers, paid for by private third parties, were allowed to enter schools once a week to provide religious instruction. Those students not wishing to participate in the program were sent to another room to continue with their class work. Attendance records were kept, and those not attending either the classes or the alternate classroom were considered truant.

Issue: Whether a school may allow outside groups to send instructors onto school grounds, during the school day, to provide students with religious instruction.

Holding: By an 8-1 vote, the Court ruled that the practice of allowing outside religious instructors into the classroom during the school day violates the Establishment Clause by providing government assistance to facilitate the mission of sectarian groups.

Reasoning: The Court found that allowing religious instruction on school grounds, during the school day, provided assistance to sectarian organizations by "providing pupils for their religious classes through use of the State's compulsory public school machinery." This arrangement was found to unconstitutionally advance religion and confer upon it symbolic government endorsement.

Majority: "To hold that a state cannot consistently with the First and Fourteenth Amendments utilize its public school system to aid any or all religious faiths or sects in the dissemination of their doctrines and ideals does not, as counsel urge, manifest a governmental hostility to religion or religious teachings." (Justice Hugo Black)

Dissent: "The prohibition of enactments respecting the establishment of religion do not bar every friendly gesture between church and state." (Justice Stanley Reed)

❖ ❖ ❖ ❖ ❖

Case 4: *Zorach v. Clausen,* 343 U.S. 306 (1952)

Facts: New York City allowed public school students to be released during the school day to religious centers located off school grounds. There, students choosing to participate would receive religious instruction and participate in devotional exercises. Attendance was kept by these religious centers and provided to the school. Students whose families chose not to participate in the release program stayed at school.

Issue: Whether voluntary "released-time" programs that allow religious instruction occurring off school grounds violate the Establishment Clause.

Holding: By a 6–3 vote, the Court held that noncoercive, off-campus "released-time" programs are permissible accommodations of the religious needs of students and do not violate the Establishment Clause.

Reasoning: The Court found New York's released-time program to be substantially different from the program in *McCollum*. In the New York program, the students were released to receive instruction off campus. "This 'released time' program involved neither religious instruction in public school classrooms nor the expenditure of public funds."

Majority: "We are a religious people whose institutions presuppose a Supreme Being. We guarantee the freedom to worship as one chooses. We make room for a wide variety of beliefs and creed as the spiritual needs of man deem necessary. We sponsor an attitude on the part of government that shows no partiality to any one group and that lets each flourish according to the zeal of its adherents and the appeal of its dogma. When the state encourages religious instruction or cooperates with religious authorities, it follows the best of our traditions." (Justice William O. Douglas)

Dissent: In his dissent, Justice Hugo Black argued that released-time programs were no different from the program struck down in *McCollum* because they "channel children into sectarian classes." He also warned against the state favoring believers over nonbelievers. "Before today, our judicial opinions have refrained from drawing invidious distinctions between those who believe in no religion and those who do believe. The First Amendment has lost much if the religious follower and the atheist are no longer to be judicially regarded as entitled to equal justice under the law."

◆   ◆   ◆   ◆   ◆

Case 5: *Engel v. Vitale*, 370 U.S. 421 (1962)

Facts: The parents of 10 pupils in New York schools challenged the constitutionality of a New York state law requiring public schools to begin each day with a state-authorized prayer drafted by the State Board of Regents. These parents argued that state-sponsored prayers in public schools violate the Establishment Clause.

Issue: Whether state legislation can require principals, teachers, and students to begin the day with prayers that are sponsored and written by the state.

Holding: In a 6–1 decision (two justices did not participate), the Court held that school officials may not require devotional religious exercises during the school day, as this practice unconstitutionally entangles the state in religious activities and establishes religion.

Reasoning: Appealing to history, the Court explained that the First Amendment protects religious liberty by keeping government from determining when and how people should pray or worship. Early Americans knew, "some of them from bitter personal experience, that one of the greatest dangers to the freedom of the individual to worship in his own way lay in the Government's placing its official stamp of approval upon one particular kind of prayer or one particular form of religious services." The Court found that the Establishment Clause prohibits the government from involving itself in devotional religious exercises. It further explained that such separation of church and state protects both government from religious domination and religion from government tyranny and abuse.

Majority: "[W]e think that the constitutional prohibition against laws respecting an establishment of religion must at least mean that in this country it is no part of the business of government to compose official prayers for any group of the American people to recite as a part of a religious program carried on by government." (Justice Hugo Black)

Dissent: "With all respect, I think the Court has misapplied a great constitutional principle. I cannot see how an 'official religion' is established by letting those who want to say a prayer say it. On the contrary, I think that to deny the wish of these school children to join in reciting this prayer is to deny them the opportunity of sharing in the spiritual heritage of our Nation." (Justice Potter Stewart)

❖   ❖   ❖   ❖   ❖

Case 6: *Abington School District v. Schempp*, 374 U.S. 203 (1963)

Facts: Pennsylvania state law required that "at least ten verses from the Holy Bible shall be read, without comment, at the opening of each public school on each school day." Two families sued, claiming this violated the Establishment Clause of the First Amendment.

Issue: Whether an official reading of Bible passages, without further comment, at the beginning of each school day violates the Establishment Clause.

Holding: By a vote of 8–1, the Court held that state-sponsored devotional Bible readings in public schools constitute an impermissible religious exercise by government.

Reasoning: The Court found that state-sponsored devotional exercises violate the Establishment Clause. The constitutional defects are not corrected by allowing an opt-out provision. The Establishment Clause constrains government from involving itself in religious matters. Therefore, government action that promotes or inhibits religion violates the Constitution. The state may not draft or conduct religious prayers in schools filled with captive audiences of children.

Majority: "In addition, it might well be said that one's education is not complete without a study of comparative religion or the history of religion and its relationship to the advancement of civilization. It certainly may be said that the Bible is worthy of study for its literary and historic qualities. Nothing we have said here indicates that such study of the Bible or of religion, when presented objectively as part of a secular program of education, may not be effected consistently with the First Amendment.

But the exercises here do not fall into those categories. They are religious exercises, required by the States in violation of the command of the First Amendment that the Government maintain strict neutrality, neither aiding nor opposing religion." (Justice Tom Clark)

◆ ◆ ◆ ◆ ◆

Case 7: *Epperson v. Arkansas*, 393 U.S. 97 (1968)

Facts: In 1965, Susan Epperson, a 10th grade biology teacher in Little Rock, Arkansas, brought suit to void a 40-year-old law forbidding the teaching of the "theory or doctrine that mankind ascended or descended from a lower order of animals." A recently adopted biology textbook included an entire chapter on the theory of evolution. Epperson argued that state law forbade teaching from this textbook; that she would be committing a crime if she did so; and that this law, therefore, violated the First Amendment.

Issue: Whether the state can constitutionally ban the teaching of evolution in public schools.

Holding: In a unanimous decision, the Court held that a state's control over the public school curriculum does not include the right to withdraw from the curriculum secular material that is at odds with certain religious beliefs. Such a selective prohibition on knowledge violates the Establishment Clause.

Reasoning: The court found that the law was passed for religious reasons. The statute's primarily religious purpose violates the First Amendment requirement of neutrality between religions, and between religion and nonreligion.

Majority: "The overriding fact is that Arkansas law selects from the body of knowledge a particular segment which it proscribes for the sole reason that it is deemed to conflict with a particular religious doctrine; that is, with a particular interpretation of the Book of Genesis by a particular religious group." (Justice Abe Fortas)

◆ ◆ ◆ ◆ ◆

Case 8: *Pickering v. Board of Education*, 391 U.S. 563 (1968)

Facts: A high school science teacher wrote a letter to the editor of a community newspaper, criticizing the board of education's allocation of funds between academics and athletics. The school board terminated the teacher, saying that the letter contained false statements that impugned the integrity of the school system. The teacher sued, claiming that the board violated his First Amendment rights by terminating him for exercising his right to freedom of speech.

Issue: Whether school officials violate the First Amendment by terminating a teacher for writing a letter to the editor that discusses important matters of public concern.

Holding: By an 8–1 vote, the Court held that school officials do violate the First Amendment when they terminate a public school teacher for speaking out as a citizen on matters of public concern.

Reasoning: Public school teachers, as public employees, are entitled to some First Amendment protections. "The problem in any case is to arrive at a balance between the interests of the teacher, as a citizen, in commenting upon matters of public concern and the interests of the State, as an employer, in promoting the efficiency of the public services it performs through its employees." In this case, the teacher was speaking more as a citizen than as an employee when he wrote the letter to the editor. The statements in the letter did not target any school official that the teacher dealt with on a daily basis.

Majority: "While criminal sanctions and damage awards have a somewhat different impact on the exercise of the right to freedom of speech from dismissal from employment, it is apparent that the threat of dismissal from public employment is nonetheless a potent means of inhibiting speech." (Justice Thurgood Marshall)

◆　　◆　　◆　　◆　　◆

Case 9: *Tinker v. Des Moines Independent Community School District*, 393 U.S. 503 (1969)

Facts: Several students planned to wear black armbands to school to protest U.S. involvement in Vietnam and mourn the dead on all sides. School officials learned of the impending protest and quickly adopted a no-armband rule, though they allowed students to wear other symbols. Nonetheless, the students wore the armbands to school. School officials suspended them for violating school policy. The students sued, claiming violation of their First Amendment rights.

Issue: Whether school officials can censor nonviolent student speech without showing that the speech will cause a material and substantial disruption of school educational activities or collide with the rights of others.

Holding: By a 7–2 vote, the Court held that school officials cannot censor student speech unless school officials reasonably forecast that the speech will cause a material and substantial disruption of school activities or collide with the rights of others. Mere apprehension of disturbance or an offense given is not enough.

Reasoning: Students do not lose their constitutional rights at the schoolhouse door. School officials' duties to provide a safe learning environment must be balanced against students' free expression rights. School officials may not censor student speech because of an "undifferentiated fear or apprehension." They must reasonably forecast that the student speech will cause a substantial disruption or invade the rights of others. In this case, "the record does not demonstrate any facts which reasonably may have led school authorities to forecast substantial disruption of or material interference with school activities, and no disturbances or disorders on the school premises in fact occurred."

Majority: "It can hardly be argued that either students or teachers shed their constitutional rights to freedom of speech or expression at the schoolhouse gate." (Justice Abe Fortas)

Dissent: This case will help usher in "a new revolutionary era of permissiveness in this country fostered by the judiciary. . . . I wish, therefore, wholly to disclaim any purpose on my part to hold that the Federal Constitution compels the teachers, parents, and elected school officials to surrender control of the American public school system to public school students." (Justice Hugo Black)

❖ ❖ ❖ ❖ ❖

Case 10: *Lemon v. Kurtzman*, 403 U.S. 602 (1971)

Facts: Pennsylvania and Rhode Island statutes provided state aid to church-related elementary and secondary schools. A group of individual taxpayers and religious liberty organizations filed suit, challenging the constitutionality of the program. They claimed that because the program primarily aided parochial schools, it violated the Establishment Clause.

Issues: Whether states can create programs that (1) provide financial support to nonpublic elementary and secondary schools by way of reimbursement for the cost of teachers' salaries, textbooks, and instructional materials in specified secular subjects (Pennsylvania), or (2) pay a salary supplement directly to teachers of secular subjects in religious schools (Rhode Island).

Holding: In a unanimous decision, the Court held that both programs violate the Establishment Clause because they create excessive entanglement between a religious entity and the state.

Reasoning: The Court looked to three factors in determining the constitutionality of the contested programs, factors that would become known as the *Lemon* test. First, the courts determined whether the legislature passed the statute based on a secular legislative purpose. The Court could find no evidence that the goal of the Pennsylvania or Rhode Island legislatures was to advance religion. Instead, the Court relied on the stated purpose that the bill was designed to improve "the quality of the secular education in all schools covered by the compulsory attendance laws."

Second, the Court questioned whether the programs had the primary effect of advancing or inhibiting religion. It bypassed this prong by examining the third prong and finding a violation there, thus obviating the need for analysis of this point.

The third factor, and the point at which the Court found the constitutional defect, was over the issue of excessive entanglement. Here, the Court held that the state's oversight and auditing requirements and the propensity for political divisiveness generated by this kind of aid program would entangle the state and the religious entity in unconstitutional ways.

Majority: "First, the statute must have a secular legislative purpose; second, its principal or primary effect must be one that neither advances nor inhibits religion; finally, the statute must not foster 'excessive entanglement with religion.' " (Chief Justice Warren Burger)

❖   ❖   ❖   ❖   ❖

Case 11: *Wisconsin v. Yoder*, 406 U.S. 205 (1972)

Facts: Members of the Old Order Amish and Mennonite religions ran afoul of Wisconsin's compulsory education law when, for religious reasons, they withdrew their children from public schools after the 8th grade. Three families brought suit, arguing the compulsory education law violated their right to freely exercise their religion.

Issue: Whether the state's interest in educating citizens outweighs the religious freedom of parents to rear their children according to the dictates of their faith.

Holding: By a vote of 6–2 (one justice did not participate), the Court ruled that the state's interest in educating children past the 8th grade does not outweigh the religious freedom of parents under the Free Exercise Clause of the First Amendment.

Reasoning: The Court was convinced that requiring Amish and Mennonite children to attend school past the 8th grade would substantially burden their religious freedom. The Court also found that the religious groups in question provided a support structure for members of their community that did not require education past the 8th grade. This addressed the state's concern that inadequately educated persons could eventually become a drain on the rest of society.

Majority: "Thus, a State's interest in universal education, however highly we rank it, is not totally free from a balancing process when it impinges on fundamental rights and interests, such as those specifically protected by the Free Exercise Clause of the First Amendment, and the traditional interest of parents with respect to the religious upbringing of their children so long as they, in the words of *Pierce*, 'prepare [them] for additional obligations.' " (Chief Justice Warren E. Burger)

Dissent: "It is the future of the student, not the future of the parents, that is imperiled by today's decision. If a parent keeps his child out of school beyond the grade school, then the child will be forever barred from entry into the new and amazing world of diversity that we have today. The child may decide that that is the preferred course, or he may rebel. It is the student's judgment, not his parents', that is essential if we are to give full meaning to what we have said about the Bill of Rights and of the right of students to be masters of their own destiny." (Justice William O. Douglas)

❖ ❖ ❖ ❖ ❖

Case 12: *Mt. Healthy City School District Board of Education v. Doyle,* 429 U.S. 274 (1977)

Facts: A nontenured high school teacher objected to a newly proposed teacher dress code. He circulated a memo from the school principal and gave it to a radio station, which reported on the dress code issue. When the teacher's contract came up for renewal, the school declined to renew it. He sued, claiming that his employment was terminated in response to his public opposition to the teacher dress code. The school board asserted that it had other valid reasons for not rehiring the teacher. These included an allegation that the teacher made an obscene gesture to two students and was involved in an argument with another teacher.

Issue: Whether a public employer can defend itself in a First Amendment retaliation claim by proving that it would have made the same employment decision in the absence of the employee's protected First Amendment activity.

Holding: In a unanimous decision, the Court held that an employer can successfully defend itself in First Amendment employee litigation by showing that it would have made the same decision in the absence of the protected speech activity.

Reasoning: An employee in a First Amendment retaliation case must show that the adverse employment action was taken in response to protected First Amendment activity. The employee must show that the employee's speech or expression played a "substantial role" in the adverse employment decision. But the employer can show that it would have made the same employment decision even if the employee had not engaged in the protected activity. This is now known as a "Mt. Healthy defense."

Majority: "The constitutional principle at stake is sufficiently vindicated if such an employee is placed in no worse a position than if he had not engaged in the conduct. A borderline or marginal candidate should not have the employment question resolved against him because of constitutionally protected conduct. But that same candidate ought not to be able, by engaging in such conduct, to prevent his employer from assessing his performance record and reaching a decision not to rehire on the basis of that record, simply because the protected conduct makes the employer more certain of the correctness of its decision." (Chief Justice William Rehnquist)

❖   ❖   ❖   ❖   ❖

Case 13: *Stone v. Graham*, 449 U.S. 39 (1980)

Facts: In 1978, the state of Kentucky enacted a law requiring the posting of the Ten Commandments in every public school classroom. Each plaque would be purchased with private contributions and would bear the following statement: "[T]he secular application of the Ten Commandments is clearly seen in its adoption as the fundamental legal code of Western Civilization and the Common Law of the United States."

Issue: Whether the Ten Commandments may be permanently and compulsorily posted in public school classrooms by state law.

Holding: By a vote of 5–4, the Court ruled that a state law requiring public schools to permanently post the Ten Commandments violates the Establishment Clause.

Reasoning: In this case, the Court issued a *per curiam* decision and reversed the lower court without hearing argument. Invoking the *Lemon* test, the Court found that there was no secular purpose behind the posting of the Ten Commandments. The Commandments are a sacred religious text, and their posting, without any connection to the curriculum, can only be for the purpose of promoting certain religious views.

Majority: "This is not a case in which the Ten Commandments are integrated into the school curriculum, where the Bible may constitutionally be used in an appropriate study of history, civilization, ethics, comparative religion, or the like. *Abington School District v. Schempp.* Posting of religious texts on the wall serves no such educational function. If the posted copies of the Ten Commandments are to have any effect at all, it will be to induce the schoolchildren to read, meditate upon, perhaps to venerate and obey, the Commandments. However desirable this might be as a matter of private devotion, it is not a permissible state objective under the Establishment Clause of the Constitution." (*Per Curiam*)

Dissent: "The Establishment Clause does not require that the public sector be insulated from all things which may have a religious significance or origin . . . Kentucky has decided to make students aware of this fact by demonstrating the secular impact of the Ten Commandments." (Justice William Rehnquist)

❖ ❖ ❖ ❖ ❖

Case 14: *Board of Education, Island Trees Union Free School District No. 26 v. Pico*, 457 U.S. 853 (1982)

Facts: After several of its members attended a conservative educational conference, an upstate New York school board determined that nine books in a high school library, including *Slaughter House Five* by Kurt Vonnegut and *Black Boy* by Richard Wright, should be removed because they were inappropriate for young people. Several students and parents challenged the school board's decision to remove these books from the library.

Issue: Whether school officials can, consistent with the First Amendment, remove books from a school library because they find the books inappropriate or objectionable.

Holding: By a 5–4 vote, the Court held that school officials cannot remove books from a school library simply because they find the ideas in the books objectionable.

Reasoning: The First Amendment protects the right to receive information and ideas. A school library is a special place, "the principal locus of such freedom." The First Amendment prohibits the suppression of material simply because government officials, including school officials, dislike the material. "Local school boards may not remove books from school library shelves simply because they dislike the ideas contained in those books and seek by their removal to 'prescribe what shall be orthodox in politics, nationalism, religion, or other matters of public opinion.'"

Majority: "[T]he special characteristics of the school library make that environment especially appropriate for the recognition of the First Amendment rights of students." (Justice William Brennan)

Dissent: The dissent argued that federal courts should not superimpose their judgments about what books should be included in school libraries. "Were this to become the law this Court would come perilously close to becoming a 'super censor' of school board library decisions." (Chief Justice Warren Burger)

❖   ❖   ❖   ❖   ❖

Case 15: *Wallace v. Jaffree*, 472 U.S. 38 (1985)

Facts: In 1981, the Alabama legislature modified a 1978 statute that had allowed a moment of silence for the purpose of "meditation." The 1981 amendment specified that the moment of silence was for the purpose of "meditation or prayer." The sponsor of the legislation went on record as stating that the sole purpose of this change was to bring prayer back into schools. When the Jaffree family brought this case to trial, the defense did nothing to rebut this description of the legislative purpose behind the revised statute.

Issue: Whether a law that authorizes a period of silence in public schools for "meditation or voluntary prayer" is a violation of the Establishment Clause.

Holding: In a 6–3 decision, the Court held that a "moment of silence" law is unconstitutional when the explicit purpose and meaning of such a statute is to promote prayer.

Reasoning: The Court distinguished between implicitly allowing students an opportunity for voluntary prayer during an "appropriate moment of silence during the school day," and a moment of silence designed explicitly to favor prayer or other religious practices. The Court pointed out that the 1978 law already protected students' rights to pray during the moment of silence and that, therefore, the only purpose for changing the statute was to highlight, endorse, and prefer prayer. For this reason, the Court found that the new law failed the first prong of the *Lemon* test—that government action must have a secular purpose.

Majority: "The addition of 'or voluntary prayer' indicates that the State intended to characterize prayer as a favored practice. Such an endorsement is not consistent with the established principle that the government must pursue à course of complete neutrality toward religion." (Justice John Paul Stevens)

Dissent: "To suggest that a moment-of-silence statute that includes the word 'prayer' unconstitutionally endorses religion, while one that simply provides for a moment of silence does not, manifests not neutrality but hostility toward religion." (Chief Justice Warren Burger)

◆   ◆   ◆   ◆   ◆

Case 16: *Bethel School District No. 403 v. Fraser*, 478 U.S. 675 (1986)

Facts: A public high school student delivered a nominating speech on behalf of another student at a student assembly. The speech contained elaborate and immature sexual innuendo. The school suspended the student for violating the school's no-disruption rule, which prohibited "obscene, profane language." The student contended that the suspension violated his First Amendment rights because his speech caused no disruption of school activities within the meaning of *Tinker.*

Issue: Whether school officials may prohibit a vulgar and lewd student speech at a student assembly even if the speech does not create a substantial disruption.

Holding: In a 7–2 decision, the Court held that school officials may prohibit student speech before a student assembly that is vulgar, lewd, and plainly offensive.

Reasoning: Public school officials have a responsibility to "inculcate values" into students. "Surely, it is a highly appropriate function of public school education to prohibit the use of vulgar and offensive terms in public discourse." The vulgar sexual allusions of the student in this case differ markedly from the pure political message of the black-armband case of *Tinker*. School officials were not censoring speech based on viewpoint. Rather, they were punishing the student for using vulgar and lewd terms at a student assembly.

Majority: "The undoubted freedom to advocate unpopular and controversial views in schools and classrooms must be balanced against the society's countervailing interest in teaching students the boundaries of socially appropriate behavior. Even the most heated political discourse in a democratic society requires consideration for the personal sensibilities of the other participants and audiences." (Chief Justice Warren Burger)

Dissent: "It does seem to me, however, that if a student is to be punished for using offensive speech, he is entitled to fair notice of the scope of the prohibition and the consequences of its violation. The interest in free speech protected by the First Amendment and the interest in fair procedure protected by the Due Process Clause of the Fourteenth Amendment combine to require this result." (Justice John Paul Stevens)

❖   ❖   ❖   ❖   ❖

Case 17: *Edwards v. Aguillard*, 482 U.S. 578 (1987)

Facts: Louisiana's "Balanced Treatment for Creation-Science and Evolution-Science in Public School Instruction" Act (Creationism Act) required any public elementary or secondary school that taught evolution also to teach "creation science." Although the act did not require evolution or creation science to be taught, it did stipulate that if either theory was presented, the other must also be taught. A group of parents, teachers, and religious leaders challenged the statute as an impermissible advancement of religion in violation of the Establishment Clause. The state officials countered that the legitimate secular purpose of the act was to protect academic freedom.

Issue: Whether a statute that requires schools teaching evolution also to provide balanced treatment of creation science violates the Establishment Clause.

Holding: In a 7–2 decision, the Court held that the Creationism Act was intended to promote religion and, therefore, violated the Establishment Clause.

Reasoning: The Court found that the act did not advance academic freedom, but instead stifled it by restricting what and how educators must teach. As this was the only stated purpose, the Court concluded that the real purpose was to promote a particular religious view of the origins of humanity, or conversely, to limit teaching about theories that are contrary to such religious views. The sponsor of the act clearly indicated that his intention in proposing this legislation was to prevent the teaching of theories that were antithetical to his own religious beliefs. For these reasons, the Court found that the "Creationism Act" violated the Establishment Clause.

Majority: "We do not imply that a legislature could never require that scientific critiques of prevailing scientific theories be taught. . . [T]eaching a variety of scientific theories about the origins of humankind to schoolchildren might be validly done with the clear secular intent of enhancing the effectiveness of science instruction. But because the primary purpose of the Creationism Act is to endorse a particular religious doctrine, the Act furthers religion in violation of the Establishment Clause." (Justice William Brennan)

Dissent: "Our task is not to judge the debate about teaching the origins of life, but to ascertain what the members of the Louisiana Legislature believed. The vast majority of them voted to approve a bill which explicitly stated a secular purpose; what is critical is not their *wisdom* in believing that purpose would be achieved by the bill, but their *sincerity* in believing it would be." (Justice Antonin Scalia)

◆　◆　◆　◆　◆

Case 18: *Hazelwood School District v. Kuhlmeier*, 484 U.S. 260 (1988)

Facts: Students produced a school newspaper as part of their journalism class. One issue was to include student-written articles about teen pregnancy and the impact of divorce on kids. The principal objected to the stories, believing they were inappropriate for the younger students and unfair to the pregnant students who might be identified from the text of the article. He also believed that the parents of the students quoted in the divorce article should have been given an opportunity to respond. He deleted the articles from the school newspaper. Three students sued, claiming a violation of their First Amendment rights under the *Tinker* standard.

Issue: Whether school officials can censor school-sponsored student publications when they believe material is inappropriate for younger students, or for reasons other than the prospect of material and substantial disruption of the educational process.

Holding: By a 5–3 vote, the Court held that school officials can censor school-sponsored student publications when they have purposes reasonably related to legitimate educational concerns. (Note: Because Justice Lewis Powell retired in 1987, there were only eight sitting justices at the time the *Hazelwood* case was argued. If the Court had reached a 4–4 split, the decision from the court of appeals, which in this case favored the students, would have stood as the final ruling.)

Reasoning: There is a fundamental difference between private student speech and student speech that occurs in school-sponsored activities. Educators have greater authority to control school-sponsored student speech because the public might reasonably believe such speech bears "the imprimatur of the school." Educators "do not offend the First Amendment by exercising editorial control over the style and content of student speech in school-sponsored expressive activities so long as their actions are reasonably related to legitimate pedagogical concerns." A publication created as part of a class is clearly school sponsored and a part of the curriculum. The school never adopted a policy whereby the publication simply became a public forum open to all views. The school administration thus properly acted as editor of the newspaper.

Majority: "A school must also retain the authority to refuse to sponsor student speech that might reasonably be perceived to advocate drug or alcohol use, irresponsible sex, or 'conduct otherwise inconsistent with the shared values of a civilized social order,' or to associate the school with any position other than neutrality on matters of political controversy." (Justice Byron White)

Dissent: The dissent argued that the majority erred in making a distinction between student-initiated and school-sponsored speech. The *Tinker* standard of material and substantial disruption should govern all student free-expression cases. "The case before us aptly illustrates how readily school officials (and courts) can camouflage viewpoint discrimination as the 'mere' protection of students from sensitive topics." (Justice William Brennan)

◆　◆　◆　◆　◆

Case 19: *Board of Education of Westside Community Schools v. Mergens,* 496 U.S. 226 (1990)

Facts: Bridget Mergens, a student at Westside High School in Nebraska, requested permission to start a Christian club. Her request was denied, and she filed suit. Mergens argued that the Equal Access Act (EAA) required the school to grant her request to form a Christian club. The act requires that secondary schools allowing "noncurriculum related clubs" to meet must also allow religious and political clubs, as long as they are student initiated and student led. The act also forbids teachers from participating in student religious clubs (except as monitors) and prohibits outside adults from directing, controlling, or regularly attending the meetings of a student religious club. School officials argued that the EAA did not apply to Westside High and that, even if it did, the act was unconstitutional.

Issue: Whether the EAA requirement that schools permitting noncurriculum related clubs must also permit student religious clubs is a violation of the Establishment Clause.

Holding: In an 8–1 decision, the Court ruled that the EAA does not violate the Establishment Clause. The purpose of the act is to avoid discrimination against student religious and political speech. Allowing student religious clubs on the same basis as other student-initiated clubs is equal treatment, not school endorsement of religion.

Reasoning: The Court found there was no Establishment Clause violation because the EAA does not promote or endorse religion, but protects student-initiated and student-led meetings. The Court noted the "crucial difference between government speech endorsing religion, which the Establishment clause forbids, and private speech endorsing religion, which the Free Speech and Free Exercise clauses protect."

Majority: "The broad spectrum of officially recognized student clubs at Westside, and the fact that Westside students are free to initiate and organize additional student clubs, counteract any possible message of official endorsement of or preference for religion or a particular religious belief." (Justice Sandra Day O'Connor)

Dissent: "Can Congress really have intended to issue an order to every public high school in the nation stating, in substance, that if you sponsor a chess club, a scuba club, or a French club—without having formal classes in those subjects—you must also open your doors to every religious, political, or social organization no matter how controversial or distasteful its views may be? I think not." (Justice John Paul Stevens)

◆　　◆　　◆　　◆　　◆

Case 20: *Lee v. Weisman*, 505 U.S. 577 (1992)

Facts: Rhode Island public schools frequently invited local clergy members to participate in graduation ceremonies at the middle and high school levels. These clergy were provided with guidelines for nondenominational and nonsectarian prayers for invocations and benedictions. The father of a student at Nathan Bishop Middle School sued, claiming that inviting a rabbi to lead prayers at the middle school graduation was a violation of the Establishment Clause.

Issue: Whether including clerical members who offer prayers as part of the official school graduation ceremony is consistent with the Religion Clauses of the First Amendment.

Holding: By a 5–4 vote, the Court held that schools may not promote religious exercises either directly or through an invited guest at graduation ceremonies.

Reasoning: The Court found that the Establishment Clause forbids government from coercing people into participating in a religious activity. Forcing students to choose between attending a graduation ceremony containing religious elements with which they disagree or avoiding the offending practices by not attending their graduation ceremony was inherently coercive and unlawful. The Court found that students who do attend are exposed to subtle coercion to appear as though they approve of or are participating in the prayer.

Majority: "The principle that government may accommodate the free exercise of religion does not supersede the fundamental limitations imposed by the Establishment Clause. It is beyond dispute that, at a minimum, the Constitution guarantees that government may not coerce anyone to support or participate in religion or its exercise, or otherwise act in a way which establishes a [state] religion or religious faith, or tends to do so." (Justice Anthony Kennedy)

Dissent: [W]hile I have no quarrel with the Court's general proposition that the Establishment Clause 'guarantees that government may not coerce anyone to support or participate in religion or its exercise,' I see no warrant for expanding the concept of coercion beyond acts backed by threat of penalty—a brand of coercion that, happily, is readily discernible to those of us who have made a career of reading the disciples of Blackstone rather than of Freud." (Justice Antonin Scalia)

❖   ❖   ❖   ❖   ❖

Case 21: *Reno v. American Civil Liberties Union,* 521 U.S. 844 (1997)
Facts: Congress passed provisions in the Communications Decency Act (CDA) of 1996 to protect minors from harmful material on the Internet. Two provisions criminalized the display of "indecent" or "patently

offensive" online communications. The American Civil Liberties Union and many other groups challenged the constitutionality of these provisions in federal court. They argued that these provisions infringed on First Amendment free speech rights. A lower federal court ruled the two provisions violated the First Amendment. The government appealed to the U.S. Supreme Court.

Issue: Whether federal laws prohibiting the display of "patently offensive" and "indecent" online speech violate the First Amendment.

Holding: By a 7–2 margin, the Court held that the two provisions did violate the First Amendment.

Reasoning: The government has a very important interest in protecting minors from harmful material. But the government cannot silence adult free speech rights simply to protect minors, and these provisions swept in sexual speech that was not obscene. "In order to deny minors access to potentially harmful speech, the CDA effectively suppresses a large amount of speech that adults have a constitutional right to receive and to address to one another."

Majority: "[O]ur cases provide no basis for qualifying the level of First Amendment scrutiny that should be applied to this medium [the Internet]." (Justice John Paul Stevens)

❖ ❖ ❖ ❖ ❖

Case 22: *Santa Fe Independent School District v. Doe*, 530 U.S. 290 (2000)

Facts: In Santa Fe, Texas, students were elected by their classmates to give pregame prayers at high school football games over the public address system. A number of students sued, arguing that such solemnizing statements or prayers constituted an endorsement of religion, violating the Establishment Clause. The district countered that the pregame invocations were a long-standing tradition in Texas communities. Moreover, the prayer came from a student, thus making it student speech and not state-sponsored speech.

Issue: Whether a student-led prayer over the public address system before high school football games violates the Establishment Clause.

Holding: In a 6–3 decision, the Court ruled that the pregame prayer given by a student at high school football games communicates a government religious endorsement and, as such, violates the Establishment Clause.

Reasoning: The Court was not persuaded by the district's arguments, finding that the student speech was not private. The control the school maintained over the content of the student speech registered government preference for religious speech or prayer. In view of the history of religious practices in the school district, the district's student election policy appeared to be designed to maintain the practice of pregame prayers.

The Court also found that the voting mechanism used by the school to determine whether a message would be given and who would give it only exacerbated the Establishment Clause issues since the different religious groups within the school now became rival political factions. Voting for the speaker ensured not only sectarian conflict, but that only the majoritarian religious voice would ever be heard.

These factors led the Court to find that the district policy on pregame messages resulted in both perceived and real endorsement of religion by the government and, therefore, was unconstitutional.

Majority: "The delivery of such a message—over the school's public address system, by a speaker representing the student body, under the supervision of school faculty, and pursuant to a school policy that explicitly and implicitly encourages public prayer—is not properly characterized as 'private' speech." (Justice John Paul Stevens)

Dissent: "The Court distorts existing precedent to conclude that the school district's student-message program is invalid on its face under the Establishment Clause. But even more disturbing than its holding is the tone of the Court's opinion; it bristles with hostility to all things religious in public life. Neither the holding nor the tone of the opinion is faithful to the meaning of the Establishment Clause, when it is recalled that George Washington himself, at the request of the very Congress which passed the Bill of Rights, proclaimed a day of 'public thanksgiving and prayer, to be observed by acknowledging with grateful hearts the many and signal favors of Almighty God.' " (Chief Justice William Rehnquist)

❖ ❖ ❖ ❖ ❖

Case 23: *Good News Club, et al. v. Milford Central School*, 533 U.S. 98 (2001)

Facts: Milford Central School, New York, enacted a community use policy whereby school facilities could be used after hours by community groups engaged in specific activities. Educational and community-oriented activities were specifically authorized. The Good News Club submitted a request to use the school's cafeteria to hold Good News Club meetings immediately following the school day. These meetings involved "a fun time of singing songs, hearing a Bible lesson and memorizing scripture" for students ages 6–12. The school district superintendent denied the request because the club activities involved religious practices that would violate school policy prohibiting the use of school facilities for worship.

Issues: (1) Whether a school violates the free speech rights of the organizers of a religious club when it denies the club access to school for an after-hours meeting. (2) Whether the Establishment Clause is violated if a public school allows a religious club involving worship to use school facilities during nonschool hours.

Holding: In a 6–3 decision, the Court held that a school district engages in viewpoint discrimination and violates the free speech rights of religious community groups when it denies them equal opportunities to use school facilities after hours on the same basis as other groups. Speech may not be excluded from a public forum because of its religious content or viewpoint. Because a religious speaker in a public forum poses no Establishment Clause problem, this could not be used as a basis for excluding the Good News Club.

Reasoning: The Court noted that the school district had created a limited public forum and, therefore, could not discriminate based on the views of the groups that wanted to use the facilities. The Court found that exclusion of the Good News Club was based on the fact that the club's educational message focused on religious matters and came from a religious viewpoint. Therefore, the school had engaged in religious viewpoint discrimination in violation of the First Amendment.

As for the Establishment Clause claim, the Court found that because the club met after school hours and was hosted by private parties and the facilities were made generally available to a number of other outside groups, no Establishment Clause violation occurred.

Majority: "When Milford denied the Good News Club access to the school's limited public forum on the ground that the Club was religious in nature, it discriminated against the Club because of its religious viewpoint in violation of the Free Speech Clause of the First Amendment." (Justice Clarence Thomas)

Dissent: "It is beyond question that Good News intends to use the public school premises not for the mere discussion of a subject from a particular, Christian point of view, but for an evangelical service of worship calling children to commit themselves in an act of Christian conversion. The majority avoids this reality only by resorting to the bland and general characterization of Good News' activity as 'teaching of morals and character from a religious standpoint.' " (Justice David H. Souter)

◆　◆　◆　◆　◆

Case 24: *Zelman v. Simmons-Harris*, 536 U.S. 639 (2002)

Facts: In an effort to address the problem of failing public schools in Cleveland, the State of Ohio enacted a voucher program that provided vouchers to low-income parents for use at participating public and private schools. Once implemented, the schools that chose to participate were overwhelmingly religious private schools, and the vast majority of participating students went to private religious schools. Local taxpayers and students in Cleveland public schools brought suit claiming that the voucher program unconstitutionally aided religious schools.

Issue: Whether Cleveland's voucher program aided private religious schools in violation of the Establishment Clause.

Holding: By a 5–4 vote, the Court held that Cleveland's voucher program provided a religiously neutral benefit that gave parents a true private choice among a number of educational venues. Therefore, the program did not violate the Establishment Clause.

Reasoning: A majority of the Court examined the Cleveland program in its totality, looking at the options available for students to go to magnet schools, receive after-school counseling, or use a voucher to go to a private school. The twin requirements of neutrality and private choice were key to the decision. Because the program was designed to provide no incentive for either religious private, secular private, or public schools, the Court found that true private choice exists, even if the participants in the program overwhelmingly chose religious schools.

Majority: "We believe that the program challenged here is a program of true private choice, consistent with *Mueller*, *Witters*, and *Zobrest*, and thus constitutional. As was true in those cases, the Ohio program is neutral in all respects toward religion. It is part of a general and multi-faceted undertaking by the State of Ohio to provide educational opportunities to the children of a failed school district." (Chief Justice William Rehnquist)

Dissent: "There is, in any case, no way to interpret the 96.6% of current voucher money going to religious schools as reflecting a free and genuine choice by the families that apply for vouchers. The 96.6% reflects, instead, the fact that too few nonreligious school desks are available and few but religious schools can afford to accept more than a handful of voucher students. . . . For the overwhelming number of children in the voucher scheme, the only alternative to the public schools is religious. And it is entirely irrelevant that the State did not deliberately design the network of private schools for the sake of channeling money into religious institutions. The criterion is one of genuinely free choice on the part of the private individuals who choose, and a Hobson's choice is not a choice, whatever the reason for being Hobsonian." (Justice David H. Souter)

Lower Court Case Summaries

Case 25: *Burnside v. Byars*, 363 F.2d 744 (5th Cir. 1966)

Facts: A group of public school students at an all-black school in Philadelphia, Mississippi, wore "freedom buttons" to school to protest racial segregation in the state. The school principal ordered the students to remove the buttons. The principal believed that the buttons would "cause commotion" and "disturb the school program." When several students continued to wear the buttons, the principal suspended them for a week.

Issue: Whether school officials could suspend students for wearing "freedom buttons."

Holding: By a 3–0 vote, a Fifth Circuit panel held that school officials could not prohibit the wearing of the "freedom buttons" because there was no evidence that the buttons would have caused a substantial disruption.

Reasoning: The record demonstrates that there was no commotion or disruption caused by the wearing of the buttons. "The record indicates only a showing of mild curiosity on the part of the other school children over the presence of some 30 or 40 children wearing such insignia." Because the wearing of buttons did not cause a disruption, the regulation preventing the wearing of such buttons is "arbitrary and unreasonable."

Majority: "But with all of this in mind we must also emphasize that school officials cannot ignore expressions of feelings with which they do not wish to contend. They cannot infringe on their students' right to free and unrestricted expression as guaranteed to them under the First Amendment to the Constitution, where the exercise of such rights in the school buildings and schoolrooms do not materially and substantially interfere with the requirements of appropriate discipline in the operation of the school." (Judge Walter Gewin)

❖ ❖ ❖ ❖ ❖

Case 26: *Scoville v. Board of Education of Joliet Township High School District 204*, 425 F.2d 10 (7th Cir. 1970)

Facts: Two public high school students in Illinois published an underground paper called *Grass High* and distributed it on campus. School officials suspended the students because they believed the content in the paper was "inappropriate and indecent." The newspapers criticized certain school policies. The students sued, claiming a violation of their First Amendment rights.

Issue: Whether school officials could suspend students without a reasonable forecast of substantial disruption.

Holding: By a 5–1 vote, the Seventh Circuit held that school officials could not punish the students for their underground newspaper unless they could reasonably forecast that it would cause a substantial disruption at school.

Reasoning: The student underground newspaper contained language that was offensive to school officials. But school officials cannot punish students for their expression unless they can show a reasonable forecast of substantial disruption. School officials failed to present any evidence of disruption.

Majority: "While recognizing the need of effective discipline in operating schools, the law requires that the school rules be related to the state interest in the production of well-trained intellects with constructive critical stances, lest students' imaginations, intellects, and wills be unduly stifled or chilled." (Judge Roger J. Kiley)

Dissent: "In my view, plaintiffs' advocacy of disregard of the school's procedure carried with it an inherent threat to the effective operation of a method the school authorities had a right to utilize for the purpose of communicating with the parents of students." (Judge Latham Castle)

❖ ❖ ❖ ❖ ❖

Case 27: *Karr v. Schmidt*, 460 F.2d 609 (5th Cir. 1972)

Facts: A male high school student with long hair sued the principal of a Texas high school after he was denied enrollment because his hair length violated the school's "good grooming" policy. This policy prohibited any male student's hair from hanging over his ears or collar, or from obstructing his vision.

Issue: Whether a public school student has a First Amendment right to wear long hair to school.

Holding: By a narrow 8–7 margin, the Fifth Circuit held that a student does not have a constitutional right to wear his hairstyle however he sees fit.

Reasoning: Observing that "the most frequently asserted basis for a constitutional right to wear long hair lies in the First Amendment," the appeals court majority stated: "For some, no doubt, the wearing of long hair is intended to convey a discrete message to the world. But, for many, the wearing of long hair is simply a matter of personal taste or the result of peer group influence."

The appeals court focused on the following statement from the Supreme Court's opinion in *Tinker*:

> The problem posed by the present case does not relate to regulation of the length of skirts or the type of clothing, to hairstyle or deportment. . . . Our problem involves direct, primary First Amendment rights akin to 'pure speech.' "

The majority reasoned that this language from *Tinker* indicates that students do not have a First Amendment right to wear any hairstyle they desire.

Majority: "For some, no doubt, the wearing of long hair is intended to convey a discrete message to the world. But for many, the wearing of long hair is simply a matter of personal taste or the result of peer group influence." (Judge Lewis Morgan)

Dissent: "I submit that under the First and Fourteenth Amendments, if a student wishes to show his disestablishmentarianism by wearing long hair or has the whim to wear long hair, antidisestablishmentarians on public school boards have no constitutional authority to prevent it." (Judge John Minor Wisdom)

❖　❖　❖　❖　❖

Case 28: *Melton v. Young*, 465 F.2d 1332 (6th Cir. 1972)

Facts: A high school in Chattanooga, Tennessee, prohibited the use of the Confederate flag and discontinued the playing of "Dixie" as the school pep song because of racial tensions. The school dress code also prohibited the wearing of "provocative symbols on clothing." The board of education specifically designated the Confederate flag as such a provocative symbol.

When a high school student was suspended for wearing a jacket with an emblem of the Confederate flag, he sued, claiming a violation of his First Amendment rights. A district court determined that the school's dress code policy was unconstitutionally vague but still upheld the suspension as valid. The student appealed.

Issue: Whether school officials could suspend a student for wearing Confederate flag clothing to school when racial tensions existed at the school the previous year.

Holding: By a 2–1 vote, a panel of the Sixth Circuit held that the school could reasonably forecast that the wearing of Confederate flag clothing would cause a substantial disruption at the school.

Reasoning: The school could reasonably forecast substantial disruption because of the history of recent racial tension at the school. Racial tensions had led to a fight at a football game and had led school officials to close school on two occasions the previous school year. Because of the "tense racial situation," the school officials were justified in suspending the student for wearing Confederate flag clothing.

Majority: "This is a troubling case; on the one hand we are faced with the exercise of the fundamental constitutional right to freedom of speech, and on the other with the oft conflicting, but equally important, need to maintain decorum in our public schools so that the learning process may be carried out in an orderly manner." (Judge Damon Keith)

Dissent: The lower court ruled that the school dress code policy prohibiting "provocative symbols" was unconstitutional. If that policy is unconstitutional, "it cannot be validly applied" to the student in this case. (Judge William E. Miller)

❖   ❖   ❖   ❖   ❖

Case 29: *Thomas v. Board of Education Granville Central School District*, 607 F.2d 1043 (2nd Cir. 1979)

Facts: Several students in a New York school published a newspaper entitled *Hard Times* that lampooned the school environment. The students created the newspaper largely on their own time and distributed the paper off campus. Nonetheless, school officials suspended the students for five days for publishing an allegedly "morally offensive, indecent, and obscene" publication.

The students sued, claiming a violation of their First Amendment rights. They argued that school officials did not have the authority to punish them for their off-campus activities. A district court sided with the school. The students then appealed.

Issue: Whether school officials can, consistent with the First Amendment, punish students for the content of publications that were created and distributed off campus.

Holding: In a unanimous panel decision, the Second Circuit ruled that the authority of school officials does not extend beyond the schoolhouse gate, certainly in the context of regulating purely expressive activity.

Reasoning: School officials must have broad discretion to oversee their many responsibilities. "But our willingness to defer to the schoolmaster's expertise in administering school discipline rests, in large measure, upon the supposition that the arm of authority does not reach beyond the schoolhouse gate." The students' publication was printed and distributed outside the school. The panel reasoned that "any activity within the school itself was 'de minimis' " or very minimal.

Majority: "When school officials are authorized only to punish speech on school property, the student is free to speak his mind when the school day ends." (Judge Irving R. Kaufman)

◆ ◆ ◆ ◆ ◆

Case 30: *Klein v. Smith*, 635 F.Supp. 1440 (Dist. Me. 1986)

Facts: A high school student in Maine made a vulgar gesture to a teacher off campus and after school hours. School officials suspended the student for ten days for "vulgar or extremely inappropriate language or conduct directed to a staff member." The student sued, claiming that the suspension violated his First Amendment free speech rights.

Issue: Whether school officials can discipline a student for engaging in vulgar behavior that occurs off campus and after school hours.

Holding: In his decision, Judge Gene Carter held that school officials lack authority to punish a student for conduct that does not occur on school grounds or during the school day. (Note: A single judge decides a case in a federal district court case.)

Reasoning: The court noted that the "conduct in question occurred in a restaurant parking lot, far removed from any school premises." The court found that the school officials could not establish that the vulgar gesture would adversely affect the orderly operation of the school.

Quote: "The First Amendment protection of freedom of expression may not be made a casualty of the effort to force-feed good manners to the ruffians among us."

❖ ❖ ❖ ❖ ❖

Case 31: *Virgil v. School Board of Columbia County*, 862 F.2d 1517 (11th Cir. 1989)

Facts: A public high school discontinued use of a textbook for a humanities course after receiving a parental complaint. The parent objected to an English translation of the Greek dramatist Aristophanes's *Lysistrata* and to English poet Geoffrey Miller's *The Miller's Tale*. The parent believed that the two works of art were too vulgar. Several other parents then sued, saying the removal of the textbook violated the First Amendment.

Issue: Whether school officials may remove a book from the curriculum because of its vulgarity and explicit sexual references.

Holding: In a 3–0 decision, an 11th Circuit panel held that school officials can remove books from the curriculum if they believe they are too vulgar for students.

Reasoning: "In matters pertaining to the curriculum, educators have been accorded greater control over expression than they may enjoy in other spheres of activity." Schools may remove books from the curriculum if they have a legitimate educational reason for doing so. Removing books because of vulgar or explicitly sexual language qualifies as such a reason.

Majority: "Like the district court, we seriously question how young persons just below the age of majority can be harmed by these masterpieces of Western literature. However, having concluded that there is no constitutional violation, our role is not to second-guess the wisdom of the Board's action." (Judge R. Lanier Anderson)

❖ ❖ ❖ ❖ ❖

Case 32: *Chandler v. McMinnville School District*, 978 F.2d 524 (9th Cir. 1992)

Facts: A group of teachers in McMinnville, Oregon, went on a lawful strike. The school district hired replacement teachers. Two students, whose fathers were striking teachers, wore buttons with the word "scab" on them. The students distributed similar buttons to their classmates.

School officials prohibited the students from wearing the buttons. The students sued, claiming a First Amendment violation. The lower court sided with the school district. The students then appealed.

Issue: Whether a lower court erred in allowing school officials to prohibit students from wearing buttons without a showing of substantial disruption.

Holding: In a 3–0 decision, a Ninth Circuit panel held that the students' wearing of the buttons could not be prohibited unless the school district could show a reasonable forecast of substantial disruption.

Reasoning: Student speech is divided into three basic categories: (1) vulgar and plainly offensive speech; (2) school-sponsored speech; and (3) speech that falls into neither of the first two categories. The buttons in this case were not vulgar and they were not school-sponsored. Thus, the school district had to show that the buttons would cause a substantial disruption of school activities. "The passive expression of a viewpoint in the form of a button worn on one's clothing is 'certainly not in the class of those activities which inherently distract students and break down the regimentation of the classroom.' " It thus falls within the *Tinker* standard.

Majority: "The schoolroom prepares children for citizenship, and the proper exercise of the First Amendment is a hallmark of citizenship in our country." (Judge John Clifford Wallace)

❖ ❖ ❖ ❖ ❖

Case 33: *DeNooyer v. Livonia Public Schools*, U.S. App. LEXIS 30084 (6th Cir. 1993)

Facts: Second grader Kelly DeNooyer was a student at McKinley Elementary School in Livonia, Michigan. Her teacher started a program where a student in her class would be "VIP of the week." This program was designed to allow students to receive special attention from classmates and be allowed special "show and tell" privileges to present before the class. The goal of this program was to give students a sense of self-confidence and poise based on their verbal presentations.

Kelly DeNooyer was chosen as VIP of the Week and was allowed to bring in an item to discuss and display to her classmates. She brought in a videotape of her performance of a religious song at a church service.

The teacher reviewed the tape and told Ms. DeNooyer that she would not be allowed to show it in class.

Issue: Whether a teacher's refusal to allow a student to show, as part of a classroom exercise, a videotape of the student singing a religious song violated that student's First Amendment rights.

Holding: In a 3–0 vote, a Sixth Circuit panel held that requiring a student to complete classroom exercises in ways that best achieve the goal of the exercise in question does not violate the free speech rights of the student.

Reasoning: The court found that school classrooms are closed forums, designed not to allow the free expression of ideas, but to create an educational environment. As such, as long as teachers have legitimate pedagogical reasons for their actions, they do not violate the Constitution when they require students to abide by the express rules as well as the goals of assignments.

Majority: "We hold that educators do not offend the First Amendment by exercising editorial control over the style and content of student speech in school-sponsored expressive activities so long as their actions are reasonably related to legitimate pedagogical concerns." (Judge Nancy G. Edmunds)

◆   ◆   ◆   ◆   ◆

Case 34: *Settle v. Dickson County School Board*, 53 F.3d 152 (6th Cir. 1995)

Facts: A teacher at Dickson County Junior High School in Tennessee assigned a research paper to students. Each student was to sign up for the topic of his or her choice, which then required approval of any changes. Brittany Settle, a student in the class, originally signed up for a paper about drama but later changed her topic to "The Life of Jesus" without approval. The teacher refused to accept Ms. Settle's paper and, when she refused to write on another topic, the student received a zero for the assignment. After exhausting the appeals process within the school system, Ms. Settle's father brought suit against the school, claiming that his daughter's free speech rights had been infringed. The teacher defended herself by providing six reasons for her decision.

Issue: Whether a teacher violated a student's free speech rights by refusing to accept her paper on "The Life of Jesus" after she was instructed to write on another topic.

Holding: In a 3–0 decision, a Sixth Circuit panel held that a teacher retains control over curriculum and assignments, and this control includes the power to determine the educational requirements of an assignment and enforcement of such requirements.

Reasoning: Teachers must retain control over their classrooms and their curricula. This includes authority over grades and assignments. A student's free speech rights are not violated by having to abide by the criteria set by the teacher. The court indicated it would only become involved in mistakes made by teachers when they indicated real intrusions on First Amendment rights.

Majority: "Teachers . . . must be given broad discretion to give grades and conduct class discussion based on the content of speech." (Judge Gilbert S. Merritt)

Concurrence: "I do not believe . . . that the majority correctly states the law in this regard by holding, 'learning is more vital in the classroom than free speech.' " (Judge Alice M. Batchelder)

❖　❖　❖　❖　❖

Case 35: *Hsu v. Roslyn School District*, 85 F.3d 839 (2nd Cir. 1996)

Facts: Emily Hsu and several other students of Roslyn High School in New York contacted school officials to request recognition of a newly forming after-school Bible club in compliance with the EAA. After months of deliberation and meetings, the school requested a club charter from the students. The charter provided to the school included a section on the requirements of officers, one of which was that all officers of the club had to be professing "Christians." After reviewing the proposed charter, the school board informed the students that they could form the Bible club only after removal of the requirement that club officers be of the Christian faith. The board claimed such provisions violated the antidiscrimination policies of the school district.

Issue: Whether denying clubs the right to form on school grounds because they limited leadership positions to members of a particular faith violates the EAA.

Holding: In a 3–0 decision, a Second Circuit panel ruled that limiting leadership of the club to particular categories of people, if relevant to the message and purpose of the club, is a form of expressive activity protected by the EAA. The school may, however, strike the religion requirement for other leadership positions not central to the identity of the club.

Reasoning: The court passed on the constitutional issues, preferring instead to look to the language and intent of statutory provisions of the EAA. The court found that the act was designed to protect religious and political speech by students, and that part of the speech protected involved forming groups for specific purposes. As long as the requirements for leadership reflected the intended speech of the student club, they were protected. For this reason, the offices of president, vice-president, and music coordinator could have religion requirements. The offices of social coordinator and secretary were not viewed as being as central to the identity and leadership of the club, and the court allowed the school to strike the religion requirements from these positions.

Majority: "[W]hen the students' desire to hold a meeting covered by the [Equal Access] Act involves a decision not to associate with other students, that decision, depending on its purpose, may constitute an exercise of the students' right of expressive association. On the one hand, an exclusion solely for reasons of hostility or cliquishness, with no direct bearing or effect on the group's speech, does not implicate the right to expressive association. But expressive association is implicated when the decision to exclude is made in order to foster the group's shared interest in particular speech." (Judge Dennis G. Jacobs)

❖ ❖ ❖ ❖ ❖

Case 36: *Pyle v. School Committee of South Hadley*, 423 Mass. 283, 667 N.E.2d 869 (1996)

Facts: Two public school students wore several "Co-ed Naked . . ." T-shirts that school officials deemed vulgar. When school officials told the students they could not wear the shirts, the students sued in federal court.

The federal appeals court eventually asked the state supreme court to interpret a state law that seemed to give students greater protection than they receive under the First Amendment.

Issue: Whether, under Massachusetts law, public high school students are free to engage in any expression they choose, even if deemed vulgar by the school, as long as the speech is neither disruptive nor school sponsored.

Holding: In a unanimous decision, the court held that Massachusetts law protects students' rights to engage in vulgar, nonschool-sponsored speech as long as it does not cause a disruption at school.

Reasoning: Massachusetts law provides: "The right of students to freedom of expression in the public schools of the commonwealth shall not be abridged, provided that such right shall not cause any disruption or disorder within the school." The state high court noted that this language is "clear and unambiguous." The statute contains no exception for vulgar or offensive expression that is not disruptive.

Majority: "Our Legislature is free to grant greater rights to the citizens of this Commonwealth than would otherwise be protected under the United States Constitution." (Judge Paul J. Liacos)

◆ ◆ ◆ ◆ ◆

Case 37: *Beussink v. Woodland R-IV School District*, 30 F.Supp. 2d 1175 (E.D. Mo. 1998)

Facts: A high school student in Missouri created a personal Web site on his own computer. His home page contained a hyperlink to the school Web site and lampooned school officials. He used vulgar language on his site. Another student showed the student's Web site to a teacher, who then showed it to the principal. The principal suspended the student for 10 days because of the content of his home page. The student sued, claiming a violation of his First Amendment rights.

Issue: Whether school officials may punish a student because they dislike the content of his personal Web site that he created off campus.

Holding: In his decision, Judge Rodney W. Sippel held that school officials may not punish a student for the content of his or her personal home page unless the material creates a substantial disruption at school. (Note: A single judge decides a case in a federal district court case.)

Reasoning: "Disliking or being upset by the content of a student's speech is not an acceptable justification for limiting student speech under *Tinker*." The student's home page did not create a substantial disruption or material interference with school activities. "Indeed, it is provocative and challenging speech, like Beussink's, which is most in need of the protections of the First Amendment."

Quote: "The public interest is not only served by allowing Beussink's message to be free from censure, but also by giving the students at Woodland High School this opportunity to see the protections of the United States Constitution and the Bill of Rights at work."

❖   ❖   ❖   ❖   ❖

Case 38: *Boring v. Buncombe Board of Education*, 136 F.3d 364 (4th Cir. 1998)

Facts: A North Carolina high school drama teacher chose the play *Independence* for her students to perform at a competition. The play depicts a dysfunctional family that includes a lesbian daughter and a daughter with an illegitimate child. The students captured top honors at a regional competition. The principal learned of the script, objected to the play, and eventually only let the students perform it with certain scenes deleted. The principal then transferred the teacher to a new school because she allegedly had failed to follow the school's "controversial materials" policy. That policy gives parents some control over what material their children are exposed to at school. The teacher alleged that the "controversial materials" policy did not cover dramatic presentations. The teacher sued on First Amendment grounds, alleging that she was retaliated against in her transfer because of the content of the play.

Issue: Whether a public school teacher has a First Amendment right to participate in the choice of the school curriculum.

Holding: By a 7–6 vote, the Fourth Circuit held that the plaintiff's selection of the play as part of the school curriculum was not protected expression under the First Amendment.

Reasoning: The majority determined that the teacher's First Amendment claim failed for two reasons: First, the court analyzed the case as a standard public employee free-speech case. In public employee free-speech cases, plaintiffs must show that their speech was a matter of public importance or public concern. The majority determined that the teacher's selection of the play did "not present a matter of public concern and is nothing more than an ordinary employment dispute."

The majority also said that the school had a legitimate educational reason for editing the play. "While we are of the opinion that plaintiff had no First Amendment right to insist on the makeup of the curriculum, even assuming that she did have, we are of the opinion that the school administration did have a legitimate pedagogical interest" for objecting to her selection of the play.

Majority: "Since plaintiff's dispute with the principal, superintendent of schools and the school board is nothing more than an ordinary employment dispute, it does not constitute protected speech and has no First Amendment protection." (Judge Hiram Widener)

Dissent: "School administrators must and do have final authority over curriculum decisions. But that authority is not wholly unfettered." (Judge Diana Motz)

◆   ◆   ◆   ◆   ◆

Case 39: *Lacks v. Ferguson Reorganized School District R-2*, 147 F.3d 718 (8th Cir. 1998)

Facts: A high school English and journalism teacher in Missouri failed to censor her students' creative writing assignments even though some of her students used profanity in their work. After a complaint, the school principal terminated the teacher for violating the school's "no-profanity" rule, which had traditionally not been applied to classroom exercises. The teacher sued, alleging a violation of her First Amendment rights. A jury sided with the teacher. The school district appealed.

Issue: Whether school officials could terminate a teacher for failing to censor her students' written work without violating her First Amendment rights.

Holding: In a 3–0 decision, an Eighth Circuit panel held that school officials did not violate the First Amendment when they terminated the teacher for allowing her students to use profanity in their classroom work.

Reasoning: The court wrote that "a school district does not violate the First Amendment when it disciplines a teacher for allowing students to use profanity repetitiously and egregiously in their written work." The majority reasoned that the school board policy against profanity was "explicit and contained no exceptions."

Majority: "We hold, as a matter of law, that the school board had a legitimate academic interest in prohibiting profanity by students in their creative writing." (Judge Richard Arnold)

◆   ◆   ◆   ◆   ◆

Case 40: *Henerey v. City of St. Charles*, 200 F.3d 1128 (8th Cir. 1999)

Facts: A Missouri high school student campaigned for junior class president. He passed out condoms to accompany his slogan "Adam Henerey, The Safe Choice." School rules provided that students must obtain prior approval for their campaign materials. The student did not obtain prior approval before passing out the condoms. School officials disqualified him from the election even though he had received a majority of the votes. The student claimed a violation of his First Amendment rights. After a district court rejected his claim, he appealed to the Eighth Circuit Court of Appeals.

Issue: Whether school officials can require students to submit campaign materials for prior approval.

Holding: In a 2–1 decision, an Eighth Circuit panel held that school officials can require students to obtain prior approval for campaign slogans during school-sponsored elections.

Reasoning: The student election was operated under the control of the school. Thus, the speech during the student election was a form of school-sponsored student speech. Under *Hazelwood*, the school can censor school-sponsored student speech if it has a legitimate educational reason. The school has a "legitimate interest in divorcing its extracurricular programs from controversial and sensitive topics, such as teenage sex." The student's actions in distributing the condoms "ran counter to the District's pedagogical concern and its educational mission."

Majority: "School districts have an interest in maintaining decorum and in preventing the creation of an environment in which learning may be impeded, an interest that was particularly strong in the present case because the condom distribution occurred within the context of a school-sponsored election." (Judge Roger L. Wollman)

Dissent: The majority should not have dismissed Henerey's First Amendment claim. "I disagree with the suggestion that safe sex among high school students is such a controversial topic that school officials may squelch its discussion in a school-sponsored school election contest." (Judge Charles R. Wolle)

◆   ◆   ◆   ◆   ◆

Case 41: *Boroff v. Van Wert City Board of Education*, 240 F.3d 465 (6th Cir. 2000)

Facts: A high school student wore a T-shirt to an Ohio school bearing the name of the shock rocker Marilyn Manson. The shirt depicted a three-faced Jesus, bearing the words "See No Truth. Hear No Truth. Speak No Truth." On the back, the shirt contained the word "BELIEVE" with the letters "LIE" highlighted.

A school official told the student that the T-shirt violated the school's dress code policy, which prohibited "clothing with offensive illustrations."

The school official ordered the student to either turn the shirt inside out or leave school. The student left and returned the next day with another Marilyn Manson T-shirt. He was again sent home. The student sued, claiming a violation of his First Amendment rights. A federal district court dismissed the suit. The student appealed to the Sixth U.S. Circuit Court of Appeals.

Issue: Whether school officials can prohibit a student from wearing T-shirts with offensive messages.

Holding: In a 2–1 vote, a Sixth Circuit panel ruled that school officials may prohibit students from wearing clothing that is vulgar or offensive.

Reasoning: The majority quoted the U.S. Supreme Court's decision in *Fraser*: "It is a highly appropriate function of public school education to prohibit the use of vulgar and offensive terms in public discourse." In addition, the court ruled that the school could prohibit student clothing which is "patently contrary to the school's educational mission."

Majority: "The standard for reviewing the suppression of vulgar or plainly offensive speech is governed by *Fraser*." (Judge Harry W. Wellford)

Dissent: The dissenting judge argued that school officials cannot forbid students from wearing T-shirts simply because they disagree with the shirt's message. "In sum, the Supreme Court's First Amendment jurisprudence prohibits school officials from telling a student that he cannot wear a particular T-shirt simply because they perceive that the T-shirt is communicating a message with which they disagree." (Judge Ronald Lee Gilman)

◆ ◆ ◆ ◆ ◆

Case 42: *Cole v. Oroville Union High School District*, 228 F.3d 1092 (9th Cir. 2000)

Facts: Ferrin Cole and Chris Niemeyer, students at Oroville High School in California, were selected to give the invocation and valedictorian graduation speeches, respectively. The district had a policy of reviewing the speeches. During this review process, the school informed the students that their messages were too sectarian and proselytizing and had to be modified. When the students refused, they were denied the opportunity to speak at graduation. The students sued, seeking damages for denial of their First Amendment right of free speech.

Issue: Whether a school's revocation of students' opportunities to give invocation and valedictorian speeches at graduation due to the religious and proselytizing nature of their messages violates the students' freedom of speech.

Holding: In a 3–0 decision, a Ninth Circuit panel ruled that a graduation ceremony is not an open speech forum but a government ceremony, and, as such, the school has a responsibility to avoid Establishment Clause violations during its graduation ceremony.

Reasoning: The court found that the close control the school exercised over every aspect of the ceremony gave the student speeches the implied endorsement of the school. Because the student messages bore the imprimatur of the school, the school had an obligation to make sure that the student messages would not violate the Establishment Clause. For these reasons, the court easily found that the graduation prayer was problematic irrelevant of its specific theological content.

The valedictorian speech posed harder problems. Yet in the end, the level of the school's control over the content of the speech indicated that the speech was not purely private student speech, but bore the significant imprimatur of the school.

Majority: "Because district approval of the content of student speech was required, allowing Niemeyer to make a sectarian, proselytizing speech as part of the graduation ceremony would have lent District approval to the religious message of the speech. Equally important, an objective observer familiar with the District's policy and its implementation would have likely perceived that the speech carried the District's seal of approval." (Judge Raymond C. Fisher)

❖ ❖ ❖ ❖ ❖

Case 43: *J.S. v. Bethlehem Area School District*, 807 A.2d 847 (Pa. 2002)

Facts: A Pennsylvania middle school student created his own Web site, which contained derogatory comments about his algebra teacher and the school principal. The site featured a picture of the teacher's head dripping with blood, showed her face morphing into Adolf Hitler, and contained language offering money to find a hit man to kill the teacher. The teacher allegedly suffered extreme distress after learning of the site. The site also contained derogatory comments about the principal.

The school suspended the student and then brought expulsion proceedings against him. The student argued that the Web site contained mere hyperbole and was not a true threat.

Issue: Whether school officials could punish a student for his derogatory and allegedly threatening online comments about a teacher.

Holding: In a 6–0 decision, the Pennsylvania Supreme Court held that school officials could punish the student because the student's Web site created a substantial disruption of school activities.

Reasoning: The state high court first reasoned that the student's comments did not constitute a true threat, finding the Web site to be a "sophomoric, crude, highly offensive and perhaps misguided attempt at humor." However, the court still ruled in favor of the school district because the student's Web site had a "demoralizing impact on the school community." First, the court determined that school officials were justified in punishing the student for his Web site, even though it was created off-campus, because there was a "sufficient nexus between the web site and the school campus to consider the speech as occurring on-campus." The court then determined that the school district's actions were protected by both the *Fraser* standard of lewd and offensive speech, and the *Tinker* standard of substantial disruption. "In sum," the court wrote, "the web site created disorder and significantly and adversely impacted the delivery of instruction."

Quote: "Unfortunately, the United States Supreme Court has not revisited this area [of First Amendment rights of public school students] for fifteen years. Thus, the breadth and contour of these cases and their application to differing circumstances continues to evolve. Moreover, the advent of the Internet has complicated analysis of restrictions on speech. Indeed, Tinker's simple armband, worn silently and brought into a Des Moines, Iowa classroom, has been replaced by J.S.'s complex multi-media web site, accessible to fellow students, teachers, and the world." (Justice Ralph J. Cappy).

◆   ◆   ◆   ◆   ◆

Case 44: *West v. Derby Unified School District No. 260*, 206 F.3d 1358 (10th Cir. 2000)

Facts: A middle school student drew a picture of the Confederate flag in his math class. Officials in his Kansas school learned of the drawing and suspended the student for violating its racial harassment and intimidation policy. That policy provided that "students shall not at school, on school property or at school activities wear or have in their possession any written material . . . that is racially divisive or creates ill-will or hatred." The student sued, claiming that the school officials violated his First Amendment rights.

Issue: Whether school officials violated the student's First Amendment rights when they suspended him for violating a racial harassment policy for drawing a picture of the Confederate flag.

Holding: In a 3–0 decision, a 10th Circuit panel held that school officials had reason to believe a student's display of the Confederate flag would cause a substantial disruption or collide with the rights of others.

Reasoning: The school district, based upon past incidents of racial tension and violence, had good reason to adopt a racial harassment and intimidation policy. School officials could reasonably believe that a student's display of the Confederate flag would cause substantial disruption of school activities or invade the rights of others. "The policy expressly prohibits any student from possessing in his own handwriting a depiction of the Confederate flag."

Majority: "To be sure, [the child's] display of the Confederate flag could well be considered a form of political speech to be afforded First Amendment protection outside the educational setting." (Judge Bobby Ray Baldock)

◆　◆　◆　◆　◆

Case 45: *Adler v. Duval*, 250 F.3d 1330 (11th Cir. 2001)

Facts: Duval County, Florida, instituted a policy for graduation ceremonies that allowed students of the senior class to vote on whether two-minute messages will be given at the beginning and end of the event, and then permitted seniors to elect a student to supply such messages. These messages were to be prepared solely by the students elected, and no school official was to have any input or review over them. The stated goal was to allow students to control their own graduation ceremony without "monitoring or review by school officials." Several Duval County students brought suit, claiming this policy had the effect of advancing religion and was a violation of the Establishment Clause.

(Note: This case originally reached the Supreme Court the same year as *Santa Fe v. Doe*. After ruling in *Santa Fe*, the Court vacated the 11th Circuit's decision and sent the case back for review in light of the *Santa Fe* decision. The 11th Circuit, using the reasoning in *Santa Fe*, reinstated their original decision.)

Issue: Whether Duval County's policy of electing student speakers to give two-minute messages constitutes a forum for true private expression of the student or is government-sponsored speech as in the *Santa Fe v. Doe* decision.

Holding: By a vote of 8–4, the court held that the Duval County policy was constitutional, even in light of *Santa Fe v. Doe*.

Reasoning: The court analyzed the policy first in light of the *Santa Fe* decision. It found the differences substantial and important enough to distinguish the two situations. The court found that the lack of oversight by administrators made the speeches the private speech of the students and that it was not transformed into government speech as in the *Santa Fe* decision. This allowed the court to proceed to analyze the policy under the *Lemon* test. As it had previously done, the court found that the policy passed muster under *Lemon*, as it had a secular purpose, did not have the effect of advancing or inhibiting religion, and did not excessively entangle the state with religion.

Majority: "While school officials may make private religious speech their own by endorsing it, schools do not endorse all speech that they do not censor. We cannot assume . . . that Duval County seniors will interpret the school's failure to censor a private student message for religious content as an endorsement of that message—particularly where the students are expressly informed as part of the election process that they may select a speaker who alone will craft any message . . . No religious result is preordained." (Judge Stanley Marcus)

Dissent: "The Supreme Court's decision on this issue renders untenable the majority's position that the Duval policy survives constitutional scrutiny. . . . Indeed, the very mechanism that the majority of this Court claims removes any impermissible coercion from the Duval policy serves to silence students espousing minority views, and forces them to participate in a state-sponsored exercise in which the message is determined by students holding majority views. The First Amendment does not permit such coercion." (Judge Phyllis A. Kravitch)

❖   ❖   ❖   ❖   ❖

Case 46: *Canady v. Bossier Parish School Board*, 240 F.3d 437 (5th Cir. 2001)

Facts: In the 1998–99 school year, a Louisiana parish school board decided to implement a mandatory school uniform policy. The school board believed the uniform policy would improve the educational process by reducing disciplinary problems. Several parents of students challenged the new dress code on First Amendment grounds. The school presented evidence that, since the adoption of the uniform policy, academic performance increased and discipline problems declined. A district court rejected the parents' lawsuit. The parents then appealed to the Fifth Circuit Court of Appeals.

Issue: Whether a mandatory school uniform policy violates students' First Amendment rights.

Holding: In a 3-0 decision, a Fifth Circuit panel held that adjusting the school's dress code by adopting a uniform policy is a constitutional means for school officials to improve the educational process if it is not directed at censoring the expressive content of student clothing.

Reasoning: The school board uniform policy in this case was passed to improve the educational process by increasing test scores and reducing discipline problems. "This purpose is in no way related to the suppression of student speech," the panel wrote. "Although students are restricted from wearing clothing of their choice at school, students remain free to wear what they want after school hours."

Majority: "The uniform requirement does not bar the important 'personal intercommunication among students' necessary to an effective educational process." (Judge Robert M. Parker)

❖ ❖ ❖ ❖ ❖

Case 47: *Chambers v. Babbitt*, 145 F. Supp. 2d 1068 (Dist. Minn. 2001)

Facts: On January 16, 2001, Elliot Chambers, a student at Woodbury High School in Minnesota, attended classes wearing a sweatshirt with the words "Straight Pride" and a symbol of a man and woman holding hands. Administrators were notified that certain students were offended by this message. The principal informed Chambers he was not to wear the shirt again.

Chambers sued, asking that the order by Principal Babbitt be declared unconstitutional and that he be allowed to wear his sweatshirt to school while the case was being litigated. The school responded by pointing to several fights and an incident of vandalism to a gay student's car on school grounds as evidence that the shirt and its message created a substantial disruption to the educational environment.

Issue: Whether school officials may prohibit a student from wearing a shirt emblazoned with a political message other students find offensive.

Holding: In his ruling, Judge Donovan W. Frank held that unless the school has a reasonable belief that the message will materially and substantially interfere with the work of the school, it cannot censor a message on a shirt merely because other students find it offensive. (Note: A single judge decides a case in a federal district court case.)

Reasoning: The court found that the *Tinker* standard requires the substantial disruptions claimed by the school to have some nexus to the student speech in question. The court granted Chamber's request for a preliminary injunction, though left open the possibility that the school could provide evidence that the "Straight Pride" sweatshirt actually caused the substantial disruption required by the *Tinker* standard.

Quote: "Maintaining a school community of tolerance includes the tolerance of such viewpoints as expressed by 'Straight Pride.' While the sentiment behind the 'Straight Pride' message appears to be one of intolerance, the responsibility remains with the school and its community to maintain an environment open to diversity and to educate and support its students as they confront ideas different from their own. The Court does not disregard the laudable intention of Principal Babbitt to create a positive social and learning environment by his decision, however, the constitutional implications and the difficult but rewarding educational opportunity created by such diversity of viewpoint are equally as important and must prevail under the circumstances."

◆ ◆ ◆ ◆ ◆

Case 48: *Lavine v. Blaine School District*, 257 F.3d 981 (9th Cir. 2001)

Facts: A Washington high school student, troubled by a recent rash of school shootings, wrote a poem, entitled "Last Words," depicting the feelings a student has after killing several classmates. The student handed the poem in to his English teacher, who had said she would be happy to review his written work.

The teacher became alarmed after reading the poem and contacted the school's counselor. The student had previously told this counselor about having suicidal feelings. The counselor also knew that the student had a fight with his father and had recently broken up with his girlfriend.

Based on the content of the poem and these other circumstances, the school officials expelled the student on an emergency basis. The student was eventually allowed to return to school after a psychologist cleared him. The student then sued, claiming that the school officials violated his First Amendment rights. A federal district court agreed with the student. The school appealed to the Ninth U.S. Circuit Court of Appeals.

Issue: Whether school officials violated the First Amendment when they expelled a student for writing a poem that depicted violence from a first-person perspective.

Holding: In a 3–0 decision, a Ninth Circuit panel held that school officials did not violate the First Amendment because they had reasonably forecasted a "potential for substantial disruption." (Note: The decision of the three-judge panel decision was appealed to all the judges of the Ninth Circuit for an en banc, or full panel, review. The Ninth Circuit then denied en banc review. Three judges dissented from the denial.

Reasoning: Schools have a duty to prevent violence to students. "*Tinker* does not require school officials to wait until disruption actually occurs before they may act," the panel wrote. "In applying *Tinker*, we look to the totality of the relevant facts."

Given the totality of the circumstances, including the "backdrop of actual school shootings," school officials could have reasonably believed that there would be substantial disruption of school activities. "Even in its most mild interpretation, the poem appears to be a 'cry for help' from a troubled teenager contemplating suicide," the court wrote.

Majority: "We review, however, with deference, schools' decisions in connection with the safety of their students even when freedom of expression is involved." (Judge Raymond C. Fisher)

◆   ◆   ◆   ◆   ◆

Case 49: *Littlefield v. Forney Independent School District*, 268 F.3d 275 (5th Cir. 2001)

Facts: A Texas school district adopted a mandatory uniform policy. The policy contained an opt-out provision for those with sincere religious or philosophical objections to the policy. A group of students and parents contended that the mandatory policy violated their First Amendment free expression rights and their free exercise of religion rights. The plaintiffs also alleged that the opt-out procedures violated the Establishment Clause by favoring certain religions over others.

Issue: Whether a public school district's mandatory uniform policy violates the First Amendment.

Holding: In a 3–0 panel decision, the Fifth Circuit ruled that the school's uniform policy was constitutional.

Reasoning: The school district passed the mandatory uniform policy "to improve student performance, instill self-confidence, foster self-esteem, increase attendance, decrease disciplinary referrals, and lower drop-out rates." The students have failed to show that the policy was intended to suppress free expression. The Free Exercise Clause claim fails because the policy's opt-out provision is neutral and does not target anyone's religious beliefs. The appeals court also summarily rejected the Establishment Clause claim because there was no endorsement of religion implied by the policy and no coercion of students to participate in religion.

Majority: "The record demonstrates that the Uniform Policy was adopted for other legitimate reasons unrelated to the suppression of student expression." (Judge Carolyn King)

❖ ❖ ❖ ❖ ❖

Case 50: *Saxe v. State College Area School District*, 240 F.3d 200 (3rd Cir. 2001)

Facts: Two high school students in Pennsylvania challenged a school district's antiharassment policy, contending it violated their First Amendment rights. The students believed that the policy prohibited them from voicing their religious belief that homosexuality was a sin.

The policy provided several examples of harassment, including: "any unwelcome verbal, written or physical conduct which offends, denigrates or belittles an individual" because of "race, religion, color, national origin, gender, sexual orientation, disability, or other personal characteristics." The district court ruled the policy constitutional. The students appealed to the Third Circuit Court of Appeals.

Issue: Whether a high school antiharassment policy that prohibits a broad range of speech offensive to others violates the First Amendment.

Holding: In a 3–0 decision, a Third Circuit panel held that such a broadly worded policy prohibits too much speech and violates the First Amendment.

Reasoning: The policy prohibits a substantial amount of speech that is neither vulgar within the meaning of the *Fraser* standard nor school-sponsored within the meaning of the *Hazelwood* standard. It even prohibits speech that harasses someone based on "clothing, physical appearance, social skills, peer group, intellect, educational program, hobbies, or values." The policy must be judged under the *Tinker* "substantial disruption" test. This policy could essentially be applied to any speech that another might find offensive. "This could include much 'core' political and religious speech," the panel wrote. "The policy, then, appears to cover substantially more speech than could be prohibited under *Tinker*'s substantial disruption test."

Majority: "No court or legislature has ever suggested that unwelcome speech directed at another's 'values' may be prohibited under the rubric of anti-discrimination." (Judge Samuel A. Alito, Jr.)

➤ PART IV ◄

RESOURCES

This part is designed to provide information about programs and organizations, education groups, and advocacy groups that address First Amendment principles and civic engagement in schools, as well as a selected bibliography.

Selected Programs and Organizations

Active Citizenship, Empowering America's Youth (www.activecitizenship.org)

There is increasing evidence that students go through school without learning the knowledge, skills, and values that are essential to becoming responsible citizens. As our government becomes more decentralized, complex social problems, such as violence, crime, poverty, and pollution, will require more active participation by informed citizens working together to solve them. This curriculum, Active Citizenship, Empowering America's Youth, teaches the rights, responsibilities, and civic values of U.S. citizenship. The curriculum includes a service learning group project in which students research and develop a solution for a real problem in their community.

Active Citizenship Today (ACT) (www.crf-usa.org/act/act.html and www.closeup.org)

ACT, sponsored jointly by the Constitutional Rights Foundation and the Close Up Foundation, involves middle and high school students in applying the knowledge and skills learned in the classroom to solving problems in their communities.

Alliance for a Media Literate America (www.nmec.org)

The mission of the alliance is to stimulate growth in media literacy education in the United States by organizing and providing national leadership, advocacy, networking, and information exchange. To help all people learn how to critically analyze and create messages using the wide variety of technological tools now available in and out of school, the alliance has brought together a diverse group of individuals and organizations to create a national nonprofit membership organization that strives to bring media literacy education to all 60 million students in the United States, their parents, their teachers, and others who care about youth.

American Bar Association Division for Public Education (www.abanet.org/publiced)

The mission of the ABA Division for Public Education is to promote public understanding of law and its role in society. Recognizing the centrality of an informed and committed citizenry, the ABA Division for Public Education affirms the value of law in a democratic society.

The American Promise (www.americanpromise.com)

The American Promise brings the American democratic system to life, letting students experience firsthand what it's like to govern and make the decisions that bind us together as a country. Since its premiere on KQED and PBS, the series has been used in more than 50,000 classrooms nationwide to provide lessons in government, civics, and history, with ideas that intrigue and inspire students.

American Society of Newspaper Editors (ASNE) High School Journalism Project (http://www.highschooljournalism.org)

ASNE wants to help scholastic journalism grow where it does not exist and flourish where it does. This project is geared toward teen journalists, their teachers and guidance counselors, and the editors and staffs of professional daily newspapers. Its goal is to encourage a diverse generation of young people to make newspaper journalism its career. Others will develop a deeper appreciation of the First Amendment and the role newspapers play in a free, informed society. This site is a place for people who care about newspapers to learn, share ideas, and celebrate hard work and success.

At the Table (www.atthetable.org)

AttheTable.org is a project of the At the Table: Youth Voices in Decision Making initiative. Hosted by the Innovation Center for Community and Youth Development, At the Table was formed to facilitate a coordinated, sustainable national youth participation movement. The project works with partners across the country to educate and inform about the value of youth participation, and to prepare youth and adults to work together to create positive change.

Bill of Rights Institute (www.billofrightsinstitute.org)

Founded in 1999, the Bill of Rights Institute's mission is to educate high school students about the Bill of Rights through classroom material and programs that teach what the Bill of Rights protects, both explicitly and implicitly; how the Bill of Rights affects our daily lives; and how the Bill of Rights shapes our society. The institute is dedicated to helping high school social studies teachers enhance their students' understanding of their rights and responsibilities as citizens, and of the historical and intellectual origins of the U.S. Constitution and the Bill of Rights.

Center for Civic Education (www.civiced.org)

The Center for Civic Education is a nonprofit, nonpartisan educational corporation dedicated to fostering the development of informed, responsible participation in civic life by citizens committed to values and principles fundamental to U.S. constitutional democracy. The center specializes in civic and citizenship education, law-related education, and international educational exchange programs for developing democracies. Programs focus on the U.S. Constitution and Bill of Rights; U.S. political traditions and institutions at the federal, state, and local levels; constitutionalism; civic participation; and the rights and responsibilities of citizens.

Center for First Amendment Rights (CFAR) (www.cfarfreedom.org)

CFAR is dedicated to increasing the understanding and appreciation of the First Amendment and the U.S. Constitution among students and the general public, particularly in Connecticut and other New England states. CFAR provides diverse educational programming and serves as a resource center for First Amendment issues and information.

Character Education Partnership (CEP) (www.character.org)

CEP is a nonpartisan coalition of organizations and individuals dedicated to developing moral character and civic virtue in the nation's youth as one means of creating a more compassionate and responsible society.

Civics in Action (www.civicsinaction.org)

Provided by Current Links in Education, Civics in Action seeks to educate and inspire students to become engaged and responsible citizens. Through its instructional program, Civics in Action brings to life and helps students understand the principles of U.S. government, the Constitution, and the virtues that are the basis of a healthy democracy. The organization provides teachers with a "turnkey" supplement to bring the social studies curriculum to life. The program is composed of biweekly lessons that use a current event or issue to reinforce a principle of U.S. government and to help students understand and develop an appreciation for virtues.

Council on Islamic Education (CIE) (www.cie.org)

Founded in 1990, CIE is a national, nonprofit resource organization composed of a diverse body of scholars of history, religion, education, and related disciplines. The mission of CIE is to contribute to the improvement of the U.S. K–12 education system, by participating in the cultivation of knowledge, critical thinking, and global awareness among the nation's young citizens. To achieve its mission, the CIE provides services, resources, and research-based tools predicated upon the highest standards of historical and social science scholarship to K–12 school textbook publishers, state education officials and policymakers, curriculum developers, and teachers.

Earth Force (www.earthforce.org)

Through Earth Force, youth discover and implement lasting solutions to environmental issues in their community. In the process they develop lifelong habits of active citizenship and environmental stewardship. Educators turn to Earth Force for innovative tools to engage young people in community problem solving. Earth Force is youth driven with a national Youth Advisory Board (YAB) made up of 15 members, ages 12–17. The YAB helps develop and implement Earth Force programs.

Educators for Social Responsibility (ESR) (www.esrnational.org)

ESR's mission is to make teaching social responsibility a core practice in education so that young people develop the convictions and skills needed to shape a safe, sustainable, democratic, and just world. ESR is nationally recognized for promoting children's ethical and social development through its leadership in conflict resolution, violence prevention, intergroup relations, and character education.

Federal Courts Community Outreach (www.uscourts.gov)

Sponsored by the Office of Public Affairs at the Administrative Office of the U.S. Courts, this program links courts to their communities through educational initiatives that increase understanding by bringing teachers, students, lawyers, community leaders, and the media into courthouses throughout the country.

First Amendment Center (firstamendmentcenter.org)

An independent affiliate of the Freedom Forum, the Center works to preserve and protect First Amendment freedoms through information and education, in part by tracking court rulings, legislation, and other events that are related to the First Amendment freedoms.

First Amendment Schools: Educating for Freedom and Responsibility (www.firstamendmentschools.org)

This national initiative of the Association for Supervision and Curriculum Development (ASCD) and the First Amendment Center seeks to reinvigorate the democratic mission of education through a comprehensive teaching and modeling of First Amendment principles across the school community.

Institute for Global Ethics (IGE) (www.globalethics.org)

IGE's Education Program promotes thinking and learning about core principles and their importance to our future as a nation and as a world community. The "Ethical Fitness" approach can help school communities come together around the core, shared values that also make constitutional government viable. "Ethical Fitness" critical thinking activities also help connect students to the content they study in school. An international nonprofit organization dedicated to "public discourse and practical action," IGE offers staff development workshops to increase awareness, define shared values, develop best practices based on those values, and develop reasoning skills to address complex ethical issues.

Journalism Education Association (JEA) (www.jea.org/)

The Journalism Education Association, Inc., is the only independent national scholastic journalism organization for teachers and advisers.

Founded in 1924, JEA is a volunteer organization that supports free and responsible scholastic journalism by providing resources and educational opportunities, by promoting professionalism, by encouraging and rewarding student excellence and teacher achievement, and by fostering an atmosphere that encompasses diversity yet builds unity.

Learn and Serve America (www.learnandserve.org)

Learn and Serve America supports service-learning programs in schools and community organizations. The organization helps nearly one million students from kindergarten through college meet community needs while improving their academic skills and learning the habits of good citizenship. Learn and Serve grants are used to create new programs or replicate existing programs, as well as to provide training and development to staff, faculty, and volunteers.

Learning In Deed (www.learningindeed.org/index.html)

Learning In Deed, a $13 million, four-year initiative, will encourage more school systems across the country to adopt service learning, making quality service-learning opportunities available to youth in every classroom in grades K–12 throughout the United States.

Let Freedom Ring Award Program
(www.jea.org/awards/freedom.html)

For the third consecutive year, the Journalism Education Association has joined the First Amendment Center, the National

Scholastic Press Association, the Columbia Scholastic Press Association, and Quill and Scroll in a national program identifying First Amendment High Schools throughout the United States.

The program, Let Freedom Ring Award: America's First Amendment High Schools, recognizes public high schools that actively support and protect First Amendment rights of their students and teachers.

Listen Up! (www.listenup.org)

Listen Up!, a project of Learning Matters Inc., encourages and facilitates a youth voice in the mass media that can contribute to a culture of free speech and social responsibility. The project seeks to create communications opportunities for youth that have traditionally been denied access to the public realm because of economic circumstances, incarceration, homelessness, or prejudice because of color, creed, or sexual orientation. Listen Up! is a network of more than 70 youth media organizations and schools nationwide whose young media makers are producing stereotype-challenging messages for the "America's Youth Speak Out" public service campaign. Since 1999, Listen Up! producers have submitted more than 600 radio, TV, and Web banner messages, increasing visibility of youth media within local communities and nationwide.

National Alliance for Civic Education (NACE) (www.cived.net)

NACE was launched in 2000 and now has more than 150 group and individual members committed to advancing civic knowledge and engagement. NACE believes the time has come to band together to ensure that the next generation of citizens understands and values democracy and participates in the ongoing work of building democracy in America.

National Conference for Community and Justice (NCCJ) (www.nccj.org)

Founded in 1927 as the National Conference of Christians and Jews, NCCJ is a human relations organization dedicated to fighting bias, bigotry, and racism in America. NCCJ promotes understanding and respect among all races, religions, and cultures through advocacy, conflict resolution, and education.

National Council for the Social Studies (NCSS) (www.ncss.org)

Founded in 1921, NCSS is the largest association in North America devoted solely to social studies education. NCSS serves as an umbrella organization for K–12 teachers of civics, history, geography, economics, political science, sociology, psychology, anthropology, and law-related education. The mission of NCSS is to provide leadership, service, and support for all social studies educators creating effective citizens. The revitalization of citizenship education is one of NCSS's highest priorities.

National Scholastic Press Association (NSPA) (www.studentpress.org/nspa/)

In 1921, NSPA began helping students and teachers to improve their publications. Today that goal remains their priority. NSPA helps students to become better reporters, writers, editors, photographers, designers, and desktop publishers, as well as advertising and business staffers. The association also helps advisers to those publications.

National Service-Learning Clearinghouse (NSLC) (www.servicelearning.org)

The Learn and Serve America NSLC supports the service-learning community in higher education, K–12, community-based initiatives and tribal programs, as well as all others interested in strengthening schools and communities using service-learning techniques and methodologies. The clearinghouse stands ready to assist with materials, references, referrals, and information. It also maintains a Web site and an ever-growing library collection that is available to Learn and Serve America grantees.

National Youth Leadership Council (NYLC) (www.nylc.org)

The council's mission is to build vital, just communities with young people through service learning. As one of the most prominent advocates of service learning and national service in the United States, NYLC is at the forefront of efforts to reform education and guide youth-oriented public policy.

Newsweek Education Program (newsweekeducation.com)

The *Newsweek* Education program is designed to help teachers and parents build bridges to real-world issues. The program recently produced a 36-page news source, *Living Up to the First Amendment*, that offers lessons on all five freedoms.

Open Society Institute (OSI) Urban Debate Program (www.soros.org/usdebate)

OSI's Urban Debate Program seeks to institutionalize competitive policy debate as an extracurricular and academic activity in urban school districts across the United States. Based on the Urban Debate League model founded by the Barkley Forum at Emory University, the Urban Debate Program has funded debate leagues in Atlanta; Baltimore; Chicago; Detroit; Kansas City; northern New Jersey; New York; Seattle; St. Louis; Tuscaloosa; Providence; the San Francisco Bay Area; southern California; and Washington, D.C. The program's primary objective is to make debate accessible to those students most in need of the skills and benefits that it generates.

Project 540 (www.project540.org)

Project 540 was created to give students a greater voice in their schools and their communities. You don't need a number 2 pencil to participate, and there won't be any tests or grades. This program is based entirely on students' insights, ideas, and dreams. This is a chance for students to imagine a better world. With 100,000 students participating nationwide, Project 540 is their turn to make a change.

Project Citizen (www.civiced.org/programs.html)

Project Citizen is a middle school civic education program designed to develop interest in public policymaking as well as the ability to participate competently and responsibly in state and local government. The program is administered by the Center for Civic Education, in cooperation with the National Conference of State Legislatures. In an assessment by Professor Kenneth Tolo, Lyndon B. Johnson School of Public Affairs, University of Texas at Austin, one conclusion reached was that "students using Project Citizen do make a difference in their communities."

Radio and Television News Directors Foundation (RTNDF) (www.rtnda.org)

RTNDF promotes excellence in electronic journalism through research, education, and training for news professionals and journalism students. RTNDF's work is supported by contributions from foundations, corporations, and individuals.

Radio Rookies (www.radiorookies.org)

Radio Rookies is a program from New York's public radio station WNYC Radio, "AM 820 and 93.9 FM," that trains young people to use words and sounds to tell true stories about themselves, their families, their communities, and the world. Through a series of 12-week workshops, each held in a new neighborhood, Radio Rookies gives teenagers the tools to become radio journalists and helps them gain the skills, confidence, and determination necessary to get their voices on the airwaves.

St. Albans School of Public Service
(www.schoolofpublicservice.org)

The St. Albans School of Public Service is a four-week summer program for high school students entering their senior year. During their time in the program, students build a strong foundation for a future in public service by gaining an understanding of the complexities of the United States government and by fine-tuning their abilities through discussions of case studies, guest speaker presentations, and study visits. Located in Washington, D.C., on the campus of the National Cathedral, the School of Public Service gives students exciting opportunities to view firsthand the preserved history and working politics at the nation's capital. Students are provided housing on the campus and have access to a full range of athletic facilities and activities.

Student Press Law Center (splc.org)

SPLC is an advocate for student free-press rights. The center provides information, advice, and legal assistance at no charge to students and the educators who work with them. Three times a year, SPLC also publishes a magazine that summarizes current cases, controversies, and legislation, and analyzes trends involving student media law.

Street Law, Inc. (streetlaw.org)

Street Law is practical, participatory education about law, democracy, and human rights. Through its philosophy and programs, Street Law empowers people to transform democratic ideals into citizen action. Street Law's programs do not end at the door of the classroom. Each student gains essential lessons that can be used for life.

USA Freedom Corps (www.usafreedomcorps.gov)

As a coordinating council housed at the White House and chaired by President George W. Bush, USA Freedom Corps is working to strengthen the United States' culture of service and help find opportunities for every American to start volunteering. In the last 30 years, community involvement has been in decline. The corps takes President Bush's challenge to foster a renewed culture of citizenship, service, and responsibility seriously, and it is bringing together the resources of the federal government with the nonprofit, business, educational, faith-based, and other sectors to begin that process and to measure results.

Youth Free Expression Network (YFEN) (www.fepproject.org)

YFEN is a project of the Free Expression Policy Project (FEPP), a think tank on artistic and intellectual freedom. YFEN works to empower youth to advocate on behalf of their own free expression rights through a speaker's bureau for young activists, a Web site, educational materials, and direct outreach to minors.

Youth Service America (www.servenet.org)

A resource center and alliance of more than 200 organizations are committed to increasing the quantity and quality of opportunities for young U.S. citizens to serve locally, nationally, or globally.

Selected Education Groups

American Association of School Administrators (AASA) (www.aasa.org)

Founded in 1865, AASA is one of the oldest professional education leadership organizations in the nation. Its more than 15,000 members across North America and in other parts of the world include top systemswide school leaders such as superintendents, other central office administrators, principals, and board members, as well as professors and others who prepare educators for leadership positions.

American Federation of Teachers (AFT) (www.aft.org)

The AFT is a 950,000-member union of public and professional employees, including public and private school teachers, paraprofessionals and school-related personnel (PSRPs), higher education faculty and professionals, employees of state and local governments, and nurses and other health professionals. The union operates at the local, state, and national level to represent its members, strengthen public education and its members' professions, and address issues that affect all children and working Americans.

American Political Science Association (APSA) (www.apsanet.org)

With more than 13,500 members residing in more than 70 countries, APSA is the world's largest professional organization for the study of politics. APSA offers an extraordinary range of programs and services for individuals, departments, and institutions, bringing together political scientists from all fields of inquiry, regions, and occupational endeavors in order to expand awareness and understanding of political life.

Association for Supervision and Curriculum Development (ASCD) (www.ascd.org)

ASCD is a unique international, nonprofit, nonpartisan association of professional educators whose jobs cross all grade levels and subject areas. In their diversity, members share a profound commitment to excellence in education. Founded in 1943, ASCD's mission is to forge covenants in teaching and learning for the success of all learners.

Compact for Learning and Citizenship, Education Commission of the States (ECS) (www.ecs.org/html/projectsPartners/clc/clc_main.htm)

The Compact for Learning and Citizenship (CLC) is a nationwide coalition of chief state school officers, district superintendents, and others who are committed to infusing service learning into the K–12 curriculum. CLC gathers and disseminates information, provides training and technical assistance, builds partnerships and networks, and serves as a national voice for creating high-quality service-learning opportunities for all students.

Council of Chief State School Officers (CCSSO) (www.ccsso.org)

CCSSO is a nationwide, nonprofit organization composed of public officials who lead the departments responsible for elementary and secondary education in the states, the U.S. extrastate jurisdictions, the

District of Columbia, and the Department of Defense Education Activity. CCSSO assists the chiefs in preparing policies and represents them on nationwide policies for education. CCSSO assists state agencies in developing leadership capacity through government- and foundation-funded projects.

Council for Spiritual and Ethical Education (CSEE) (www.csee.org)

The council serves as a national resource for schools to encourage the moral, ethical, and spiritual development of young people. It also promotes community service, providing resources and a network for schools' involvement in community service and service learning. CSEE's programs and services are developed to encourage a school climate of open ethical and religious inquiry and expression. The council supports instruction in world religions and ethics as essential components of a complete education.

National Association of Elementary School Principals (NAESP) (www.naesp.org)

Established in 1921, NAESP serves 27,000 elementary and middle school principals nationwide. Dedicated to educational excellence and high professional standards among K–8 educators, NAESP works at the national, state, and local levels to help school leaders provide the best possible education to the children and youth in their schools. Headquartered in the Washington, D.C., metropolitan area, NAESP has an affiliate in every state and the District of Columbia.

National Association of Independent Schools (NAIS) (www.nais.org)

NAIS, governed by a board of directors, represents more than 1,100 independent schools and associations in the United States and abroad. The association offers a broad variety of services to member schools and associations. NAIS membership includes day schools, boarding schools, and combination boarding and day schools.

National Association of Secondary School Principals (NASSP) (www.principals.org)

Established in 1916, NASSP has grown to more than 42,000 members and is now the nation's largest school leadership organization for middle level and high school administrators. Its membership includes principals, assistant superintendents, deans of students, and college and university professors. NASSP focuses on professional development programs to help school leaders become more proficient in serving middle level and high school students in the United States. NASSP does this through a national convention, multiday single-topic seminars, workshops, and publications. The association also promotes the interest of education in Congress, conducts research, and provides consultant services to members. NASSP founded and administers the National Honor Society and the National Association of Student Councils with a combined membership of more than 2 million students.

National Association of State Boards of Education (NASBE) (www.nasbe.org)

NASBE is a nonprofit, private association that represents state and territorial boards of education. Its principal objectives include strengthening state leaders in educational policymaking, promoting excellence in the education of all students, advocating equality of access to educational opportunity, and assuring continued citizen support for public education. The association services more than 600 individuals, including members of state boards, state board attorneys, and state board executive secretaries. These members are responsible for the educational interests of more than 40 million students in public schools and more than 3 million students in postsecondary institutions.

National Education Association (NEA) (www.nea.org)

The NEA is America's oldest and largest organization committed to advancing the cause of public education. Founded in 1857 in Philadelphia and now headquartered in Washington, D.C., NEA has 2.5 million members who work at every level of education, from preschool to university graduate programs. NEA has affiliates in every state as well as in more than 13,000 local communities across the United States.

National School Boards Association (NSBA)

NSBA is the nationwide advocacy organization for public school governance. NSBA's mission is to foster excellence and equity in public elementary and secondary education in the United States through local school board leadership. Founded in 1940, NSBA is a not-for-profit federation of state associations of school boards across the United States and the District of Columbia, Guam, Hawaii, Puerto Rico, and the U.S. Virgin Islands. NSBA represents the nation's 95,000 school board members. These board members govern 14,722 local school districts that serve more than 45 million public school students—approximately 90 percent of all elementary and secondary school students in the nation.

National PTA (www.pta.org)

The National PTA is the oldest and largest volunteer association in the United States, working exclusively on behalf of children and youth for more than 100 years. The National PTA consists of more than 6.5 million members; 26,000 local units in 50 states, District of Columbia, and Pacific Congress and European Congress, which serve Department of Defense schools overseas. Members include parents, teachers, students, and other child advocates.

U.S. Department of Education (www.ed.gov)

The U.S. Department of Education has issued guidelines on prayer in public schools. These guidelines are related to No Child Left Behind Act of 2001. Although mostly consistent with guidelines distributed during the Clinton administration, there are new interpretations of current law. Moreover, the failure of a school district to comply with the guidance could result in the loss of federal funding. Guidelines may be found at http://www.ed.gov.inits/religionandschools/prayer guidance.html.

Selected Advocacy Groups

American Booksellers Foundation for Free Expression (ABFFE) (www.abffe.org)

ABFFE is the bookseller's voice in the fight against censorship. Founded by the American Booksellers Association in 1990, ABFFE's mission is promote and protect the free exchange of ideas, particularly those contained in books, by opposing restrictions on the freedom of speech; issuing statements on significant free expression controversies; participating in legal cases involving First Amendment rights; collaborating with other groups with an interest in free speech; and providing education about the importance of free expression to booksellers, other members of the book industry, politicians, the press, and the public.

American Center for Law and Justice (ACLJ) (www.aclj.org)

ACLJ engages in litigation, provides legal services, renders advice and counsels clients, and supports attorneys who are involved in defending the religious and civil liberties of U.S. citizens. The center has a national network of attorneys who are committed to the defense of Judeo-Christian values. ACLJ also cooperates with other organizations that are committed to a similar mission, and serves the public through educational efforts regarding First Amendment and religious freedom issues as well as profamily and prolife concerns.

American Civil Liberties Union (ACLU) (www.aclu.org)

Since its founding in 1920, the ACLU has worked to fight civil liberties violations wherever and whenever they occur. The ACLU works daily in courts, legislatures, and communities to defend and preserve the individual rights and liberties guaranteed to all people in this country by the Constitution and laws of the United States.

American Jewish Committee (www.ajc.org)

AJC has a three-part mission: to safeguard the welfare and security of Jews in the United States, in Israel, and throughout the world; to strengthen the basic principles of pluralism around the world, as the best defense against anti-Semitism and other forms of bigotry; and to enhance the quality of Jewish life in the United States by helping to ensure Jewish continuity and deepen ties between U.S. and Israeli Jews.

American Jewish Congress (AJCongress) (www.ajcongress.org)

The mission of the AJCongress is to protect fundamental constitutional freedoms and U.S. democratic institutions, particularly the civil and religious rights and liberties of all U.S. citizens and the separation of church and state; advance the security and prosperity of the State of Israel and its democratic institutions, and to support Israeli's search for peaceful relations with its neighbors in the region; advance social and economic justice, women's equality, and human rights at home and abroad; remain vigilant against anti-Semitism, racism, and other forms of bigotry, and to celebrate cultural diversity and promote unity in U.S. life; and invigorate and enhance Jewish religious, institutional, communal and cultural life at home and abroad, and seek creative ways to express Jewish identity, ethics, and values.

American Library Association (ALA) Office of Intellectual Freedom (www.ala.org/alaorg/oif)

The Office for Intellectual Freedom is charged with implementing ALA policies concerning the concept of intellectual freedom as embodied in the Library Bill of Rights, the association's basic policy on free access to libraries and library materials. The goal of the office is to educate librarians and the general public about the nature and importance of intellectual freedom in libraries. To meet its educational goals, the office undertakes information, support, and coordination activities.

Americans United for Separation of Church and State (AU) (www.au.org)

Since 1947, AU has worked to protect the constitutional principle of church-state separation, a vital cornerstone of religious liberty. Citizens of many faiths and political viewpoints, individuals from all walks of life, have come together to defend freedoms. According to AU, mandatory prayer in public schools, tax dollars for parochial schools, government intrusion into religious affairs, and meddling in partisan politics by religious groups are among the troubling issues that threaten the protective wall between church and state. Daily, on members' behalf, AU confronts these problems and those who seek to force their religious views on the public.

Anti-Defamation League (ADL) (www.adl.org)

The mission of ADL is to expose and combat the purveyors of hatred in our midst, responding to whatever new challenges may arise. Where once ADL protested admissions quotas at leading graduate schools, today it exposes Internet sites devoted to Holocaust denial and white-supremacist propaganda. The particulars may change, but the goal remains the same: to stand up for the core values of the United States against those who seek to undermine them through word or deed. ADL looks to its past record for inspiration as it goes forward into the new millennium and its second century.

Baptist Joint Committee (BJC) (www.bjcpa.org)

The mission of the BJC is to defend and extend God-given religious liberty for all, while bringing a uniquely Baptist witness to the principle that religion must be freely exercised, neither advanced nor inhibited by government.

Catholic League for Religious and Civil Rights (www.catholicleague.org)

The Catholic League is the nation's largest Catholic civil rights organization. Founded in 1973 by the late Father Virgil C. Blum, S.J., the league defends the right of Catholics—lay and clergy alike—to participate in U.S. public life without defamation or discrimination. Motivated by the letter and the spirit of the First Amendment, the league works to safeguard both the religious freedom rights and the free speech rights of Catholics whenever and wherever they are threatened.

Christian Legal Society (CLS) (www.clsnet.org)

CLS is a national, nondenominational membership organization of attorneys, judges, law professors, and law students, working in association with others, to follow Jesus's command "to do justice with the love of God." (Luke 11:42; Matthew 23:23). Acting through its national staff, its member volunteers, and its attorney and law student chapters, the society's mission is to identify, equip, and mobilize "a national grassroots network of lawyers and law students committed to proclaiming, loving and serving Jesus Christ, through all we do in the practice of law, and by advocating biblical conflict reconciliation, public justice, religious freedom and the sanctity of human life."

Family Resource Council (FRC) (www.frc.org)

FRC champions marriage and family as the foundation of civilization, the seedbed of virtue, and the wellspring of society. The council shapes public debate and formulates public policy that values human life and upholds the institutions of marriage and the family. Believing that God is the author of life, liberty, and the family, FRC promotes the Judeo-Christian worldview as the basis for a just, free, and stable society.

The Gay, Lesbian and Straight Education Network (GLSEN) (www.glsen.org)

GLSEN is the leading national organization fighting to end antigay bias in K–12 schools. Because GLSEN holds that homophobia and heterosexism undermine a healthy school climate, it works to educate teachers, students, and the public at large about the damaging effects these forces have on youth and adults alike. The network recognizes that forces such as racism and sexism have similarly adverse impacts on communities, and it supports schools in seeking to redress all such inequities. GLSEN seeks to develop school climates where difference is valued for the positive contribution it makes in creating a more vibrant and diverse community. GLSEN welcomes as members any and all individuals, regardless of sexual orientation or gender identity, expression, or occupation, who are committed to seeing this philosophy realized in K–12 schools.

People for the American Way Foundation (PFAWF) (www.pfaw.org)

PFAWF is committed to defending democracy and bringing the ideals of community, opportunity, diversity, equality, and fairness together to form a strong, united voice. To achieve this, PFAWF conducts research, legal, and education work; it monitors and researches the religious right movement and its political allies. The organization is a premier source of vital information for policymakers, scholars, and activists nationwide.

Religious Action Center (RAC) (www.rac.org)

RAC has been the hub of Jewish social justice and legislative activity in the nation's capital for more than 40 years. It has educated and mobilized the U.S. Jewish community on legislative and social concerns as an advocate in the Congress of the United States on issues ranging from Israel and Soviet Jewry to economic justice and civil rights, to international peace and religious liberty. RAC is the Washington office of the Union of American Hebrew Congregation (UAHC) and the Central Conference of American Rabbis (CCAR), representing 1.5 million Reform Jews and 1,700 Reform rabbis in 900 congregations throughout North America.

The Thomas Jefferson Center for the Protection of Free Expression (www.tjcenter.org)

The Thomas Jefferson Center for the Protection of Free Expression is an organization devoted solely to the defense of free expression in all its forms. Although its charge is sharply focused, the center's mission is broad. The center is as concerned with the musician as with the mass media, with the painter as with the publisher, and as much with the sculptor as with the editor. Its programs cover issues of education, public policy, and the arts. The center enjoys close ties to the University of Virginia but is an autonomous, not-for-profit entity.

Selected Bibliography

Abell, A. (1999, October). Against the odds. *Washingtonian*, p. 72.

Al-Hibri, A. Y., Elshtain, J. B., & Haynes, C. C. (2001). *Religion in American public life: Living with our deepest differences.* New York: W. W. Norton.

American Jewish Congress, Christian Legal Society, and First Amendment Center. (1999). *Public schools and religious communities: A First Amendment guide:* Authors.

Blum, J. (2002, May 31). D.C. charter school learns and grows. *Washington Post.*

Butler, J., & Stout, H. S. (Eds.). (1999). *Religion in American life.* New York: Oxford University Press.

Calvert, C. (2000). Free speech and public schools in a post-Columbine world: Check your speech rights at the schoolhouse metal detector. *Denv. L. Rev., 77*, 739.

Center for Civic Education. (1994). *National standards for civics and government.* Calabasas, CA: Author.

Clark, T. (1999). Rethinking civic education for the 21st century. In D. Marsh (Ed.), *1999 ASCD yearbook.* Alexandria, VA: Association for Supervision and Curriculum Development.

Cogan, N. (Ed.). (1997). *The complete Bill of Rights: The drafts, debates, sources, and origins.* New York: Oxford University Press.

Easton, L. B. (2002). *The other side of curriculum: Lessons from learners.* Portsmouth, NH: Heinemann.

Education Commission of the States. (2000). *Every student a citizen: Creating the democratic self.* Denver, CO: Author.

Education Commission of the States. (1999). *Service-Learning: Every child a citizen.* Denver, CO: Author.

First Amendment Center. (2001). *A teacher's guide to religion in the public schools* (pamphlet). Nashville, TN: Author.

Fischer, L., Schimmel, D., & Stellman, L. (2002). *Teachers and the law.* Boston: Allyn & Bacon.

Fiske, E. B., & the National Commission on Service-Learning. (2001). *Learning in deed: The power of service-learning for American schools.* Battle Creek, MI: W. K. Kellogg Foundation.

Gaustad, E. S. (1999). *Church and state in America*. New York: Oxford University Press.

Giles, D. E., & Eyler, J. (1999). *Where's the learning in service-learning?* San Francisco: Jossey-Bass.

Glickman, C. D. (1998). *Revolutionizing America's schools*. San Francisco: Jossey-Bass.

Goldwin, R. A. (1997). *From parchment to power: How James Madison used the Bill of Rights to save the Constitution*. Washington, DC: AEI Press.

Halaby, M. H. (2000). *Belonging: Creating community in the classroom*. Cambridge, MA: Brookline Books.

Haynes, C. C., & Thomas, O. (2001). *Finding common ground: A guide to religious liberty in public schools*. Nashville, TN: First Amendment Center.

Hoppman, K. B. (1997). Concern with public concern: Toward a better definition of the Pickering/Connick Threshold Test, *V & L. Rev.*, 50, 993.

Hudson, D. L., Jr. (2002). Balancing act: Public employees and free speech. Nashville, TN: First Amendment Center.

Hudson, D. L., Jr. (2002). *The Bill of Rights*. Berkeley Heights, NJ: Enslow.

Hudson, D. L., Jr. (2002). *The Fourteenth Amendment*. Berkeley Heights, NJ: Enslow.

Hudson, D. L., Jr. (2000). Censorship of student Internet speech: The effect of diminishing student rights, fear of the Internet and Columbine. *L. Rev. M.S.U.-D.C.L*, 199, 209–210.

Hudson, D. L., Jr., & Ferguson, J. E., Jr. (2002). The courts' inconsistent treatments of *Bethel v. Fraser* and the curtailment of student rights. 36 J. Marshall L. Rev. 181–209.

Kinsley, C. W., & Gomez, B. (1999). *Service learning* (professional inquiry kit). Alexandria, VA: Association for Supervision and Curriculum Development.

Kinsley, C. W., & McPherson, K. (1998). *Enriching the curriculum through service learning*. Alexandria, VA: Association for Supervision and Curriculum Development.

Lappé, F. M., & Du Bois, P. M. (1994). *The quickening of America: Rebuilding our nation, remaking our lives*. San Francisco: Jossey-Bass.

Ma, P. (1996). Public employee speech and public concern: A critique of the U.S. Supreme Court's threshold approach to public employee speech cases. *John Marshall L. Rev., 30,* 121.

McFarland, S. T. (1996). A religious equality amendment? The necessity and impact of the proposed religious equality amendment. *B.Y.U.L. Rev.,* 627.

Monk, L. R. (1995). *The Bill of Rights: A user's guide.* Alexandria, VA: Close Up Publishing.

Nisbet, M. (1998). Public access to student publications: Does the rejection of a political advertisement violate the right to free speech? *J.L. & Educ. 27,* 323.

Nord, W. A. (1995). *Religion and American education: Rethinking a national dilemma.* Chapel Hill, NC: University of North Carolina Press.

Nord, W. A., & Haynes, C. C. (1998). *Taking religion seriously across the curriculum.* Alexandria, VA: Association for Supervision and Curriculum Development; and Nashville, TN: First Amendment Center.

Oakes, J., Quartz, K. H., Ryan, S., & Lipton, M. (2000). *Becoming good American schools: The struggle for civic virtue in education reform.* San Francisco: Jossey-Bass.

O'Neill, K. F. (2000). A First Amendment compass: Navigating the speech clause with a five-step analytical framework. *SW Univ. L. Rev., 29,* 223, 284–289.

Pearson, S. S. (2002). *Finding common ground: Service-Learning and education reform—A survey of 28 leading school reform models.* Washington, DC: American Youth Policy Forum.

Raskin, J. B. (2000). *We the students: Supreme Court decisions for and about students.* Washington, DC: Congressional Quarterly Press.

Ray, A. (1995). A nation of robots? The unconstitutionality of public school uniform codes. *J. Marshall L. Rev., 28,* 645.

Rothman, J. E. (2001). Freedom of speech and true threats. *Harv. J. L. & P.P., 25,* 283.

Schoen, R. B. (1999). Pickering plus thirty years: Public employees and free speech. *Tex. Tech L. Rev., 30,* 5.

Schudson, M. (1998). *The good citizen: A history of American civic life.* New York: Martin Kessler Books.

Silva, P. C., & Mackin, R. A. (2002). *Standards of mind and heart: Creating the good high school*. New York: Teachers College Press.

Soder, R., Goodlad, J. I., & McMannon, T. J. (Eds.). (2001). *Developing democratic character in the young*. San Francisco: Jossey-Bass.

Stein, R., Richin, R., Banyon, R., Banyon, F., & Stein, M. (2000). *Connecting character to conduct: Helping students do the right things*. Alexandria, VA: Association for Supervision and Curriculum Development.

Student Press Law Center. (1994). *Law of the student press*. (2nd ed.). Washington, DC: Author.

U. S. Department of Education (1999, September). *Religious expression in public schools*. Available in Pearson, S. S., *Finding common ground: service-learning and education reform—A survey of 28 leading school reform models* (2002).

Van Alstyne, W. W. (2002). *The American First Amendment in the twenty-first century: Cases and materials*. New York: Foundation Press.

Wagman, R. J. (1991). *The First Amendment book*. New York: World Almanac.

Watkins, W. D., & Hooks, J. S. (1999). The legal aspects of school violence: Balancing school safety with students' rights. *Miss. L.J.*, 69, 641, 642–643.

Wood, G. H. (1998). *A time to learn: Creating community in America's high schools*. New York: Dutton.

INDEX

Note: An *f* after a page number indicates a reference to a figure. An *n* and a number after a page number indicates a reference to an endnote.

AASA. *See* American Association of School Administrators

ABFFE. *See* American Booksellers Foundation for Free Expression

Abington School District v. Shempp, 51, 124–125, 131

ACLJ. *See* American Center for Law and Justice

ACLU. *See* American Civil Liberties Union

ACLU, Reno v., 81

ACT. *See* Active Citizenship Today

Active Citizenship, Empowering America's Youth, 167

Active Citizenship Today (ACT), 167–168

ADL. *See* Anti-Defamation League

Adler v. Duval, 46, 160–161

Administrative Office of the U.S. Courts, Office of Public Affairs, 171

administrators, school. *See* educators

The Adventures of Huckleberry Finn (Twain), 106, 107*f*

advertisements in student newspapers, 91–92

African American heritage, as defense, 77

AFT. *See* American Federation of Teachers

Aguillard, Edwards v., 134–135

AJCongress. *See* American Jewish Congress

ALA. *See* American Library Association

alcohol, 73

Alito, Samuel A., 166

Alliance for a Media Literate America, 168

American Association of School Administrators (AASA), 177

American Bar Association Division for Public Education, 168

American Booksellers Foundation for Free Expression (ABFFE), 181

American Center for Law and Justice (ACLJ), 181–182

American Civil Liberties Union (ACLU), 182
  and Children's Internet Protection Act, 84, 85
  and Communications Decency Act, 81

American Civil Liberties Union v. Reno, 81, 138–139

American Federation of Teachers (AFT), 177–178

American Jewish Committee, 182

American Jewish Congress (AJCongress), 181

American Library Association (ALA)
  and censorship of school libraries, 106, 182–183
  and Children's Internet Protection Act, 84, 85
  most frequently challenged books, 107*f*

American Library Association v. United States, 84

American Political Science Association (APSA), 178

American Society of Newspaper Editors (ASNE) High School Journalism Project, 168–169

Americans United for Separation of Church and State (AU), 183

America Online, Inc. (AOL) content filters, 85

Amish, Old Order, 128–129

Anderson, R. Lanier, 148

Anti-Defamation League (ADL), 183

Antifederalists, 11

AOL. *See* America Online, Inc.

appeals
  for *en banc* review, 3–4
  to United States Supreme Court, 4

appellate courts, 2
APSA. *See* American Political Science Association
Arkansas, Epperson v., 125
armbands, 59–60, 126
Arnold, Richard, 155
Articles of Confederation, 10–11
ASCD. *See* Association for Supervision and Curriculum Development
ASNE. *See* American Society of Newspaper Editors
Association for Supervision and Curriculum Development (ASCD), viii, 1, 171, 178
At the Table, 169
AU. *See* Americans United for Separation of Church and State

Babbitt, Chambers v., 162–163
baccalaureate services, 46
Badger Herald (University of Wisconsin), 91
Balanced Treatment for Creation-Science and Evolution-Science in Public School Instruction Act (Louisiana). *See* Creationism Act
Baldock, Bobby Ray, 160
Baptist Joint Committee (BJC), 183
Batchelder, Alice M., 151
Belyeu v. Coosa County Board of Education, 96–97
Bethel School District No. 403 v. Fraser
    as precedent, 157, 159, 165
    as standard for offensive speech, 61–62, 64–66, 72–73, 103, 133–134
    and student dress, 77–78, 80
Bethlehem Area School District, J.S. v., 83, 158–159
Beussink v. Woodland R-IV School District, 153
Bible, reading in schools, 43, 124–125
Bill of Rights
    education about, vii–ix. *See also* civic education, curricula
    history of, 10–15
    and ratification of Constitution, 11
Bill of Rights Institute, 169
BJC. *See* Baptist Joint Committee
Black Boy (Wright), 131
Black, Hugo
    on prayer in schools, 124
    on released time programs, 123
    on separation of church and state, 121, 122
    on students' freedom of speech, 127
Blaine School District, Lavine v., 68, 163–164
Bluestem Unified School District, Boman v., 68

Board of Education, East Hartford Education Association v., 99
Board of Education, Island Trees Union Free School District No. 26 v. Pico, 104–105, 131–132
Board of Education, McCollum v., 121–122, 123
Board of Education, Pickering v., 93–94, 96, 125–126
Board of Education Granville Central School District, Thomas v., 6, 146–147
Board of Education of Ewing Township, Everson v., 120–121
Board of Education of Joliet Township High School District 204, Scoville v., 144
Board of Education of Westside Community Schools v. Mergens, 47–48, 136–137
Boman v. Bluestem Unified School District, 68
Boring v. Buncombe Board of Education, 154–155
Boroff v. Van Wert City Board of Education, 156–157
Bossier Parish School Board, Canady v., 161–162
Brennan, William
    on Bill of Rights education, vii
    on censorship in school libraries, 132
    on censorship of school newspapers, 135–136
    on Creationism as religious doctrine, 135
Bridge to Terabithia (Paterson), 107f
Buddhists, 74
bullying in school, 69–71
Buncombe Board of Education, Boring v., 154–155
Burger, Warren
    on censorship in school libraries, 132
    on compulsory education, 129
    on *Lemon* test, 128
    on moment of silence, 133
    on vulgarity in student speech, 134
Burnside v. Byars, 143–144
Bush, George W., 177
Butler Middle School (Salt Lake City, UT), 26–27
buttons, worn by students, 65–66, 143–144, 148–149
Byars, Burnside v., 143–144

California, Cohen v., 72
Canady v. Bossier Parish School Board, 161–162
Cappy, Ralph J., 159
Carter, Gene, 147–148
Castle, Latham, 144
The Catcher in the Rye (Salinger), 107f

Catholic League for Religious and Civil
    Rights, 183–184
Cavalier Daily (University of Virginia), 91
CCSSO. *See* Council of Chief State School
    Officers
CDA. *See* Communications Decency Act
censorship
    of Internet, 81–86, 138–139, 153,
        158–159
    opposition to
        American Booksellers Foundation
            for Free Expression and, 181
        American Library Association and,
            182–183
    in school libraries, 104–106, 131–132
    of school newspapers, 62–63, 86–90, 88*f*,
        135–136
    of student dress, 74–80, 162–163
    of student (underground) newspapers,
        90, 143–144, 146–147
    of student work, 67–68, 102–103,
        114*n*206, 155
    of textbooks, 148
    of yearbooks, 86
Center City School (Salt Lake City, UT),
    28–29
Center for Civic Education, 169
Center for First Amendment Rights (CFAR),
    169–170
Center for Racial Reconciliation (University
    of Mississippi), 33
CEP. *See* Character Education Partnership
ceremonial deism, 67
certiorari, writ of, 4
Cesar Chavez Public Charter High School
    for Public Policy (Washington, DC), 29–30
CFAR. *See* Center for First Amendment
    Rights
Chambers v. Babbitt, 162–163
Champaign (Illinois) County Board of
    Education, 121
Chandler v. McMinnville School District,
    148–149
Character Education Partnership (CEP), 55,
    170
character education *versus* religious education,
    55
Child Online Protection Act (COPA),
    112*n*144
Children's Internet Protection Act (CIPA),
    83–85
The Chocolate War (Cormier), 107*f*
Christian Legal Society (CLS), 184
Christmas. *See* religious holidays

CIE. *See* Council on Islamic Education
circuit courts of appeals
    contacts at, 5*f*
    decisions, how to find, 5
    definition of, 2
    geographic boundaries of, 2, 3*f*
citations, legal
    abbreviations used in, 7–8
    interpretation of, 4–7
    in locating decisions, 4–7
City of St. Charles, Henery v., 155–156
civic education
    curricula on
        Active Citizenship, Empowering
            America's Youth and, 167
        The American Promise and, 168
        Bill of Rights Institute and, 169
        Center for Civic Education and,
            169
        Center for First Amendment Rights
            and, 169–170
        Civics in Action and, 170
        Council for Spiritual and Ethical
            Education and, 179
        Project Citizen and, 175
        St. Albans School of Public Service
            and, 176
    and educators
        Educators for Social Responsibility
            and, 171
        Institute for Global Ethics and,
            171–172
        National Council for the Social
            Studies and, 174
    and public life, 20
        National Alliance for Civic
            Education and, 173
    versus religious education, 55
civics. *See* civic education
Civics in Action, 170
Clark, Tom, 125
class codes, 26–27
Clausen, Zorach v., 59, 122–123
CLC. *See* Compact for Learning and
    Citizenship
Clinton, William J., 78
Close Up Foundation, 167
clothing. *See* dress codes; religious clothing;
    shirts
CLS. *See* Christian Legal Society
clubs, student. *See* political clubs; religious
    clubs
cluster model of school architecture, 31–32
Cohen v. California, 72

Cohn, Carl A., 75
Cole v. Oroville Union High School District,
    157–158
Columbia Scholastic Press Association, 173
Columbine High School (Littleton, CO), 67,
    71, 83
Communications Decency Act (CDA), 81,
    138–139
community
    interest in democratic freedoms of, 20–21
    role in First Amendment Schools of,
        22–23, 27–28, 32
    youth activities in
        Active Citizenship Today and,
            167–168
        Earth Force and, 170–171
        Federal Courts Community
            Outreach and, 171
        Learn and Serve America and, 169
        Learning in Deed and, 169
        National Service-Learning
            Clearinghouse and, 174
        National Youth Leadership Council
            and, 174
        Project 540 and, 175
        At the Table and, 169
        USA Freedom Corps and, 177
community group use of school facilities,
    57–58
Compact for Learning and Citizenship
    (CLC), 178
compelling interest test, 38–41
condoms, 155
Confederate flag, 64–65, 79–80, 145–146,
    159–160
Constitution, United States
    Amendments to. *See specific amendments*
    ratification of, 11–14
    success of, 9–10
Constitutional Convention, 10–12
Constitutional Rights Foundation, 167
Consumer Reports, 85
Coosa County Board of Education, Belyeu v.,
    96–97
COPA. *See* Child Online Protection Act
Council for Spiritual and Ethical Education
    (CSEE), 179
Council of Chief State School Officers
    (CCSSO), 178–179
Council on Islamic Education (CIE), 170
courts. *See also* circuit courts of appeals;
    district courts; Supreme Court
    decisions of
        applicability of, 4

courts *(cont'd)*
    decisions of *(cont'd)*
        citations used to locate, 4–7
        key First Amendment cases,
            117–119
        student run, 25
        system of, levels and jurisdiction in, 2, 4
Creationism Act (Louisiana), 134–135
creation science, 134–135
CSEE. *See* Council for Spiritual and Ethical
    Education
curriculum
    on civics education. *See* civic education,
        curricula on
    development of
        at Center City School, 28
        democratic freedoms in, 20
        at Edith Bowen Laboratory School,
            24
        at Federal Hocking High School, 30
        teacher involvement in, 101–102,
            154–155
    on law. *See* law, curricula
    on media literacy, 168
    religious exemption from, 40
    school officials authority over, 105–106
    state control of, 125
    student newspapers in, 88*f*, 89
    study about religion in, 52–53
    teacher adherence to, 102

Daddy's Roommate (Willhoite), 107*f*
Darden, Edward, 82–83
decisions of courts
    applicability of, 4
    publication of, 4–6
Declaration of Rights (Mason), 11
defendant, definition of, 6
democracy in schools, 19
DeNooyer v. Livonia Public Schools, 149
Derby Unified School District No. 260, West v.,
    159
*Des Moines Independent Community School
    District, Tinker v. See Tinker v. Des Moines
    Independent Community School District*
Dickson County School Board, Settle v., 150–151
dietary restrictions of students, 42
disruption, threat of, and student speech. *See
    Tinker v. Des Moines Independent Community
    School District*
distinguished precedent, 4
district courts
    decisions, how to find, 5
    definition of, 2

District of Columbia Public Charter School
    Resource Center, 29
diversity in schools, 25–28
Doe, Santa Fe Independent School District v., 45,
    139–140, 160–161
Douglas, William O.
    on compulsory education, 129
    on released time programs, 123
*Doyle, Mt. Healthy City School District Board of
    Education v.*, 97–98, 129–130
dress codes. *See also* school uniforms
    arguments for and against, 75–77
    exemption of Jews from, 41
    for students, 74–80, 126–127, 145–146,
        156–157
    for teachers, 129–130
Duval, Adler v., 46

EAA. *See* Equal Access Act
earrings, worn by male students, 76
Earth Force, 170–171
*East Hartford Education Association v. Board of
    Education*, 99
Edith Bowen Laboratory School (Logan,
    UT), 24
Edmunds, Nancy G., 150
education, compulsory, 128–129
Education Amendments of 1972, Title IX, 70
Education Commission of the States. *See*
    Compact for Learning and Citizenship
Education Department, and school uniforms,
    78
educators. *See also* teachers
    censorship by
        of school newspapers, 62–63, 86–90,
            88*f*, 135–136
        of student dress, 74–80, 162–163
        of student (underground)
            newspapers, 90, 144, 146–147
        of student work, 67–68, 102–103,
            114*n*, 206, 155
    and civic education, Educators for Social
        Responsibility and, 171
    control limited to school grounds,
        71–72
    editorial control of school newspapers,
        62–63, 86–90, 135–136
    neutrality required of, 36–37, 65,
        103–104, 142
    professional activity of
        American Association of School
            Administrators and, 177
        Council of Chief State School
            Officers and, 178–179

educators *(cont'd)*
    professional activity of *(cont'd)*
        Educators for Social Responsibility
            and, 171
        National Association of Elementary
            School Principals and, 179
        National Association of Secondary
            School Principals and, 179–180
        National Association of State
            Boards of Education and, 180
        National School Boards Association
            and, 180–181
    and promotion of democratic freedoms,
        20–21
    rights and responsibilities of, 92–104
    and student journalism
        Journalism Education Association
            and, 172
        National Scholastic Press
            Association and, 174
Educators for Social Responsibility (ESR), 171
Edwards v. Aguillard, 134–135
Employment Division v. Smith, 39–40
en banc, definition of, 2
Engel v. Vitale, 123–124
Epperson v. Arkansas, 125
Equal Access Act (EAA)
    constitutionality of, 136–137
    and student clubs, 47–48, 50, 136–137,
        151–152
equal time for all faiths, 53
ESR. *See* Educators for Social Responsibility
establishment clause. *See* religion,
    establishment of
ethics education. *See* civic education
events. *See* school events
*Everson v. Board of Education of Ewing
    Township*, 120–121
evolution, theory of, 102, 125, 134

Fairview Elementary School (Modesto, CA),
    24–25
Family Resource Council (FRC), 184
Federal Communications Commission (FCC)
    and Internet, 84
federal courts
    cases heard by, 2
    jurisdictions of, 2, 3*f*
    and state law, 4
Federal Courts Community Outreach, 171
Federal Hocking High School (Stewart, OH),
    30–31
Federalists, 11
Federal Reporter, 5–6

Federal Supplement, 5
FEPP. *See* Free Expression Policy Project
Ferguson Reorganized School District R-2, Lacks v., 155
filtering software for Internet, 83–86
Finding Common Ground (Haynes & Thomas), 52–53
First Amendment
   application of
      to public schools, 35
      to states, 14, 34–35
   debate over contents of, 13–14
   development of, 12–15
   early drafts of, 13
   education about, vii–ix. *See also* civic education
   importance of, ix–x, 10, 18
   ratification of, 14–15
   teaching and modeling in schools, 18–21, 30
First Amendment Center
   and Bill of Rights education, viii, 171, 172
   and religion in public schools, 40
   and school reform, 1
First Amendment Schools: Educating for Freedom and Responsibility
   community involvement in, 22–23
   definition of, ix, 1, 23, 171
   goals of, 17
   implementation of, 22
   as national resource, vii–x, 21
   school participation in
      elementary schools and, 24–26
      high schools and, 29–33
      middle schools and, 26–29
   success of, 23
   vision statement of, 18–21
   web resources of, 21, 23
First Amendment Schools Grant Award Program, 21–22
First Congress, and First Amendment, 12–15
Fisher, Raymond C.
   on school control of student speech, 157–158
   on student safety *versus* freedom of speech, 164
flag salute, 119–120
Forever (Blume), 107*f*
Forney Independent School District, Littlefield v., 164–165
Fortas, Abe
   on students' freedom of speech, 60, 127
   on teaching of evolution, 125

Fourteenth Amendment
   due process clause of, 14, 34–35, 76
   and parental rights in rearing children, 75–77
Frank, Donovan W., 163
Frankfurter, Felix, 120
Fraser, Bethel School District No. 403 v. See Bethel School District No. 403 v. Fraser
FRC. *See* Family Resource Council
freedom buttons, 143–144
Freedom Forum, 171
freedom of press. *See* freedom of speech
freedom of speech
   and class assignments, 149–151
   and Confederate flag, 64, 79–80, 159–160
   outside school grounds, 71–72
   and Pledge of Allegiance, 119–120
   and private speech of students, 37
   restriction of, by state courts, 34
   school control of student, 65, 158–159, 160–161
   in school newspapers, 91–92, 135–136, 144, 146–147
   and speech codes, 69–73
   and student dress codes, 74–80, 126–127, 145–146, 157–158
   and student Web sites, 72, 82–83, 153, 158–159
   and teacher dress codes, 129–30
   and use of school facilities, 140–142
   and wearing of buttons, 65–66, 143–144, 148–149
free exercise of religion
   compulsory education and, 128–129
   limits on, 38
   protection of, 38–42, 119–120
Free Expression Policy Project (FEPP), 177
free expression rights of students. *See also* freedom of speech; students, free speech of
   legal standards for. *See Bethel School District No. 403 v. Fraser; Hazelwood School District v. Kuhlmeier; Tinker v. Des Moines Independent Community School District*
   The Thomas Jefferson Center for the Protection of Free Expression and, 185

The Gay, Lesbian and Straight Education Network (GLSEN), 184
gay students
   and dates at school events, 51
   and straight pride shirt, 162–163
Gewin, Walter, 143–144

Gilman, Ronald Lee, 156–157
Gitlow v. New York, 34–35
GLSEN. *See* The Gay, Lesbian and Straight
   Education Network
Gobitis, Minersville School District v., 35
Goldberg, Arthur, 91
Good News Club, et al. v. Milford Central School,
   58, 140–142
graduation exercises
   prayer at, 44–46, 157–158
   student speech at, 157–158, 160–161
Graham, Stone v., 130–131
Grass High (student newspaper), 144
guest speakers in classroom, 54

hair, student, length or color of, 79, 144–145
Halloween. *See* religious holidays
Hansen, Chris, 84
Hanukkah. *See* religious holidays
harassment. *See* school policy; sexual
   harassment
Hard Times (student newspaper), 146–147
"harmful to minors," definition of, 84–85
Harmony High (Bloomington, IN), 31
Hazelwood School District v. Kuhlmeier
   and censorship of student publications,
      86–90, 88*f*, 135–136
   as precedent, 4, 156, 165
   as standard for school-sponsored speech,
      62–64, 81–82, 86–87, 135–136
   and teachers' in-class speech, 94
Heather Has Two Mommies (Newman), 107*f*
Henery v. City of St. Charles, 155–156
hip-hop, fashion and lifestyle, 77
holidays. *See* religious holidays
Holmes, Oliver Wendell, 92
homosexuality. *See* gay students; lesbians
Hsu v. Roslyn School District, 151–152
Hudson High School (Hudson, MA), 31–32

Idem (Id.), definition and use, 7
IGE. *See* Institute for Global Ethics
I Know Why the Caged Bird Sings (Angelou),
   106, 107*f*
illegitimacy depicted in school materials, 154
Independence (play), 154
"In God We Trust," 106–107
Institute for Global Ethics (IGE), 171–172
Internet. *See also* Web sites
   censorship of, 81–86, 138–139, 153,
      158–159
   filtering software for, 83–86
   student license to use, 86
   and use outside school, 82–83

invocation. *See* school events, prayer at
Islam. *See* Council on Islamic Education;
   Muslims

Jackson, Robert, 35, 119
Jackson Municipal Separate, McGlothlin v.
   School District, 99
Jacobs, Dennis G., 152
Jaffree, Wallace v. See Wallace v. Jaffree
JEA. *See* Journalism Education Association
Jefferson, Thomas
   on Bill of Rights, 11–12
   on establishment of religion, 36, 121
Jehovah's Witnesses
   excuse of, from celebrations, 41
   and refusal to salute flag, 35, 66, 98, 119
jewelry. *See* buttons; earrings; religious
   jewelry; rosaries
Jews
   activities for protection of
      American Jewish Committee and,
         181
      American Jewish Congress
         (AJCongress) and, 181
      Anti-Defamation League and, 183
      Religious Action Center and, 185
   exemption from dress codes, 41
journalism, student. *See* school newspapers
Journalism Education Association (JEA), 172
J.S. v. Bethlehem Area School District, 83,
   158–159
jurisdictions of federal courts, 2, 3*f*

Karr v. Schmidt, 144–145
Katz v. McAulay, 50
Kaufman, Irving R., 147
Keith, Damon, 146
Kennedy, Anthony, 138
Kiley, Roger J., 144
King, Carolyn, 165
Klein v. Smith, 147–148
Kravitch, Phyllis A., 161
Kurtzman, Lemon v., 127–128

*Lacks v. Ferguson Reorganized School District
   R-2*, 155
Lanier High School (Jackson, MS), 32–33
Last Words (Lavine), 68, 163
Lavine v. Blaine School District, 68, 163–164
law
   advocacy for
      American Center for Law and
         Justice and, 181–182
      Christian Legal Society and, 184

law *(cont'd)*
    curricula on
        American Bar Association Division
           for Public Education and, 168
        Street Law and, 176
Lawyers' Edition United States Supreme Court Reporter, 6
Learn and Serve America, 172
Learning in Deed, 172
Learning Matters, Inc., 173
Lee v. Weisman, 44–46, 137–138
legal citations. *See* citations, legal
Lemon test, 128, 131, 133, 161
Lemon v. Kurtzman, 127–128
lesbian issues. *See* Gay, Lesbian and Straight Education Network
lesbians
    depiction in school materials, 154
    and student dates at school events, 51
Let Freedom Ring Award Program, 172–173
Liacos, Paul J., 153
libraries. *See* public libraries; school libraries
"limited open forum"
    definition of, 47
    school control of, 48
Listen Up!, 173
literature. *See* political literature; religious literature
Littlefield v. Forney Independent School District, 164–165
Littleton, CO, shootings at, 67, 71, 83
Living Up to the First Amendment (*Newsweek* Education Program), 174–175
Livonia Public Schools, DeNooyer v., 149
Long Beach Unified School District, 75
Lysistrata (Aristophanes), 106, 148

Madison, James
    in Constitutional Convention, 11–12
    in First Congress, 12–15
Marcus, Stanley, 161
Marshall, Thurgood, 93, 126
Mason, George, 11
McAulay, Katz v., 50
McCollum v. Board of Education, 121–122, 123
McGlothlin v. Jackson Municipal Separate School District, 99
McKinley Elementary School (Livonia, MI), 149
McMinnville School District, Chandler v., 148–149
media literacy curricula, 168
Melton v. Young, 145–146
Mennonites, 128–129

Mergens, Board of Education of Westside Community Schools v., 47–48, 136–137
Merritt, Gilbert S., 151
Of Mice and Men (Steinbeck), 107*f*
Milford Central School (Milford, NY), 140
Milford Central School, Good News Club, et al. v., 58, 140–142
Miller, William E., 146
The Miller's Tale (Chaucer), 106, 148
Minersville School District v. Gobitis, 35
moment of silence, 44, 132–133
Monroe, James, 12
Morgan, Lewis, 145
Motz, Diana, 154
Mt. Healthy City School District Board of Education v. Doyle, 97–98, 129–130
Mt. Healthy defense, 97–98, 130
Murray v. Pittsburgh Board of Education, 101
Muslims
    and prayer at school, 41
    and right to distribute literature, 74
    and right to wear religious clothing, 99–100

NACE. *See* National Alliance for Civic Education
NAESP. *See* National Association of Elementary School Principals
NAIS. *See* National Association of Independent Schools
NASBE. *See* National Association of State Boards of Education
NASSP. *See* National Association of Secondary School Principals
Nathan Bishop Middle School (RI), 138
National Alliance for Civic Education (NACE), 173
National Association of Elementary School Principals (NAESP), 179
National Association of Independent Schools (NAIS), 179
National Association of Secondary School Principals (NASSP), 179–180
National Association of State Boards of Education (NASBE), 180
National Conference for Community and Justice (NCCJ), 173
National Council for the Social Studies (NCSS), 174
National Education Association (NEA), 180
National PTA, 40, 181
National Scholastic Press Association (NSPA), 172–173, 174

National School Boards Association (NSBA), 82–83, 180–181
National Service-Learning Clearinghouse (NSLC), 174
National Youth Leadership Council (NYLC), 174
NCCJ. *See* National Conference for Community and Justice
NCSS. *See* National Council for the Social Studies
NEA. *See* National Education Association
newspapers. *See* school newspapers; underground newspapers
Newsweek Education Program, 174–175
New York, Gitlow v., 34–35
New York State Board of Regents, 123
The New York Times Co. v. Sullivan, 91
noncurriculum related student groups. *See also* political clubs; religious clubs
    definition of, 47–48
    exclusion of, 49–50
Northwest Middle School (Salt Lake City, UT), 27–28
NSBA. *See* National School Boards Association
NSLC. *See* National Service-Learning Clearinghouse
NSPA. *See* National Scholastic Press Association
Nursery Road Elementary School (Columbia, SC), 25–26
NYLC. *See* National Youth Leadership Council

O'Brien, United States v., 78
O'Connor, Sandra Day, 137
offensive language. *See* profanity; vulgarity
Open Society Institute (OSI), 175
Oroville High School (Oroville, CA), 157–158
Oroville Union High School District, Cole v., 157–158
OSI. *See* Open Society Institute
outside groups, religious instruction by, 121–122
Owens, Bill, 69

parents. *See also* National PTA
    and civic education, 20
    and religion in schools, 40
A Parent's Guide to Religion in the Public Schools, 40
Parker, Robert M., 162
parochial schools. *See* private schools
PBS. *See* Public Broadcasting System

People for the American Way Foundation (PFAWF), 185
Perry Education Association v. Perry Local Educators' Association, 89
Perry Local Educators' Association, Perry Education Association v., 89
PFAWF. *See* People for the American Way Foundation
Pickering v. Board of Education, 93–94, 96, 125–126
Pico, Board of Education, Island Trees Union Free School District No. 26 v., 104–105, 131–132
Pink Floyd — The Wall, 101
Pittsburgh Board of Education, Murray v., 101
Pittsburgh Board of Public Education, Sanguigni v., 95
plaintiff, definition of, 6
Pledge of Allegiance, 66–67, 98, 119–120
political clubs
    in elementary schools, 50
    in secondary schools, 47
political literature distributed in schools, 73–74
political science. *See* American Political Science Association
prayer in schools. *See* school prayer
precedent, definition of, 4
private schools, transportation of students of, 120–121
profanity, 72–73
professional associations. *See* educators; teachers
Project 540, 175
Project Citizen, 175
proselytizing. *See* religion
PTA. *See* National PTA
Public Broadcasting System (PBS), 168
public employees, rights of, 92–93
public forum
    classroom as, 100–101
    and school publications, 87–89
public libraries, censorship of Internet in, 84
public policy taught in schools, 29–30
public schools
    and democratic freedoms, 1, 19–20
    neutrality required of, 58–59
Pyle v. School Committee of South Hadley, 152–153

RAC. *See* Religious Action Center
racial tension, 80, 96–97, 145–146, 159–160

radio, student produced. *See* Listen Up!;
   Radio and Television News Directors
   Foundation; Radio Rookies
Radio and Television News Directors
   Foundation (RTNDF), 175–176
Radio Rookies, 176
Reed, Stanley, 122
Rehnquist, William
      on prayer at school events, 140
      on school vouchers, 142
      on teacher dress codes, 130
      on Ten Commandments, 131
released time programs, 59, 122–123
religion. *See also* free exercise of religion
   establishment of
         Americans United for Separation of
            Church and State and, 183
         and ban on teaching evolution,
            125
         and Bible reading, 124–125
         and creation science, 134–135
         and "In God We Trust," 106–107
         and public schools, 35–39
         and released time programs, 59,
            122–123
         and religious clubs, 136–137
         and religious holiday-related
            activity, 55–56
         and school uniforms, 75–76, 80,
            164–165
         and school vouchers, 142–143
         and state aid to religious schools,
            127–128
         and state authorized prayer,
            123–124, 137–138
         versus teaching about religion, 52
         and Ten Commandments, 130–131
         tests concerning, 36, 37–38
         and third party religious instruction,
            121–122
         and transportation cost
            reimbursement, 120–121
         and use of school facilities, 57–58,
            140–142
      freedom of. *See also* free exercise of
         religion
         Baptist Joint Committee and, 183
         Catholic League for Religious and
            Civil Rights and, 183–184
         definition of, 36
         and free exercise clause, 38–42
      of students
         accommodation by schools, 39–42
         in clubs and activities, 47–51

religion *(cont'd)*
   of students *(cont'd)*
         and exemption from class activity,
            40–41
         limits on expression of, 42–47,
            140–141, 150–151, 157–158
      teaching about
         versus character education, 55
         constitutionality of, 51–55
         Council of Islamic Education and,
            170
         definition of, 52
         guest speakers and, 54, 121–122
Religious Action Center (RAC), 185
religious clothing, teacher's right to wear,
   99–100
religious clubs
   in elementary schools, 50
   religious leader participation in, 49
   school regulation of, 151–152
   in secondary schools, 47, 136–137
   teacher participation in, 48–49
   use of school facilities by, 140–142
   use of school media by, 49
religious groups and public schools, 58–59
religious holidays
   school activity relating to, 55–56
   student absence on, 42, 56–57
religious instruction in public schools, 121
religious jewelry, teacher's right to wear, 100
religious leaders' participation in religious
   clubs, 49
religious literature distributed in schools,
   73–74
religious schools, state aid to, 127–128
Reno v. American Civil Liberties Union, 81,
   138–139
reporters, 4–6. *See also specific reporter*
respondent, definition of, 6
retaliation by employers in First Amendment
   cases. *See* Mt. Healthy defense
Rights, Responsibilities, Respect (3 R's
   project), 26–28
Roger Williams Award, 27
rosaries, worn by students, 76
Roslyn High School (Roslyn, NY), 151–152
Roslyn School District, Hsu v., 151–152
RTNDF. *See* Radio and Television News
   Directors Foundation
Rutledge, Wiley B., 121

safe sex, 155–156
safety. *See* students, safety of
St. Albans School of Public Service, 176

Sanguigni v. Pittsburgh Board of Public Education, 95
Santa Fe Independent School District v. Doe
    as precedent in *Adler v. Duval*, 160–161
    and student prayer at football games, 45, 139–140
Saxe v. State College Area School District, 70, 165–166
scab buttons, 148–149
Scalia, Antonin
    on prayer at school events, 138
    on teaching creation science, 135
Scary Stories (Schwartz), 107*f*
Schmidt, Karr v., 144–145
School Board of Columbia County, Virgil v., 148
School Committee of South Hadley, Pyle v., 152–153
school events
    gay or lesbian dates at, 51
    prayer at, 42–47, 123–124, 137–138, 139–140
school facilities used by outside groups, 57–58, 121–122, 140–141
school grounds, limit of educator control to, 71–72
school libraries, censorship of books in, 104–105, 131–132
school newspapers
    censorship of, 86–92, 135–136, 144, 146–147
    support for
        American Society of Newspaper Editors High School Journalism Project and, 168–169
        Journalism Education Association and, 172
        National Scholastic Press Association and, 174
school policy
    on controversial materials, 154–155
    democratic freedoms in, 20
    on harassment and intimidation, 69–71, 159–160, 165–166
    on Internet use, 86
    on moment of silence, 44, 132–133
    on school uniforms, 74–79, 161–162, 164–165
    and speech codes, 69–73
    on student hair length or color, 79, 144–145
    on student speech at ceremonies, 157–158, 160–161
school prayer. *See also* school events, prayer at
    legality of, 42, 123–124, 137–138
    limitations on, 42–47, 132–133

school shootings, 67
school uniforms
    arguments for and against, 25, 75–77
    mandatory wearing of, 74–79, 161–162, 164–165
    religious objection to, 76, 79–80
school vouchers, 142–143
Scoville v. Board of Education of Joliet Township High School District 204, 144
separation of church and state. *See* religion, establishment of
service-learning. *See* community, youth activities in
Settle v. Dickson County School Board, 150–151
sexual harassment, 69–70
Shempp, Abington School District v., 51, 124–125, 131
Sherbert test. *See* compelling interest test
Sherbert v. Verner, 38–39
shirts, controversial, worn by students, 61–62, 77–78, 152–153, 156–157, 162–163
Sikhs, 100
Simmons-Harris, Zelman v., 142–143
Sippel, Rodney W., 153
Slaughterhouse-five (Vonnegut), 131
Smith, Employment Division v., 39–40
Smith, Klein v., 147–148
solicitation of funds at school, student right of, 50
Souter, David
    on religious club use of school facilities, 141
    on school vouchers, 142–143
The Spectrum (school newspaper), 62, 86
speech. *See* freedom of speech
speech codes. *See* school policy
Springfield, OR, shootings at, 67
state aid to religious schools, 127–128
State College Area School District, Saxe v., 70, 165–166
state courts, 2, 4
state laws and student publications, 89–90
Stevens, John Paul
    on censorship of the Internet, 139
    on moment of silence, 133
    on prayer at school events, 140
    on religious clubs, 137
    on vulgarity in student speech, 134
Stewart, Potter, 124
Stone v. Graham, 130–131
straight pride, 162–163
Street Law, 176
Student Press Law Center, 92, 176

students
  disabled, 25
  free speech of
    and armbands, 59–61, 65–66,
      126–127
    and class assignments, 149–151,
      163–164
    and Confederate flag, 64–65, 79–80,
      145–146, 159–160
    and creation of Web sites, 72, 153,
      158–159
    and dress codes, 74–80, 126–127,
      145–146, 157–158
    and harassment, 69–71
    outside school grounds, 71–72
    and religious expression, 37
    restriction of, by state courts, 34
    in school ceremonies, 157–158,
      160–161
    in school newspapers, 86–90, 88f,
      135–136, 176
    and school uniforms, 74–79,
      161–162, 164–165
    in underground newspapers, 73, 90,
      144, 146–147
    and vulgarity, 72–73, 133, 147–148,
      152–153
    and wearing of buttons, 65–66,
      143–144, 148–149
  hair length and color of, 79, 144–145
  and learning democratic freedoms, 20
  minority, 25
  religious needs of, 39–42
  respect among, 26–27
  safety of, versus freedoms of, 67–69, 71,
    163–164
Sullivan, The New York Times Co. v., 91
Supreme Court, United States
  appeals to, 4
  decisions, how to find, 5–6
  key First Amendment cases of,
    117–118

teachers
  free speech of
    and censorship of student work,
      102–103, 114n206, 155
    and dress codes, 98–99, 129–130
    in matters of public concern, 93,
      95–98, 125–126
    and religious beliefs, 102, 104
  legal protection of, 93–94
  mailboxes of, 89
  National PTA and, 181

teachers (cont'd)
  participation in curriculum development,
    154–155
  participation in religious clubs, 48–49
  and Pledge of Allegiance, 98
  professional activity of
    American Federation of Teachers
      and, 177–178
    National Education Association
      and, 180
  rights and responsibilities of, 92–104
  and salary subsidies in religious schools,
    127–128
television, student produced. See Radio and
  Television News Directors Foundation
Ten Commandments, 130
Ten Reasons Why Reparations for Slavery Is a
  Bad Idea (Horowitz), 91
textbooks, censorship of, 148
Thomas, Clarence, 141
The Thomas Jefferson Center for the
  Protection of Free Expression, 185
Thomas v. Board of Education Granville Central
  School District, 6, 146–147
threat, speech as, 71–72
Three R's project (Rights, Responsibilities,
  Respect), 26–28
Tinker v. Des Moines Independent Community
  School District
  and censorship of student speech, 59–61,
    81, 86–90, 88f, 103, 126–127
  as precedent, 61, 133–134, 145, 149,
    153, 159, 163, 164, 166
  as standard for student rights of
    expression, 59–61, 64–68, 74, 77,
    80
  and student dress, 77
Tocqueville, Alexis de, 9–10
transportation of students, reimbursement
  for, 120–121
T-shirts. See shirts

underground newspapers, 73, 90, 143–144,
  146–147
uniforms. See school uniforms
United States, American Library Association v.,
  84
United States, Department of Education, and
  school uniforms, 78
United States Reports, 5–7
United States Supreme Court Reporter, 6–7
United States v. O'Brien, 78
Urban Debate Program, 175
USA Freedom Corps, 177

Utah, State of, Elementary Education
Department, 24
Utah State University, 24

valedictorian speech. *See* graduation exercises
Valentine's Day. *See* religious holidays
Van Wert City Board of Education, Boroff v.,
156–157
Verner, Sherbert v., 38–39
Vietnam War protests, 60, 65, 126
Virgil v. School Board of Columbia County, 148
Virginia, 77, 79, 101
VISTA Service Learning Democracy Project,
31
Vitale, Engel v., 123–124
Voodoo & Hoodoo, 105
vouchers. *See* school vouchers
vulgarity in student speech or gesture, 72–73,
133, 147–148, 157

Wallace, John Clifford, 149
Wallace v. Jaffree
citation for, explained, 6–7
and moment of silence law, 44, 132–133
Warrior Times (Northwest Middle School), 28
Washington, George, 14
Web sites, 72, 81–86, 153, 158–159. *See also*
Internet
Weisman, Lee v., 44–46, 137–138
Wellford, Harry W., 156–157

Westside High School (Westside, NE),
136–137
West v. Derby Unified School District No. 260,
159
*West Virginia State Board of Education v.
Barnette*, 35, 66–67, 98, 110n71, 119–120
White, Byron, 135–136
Widener, Hiram, 154
Wisconsin v. Yoder, 128–129
Wisdom, John Minor, 145
Wolle, Charles R., 156
Wollman, Roger L., 156
Wood, George, 30–31
Woodbury, Sonia, 28–29
Woodbury High School (Woodbury, MN),
162
Woodland High School (Woodland, MO),
153
Woodland R-IV School District, Beussink v., 153
writ of *certiorari*, 4

yearbooks, censorship of, 86–88, 112n147
YFEN. *See* Youth Free Expression Network
Yoder, Wisconsin v., 128–129
Young, Melton v., 145–146
youth court, student run, 25
Youth Free Expression Network (YFEN), 177

Zelman v. Simmons-Harris, 142–143
Zorach v. Clausen, 59, 122–123

ABOUT THE AUTHORS

Charles C. Haynes is senior scholar at the First Amendment Center and director of the center's education programs in schools. The First Amendment Center, with offices in Virginia and Tennessee, works to preserve and protect First Amendment freedoms through information and education. Haynes was one of the principal organizers and drafters of a series of consensus guidelines on religious liberty in public education endorsed by a broad range of major religious and educational organizations. In 2000, the U.S. Department of Education distributed three of these guides to every public school in the United States.

Haynes is the author or co-author of six books, including *Religion in American History: What to Teach and How*, *Finding Common Ground: A Guide to Religious Liberty in Public Schools*, *Religion in American Public Life: Living With Our Deepest Differences* and *Taking Religion Seriously Across the Curriculum*. His bi-monthly column *Inside the First Amendment* appears in newspapers nationwide.

An educator for more than 20 years, Haynes served as executive director of First Liberty Institute at George Mason University in Fairfax, Va. Haynes holds a master's degree in religion and education from Harvard Divinity School and a doctorate in theological studies from Emory University. He presently serves as president of the Character Education Partnership.

Sam Chaltain is the coordinator of the First Amendment Schools project at the First Amendment Center. He came to the First Amendment Center from the public and private school systems of New York City, where he spent five years teaching high school history, English, and journalism, and coaching soccer and basketball.

Since joining the First Amendment Center, he has written articles for *Teaching Tolerance, Educational Leadership, ABA Insights*, and *Learning Magazine*, among others. Chaltain has a master's degree in American studies from the College of William and Mary, with an emphasis on 20th century social and cultural history. He received his undergraduate degree from the University of Wisconsin at Madison, where he graduated with a double major in African American studies and history.

John E. Ferguson Jr. is the education coordinator for the First Amendment Center at Vanderbilt University. While at the First Amendment Center, Ferguson authored several articles for legal and educational journals, and acted as associate editor on the newest revisions of *Finding Common Ground: A Guide to Religious Liberty in Public Schools*. He also travels around the nation speaking to educators and civic groups about religious liberty in the public schools.

Ferguson is a graduate of Vanderbilt University's Law and Divinity schools, earning his Juris Doctor and Master of Theological Studies. He is a member of the Tennessee and Washington, D.C., bars. He graduated summa cum laude from Howard Payne University with a Bachelor of Arts with a double major in practical theology and academy of freedom.

David L. Hudson Jr. is a research attorney at the First Amendment Center at Vanderbilt University in Nashville, Tennessee. He is a First Amendment contributing editor to the American Bar Association's *Preview of United States Supreme Court Cases*. He also is the author of two books for young people: *The Bill of Rights: The First Ten Amendments of the Constitution* and *The Fourteenth Amendment: Equal Protection Under the Law*. He has written several law review articles dealing with the First Amendment rights of public school students. Hudson received his law degree from Vanderbilt University and his undergraduate degree from Duke University.

Oliver Thomas is a lawyer, minister, author and school board member. He serves as director of the Niswonger Foundation, a private operating foundation designed to provide educational opportunities in Southern Appalachia.

Thomas has written and lectured extensively on the subject of religion and public education and has consulted with hundreds of school districts. He has been involved in litigation at every level of state and federal court including the U. S. Supreme Court. Thomas's clients have included the National Council of Churches and the Baptist Joint Committee.

In addition to representing several Evangelical groups, Thomas co-authored the ACLU handbook on church-state law. Before returning to his native Tennessee, he taught at Georgetown University Law Center.

Thomas is a graduate of the University of Tennessee, University of Virginia, and New Orleans Baptist Theological Seminary, where he was chosen as the most outstanding divinity graduate.

Related ASCD Resources: The First Amendment and Schools

At the time of publication, the following ASCD resources were available; for the most up-to-date information about ASCD resources, go to www.ascd.org. ASCD stock numbers are noted in parentheses.

Audiotapes
First Amendment Schools: Education for Freedom and Responsibility by Charles C. Haynes (#202165)

Networks
Visit the ASCD Web site (www.ascd.org) and search for "ASCD Networks" for information about professional educators who have formed groups around topics like "Religion and Public Education." Look in the "Network Directory" for current facilitators' addresses and phone numbers.

Print Products
Finding Common Ground: A Guide to Religious Liberty in Public Schools by Charles C. Haynes and Oliver Thomas (#303106)
Schools and the Law (December 2001/January 2002) *Classroom Leadership* (#102104)
The Spirit of Education (December 1998/January 1999) *Educational Leadership* (#198262)
Student Engagement (February 2002) *Infobrief* (#102284)
Understanding the Law (December 2001/January 2002) *Educational Leadership* (#102274)

For more information, visit us on the World Wide Web (http://www.ascd.org), send an e-mail message to member@ascd.org, call the ASCD Service Center (1-800-933-ASCD or 703-578-9600, then press 2), send a fax to 703-575-5400, or write to Information Services, ASCD, 1703 N. Beauregard St., Alexandria, VA 22311-1714 USA.

About the First Amendment Center

The First Amendment Center serves as a forum for the study and exploration of the five freedoms protected by the First Amendment. The center conducts programs and events nationwide and has offices in Nashville, Tennessee, and Arlington, Virginia. Programs and resources include

First Amendment Center Online—Your first stop for news and information about the First Amendment. Visit www.firstamendmentcenter.org.

Inside the First Amendment—A syndicated newspaper column by Ken Paulson and Charles C. Haynes, available for your community newspaper free of charge. Contact Gene Policinski at 615-727-1303.

Speaking Freely—A television program on free expression and the arts, shown nationwide on public television. Visit www.speakingfreely.com.

Media Commentary—Commentary on and analysis of newsworthy First Amendment issues. Contact Gene Policinski at 615-727-1303.

First Amendment Schools—A multiyear project, cosponsored by ASCD, designed to transform how schools teach and apply the guiding principles of the First Amendment. Visit www.firstamendmentschools.org.

Freedom Sings—A critically acclaimed multimedia experience featuring an all-star cast of musicians, now playing on campuses throughout the United States. Contact Jenny Atkinson at 615-727-1325.